Supernatural

Supernatural

Death, Meaning, and the Power of the Invisible World

CLAY ROUTLEDGE

OXFORD
UNIVERSITY PRESS

OXFORD
UNIVERSITY PRESS

Oxford University Press is a department of the University of Oxford. It furthers
the University's objective of excellence in research, scholarship, and education
by publishing worldwide. Oxford is a registered trade mark of Oxford University
Press in the UK and certain other countries.

Published in the United States of America by Oxford University Press
198 Madison Avenue, New York, NY 10016, United States of America.

Library of Congress Cataloging-in-Publication Data
Names: Routledge, Clay, author.
Title: Supernatural : death, meaning, and the power of the invisible world /
Clay Routledge. Description: New York : Oxford University Press, 2018. |
Includes bibliographical references and index.
Identifiers: LCCN 2017041795 | ISBN 9780190629427 (jacketed hardcover : alk. paper)
Subjects: LCSH: Supernatural. | Religion. | Occultism.
Classification: LCC BL100 .R68 2018 | DDC 200.1/9—dc23
LC record available at https://lccn.loc.gov/2017041795

9 8 7 6 5 4 3 2 1

Printed by Sheridan Books, Inc., United States of America

This book is dedicated to my mother and late father. I don't have the words to thank them for all they have done for me.

TABLE OF CONTENTS

ACKNOWLEDGMENTS

I would like to thank my editor Abby Gross and my publisher Oxford University Press. I would like to give a special thanks to my literary agent Nathaniel Jacks of Inkwell Management who played a vital role in helping me shape a coherent vision for this book. I would also like to thank the John Templeton Foundation, which funded some of my research on meaning-motivated supernatural beliefs discussed in this book. Most importantly, I would like to thank my wife, Jenny Routledge, for her constant support and feedback in life, generally, and on this book, specifically.

My son is a high school swimmer and, for reasons that remain a mystery to me, at a recent meet decided to collect and combine the bottles of juice, sports beverages, and smoothies various members of his team were consuming in order to make a super sugary cocktail. After preparing his mix, which he named "The Juice," he insisted that every swimmer on the team take a swig (or more) prior to their next race. What did the exercise in improvisational mixology accomplish? Evidently, a lot as everyone who consumed this nectar of the Gatorade Gods improved their race times. And by being the one who engineered this magical athletic elixir, my son was nicknamed "The Juice" and charged with the duty of concocting "the juice" at every swim meet for the rest of the season.

These kinds of superstitious behaviors in sports are common. Michael Jordan, often considered the best basketball player of all time, admitting to wearing his old University of North Carolina shorts underneath his NBA uniform because he thought doing so would bring him good luck. Jordan was a dominant player during his career, and yet he still thought it prudent to keep the magical ritual going. And he is not alone. Many top level professional athletes have confessed to a range of superstitious behaviors during competition. Many sports fans also employ a variety of superstitious rituals in order to make their magical contribution to their favorite team's success.

Have you ever had a goal blocked such as getting that coveted promotion at work you desperately wanted or buying that perfect house in the ideal neighborhood that you put an offer on? When the outcome you wanted did not occur did someone offer the condolence of "I guess it wasn't meant to be"? Or did you think that yourself? Can you think of an experience involving a positive outcome such as meeting the love of your life that felt destined to be? Or have you had a close call of some variety, trivial or serious, that made you feel like someone or something up above was watching out for you?

I remember seeing an interview once with an environmental activist who was arguing that recent extreme weather trends were the result of Mother Nature being angry with humans for polluting the Earth and wasting its resources. She was not simply saying that human behavior was causing changes in the climate. She was going a step further and asserting that we have caused the Earth pain and suffering and have angered it. And now we are facing the wrath of this vengeful living organism.

Every day, through the act of prayer, millions of people talk to a deity they have never seen. People have spent time and money fighting to preserve their right to this activity in public spaces. Political elections are sometimes swayed by whether or not a candidate is believed to be a supporter of prayer and someone who prays. Many people around the globe are confident that God is listening and responding to their prayers, even if they are not able to understand his wisdom.

I recently gave a talk at a universalist church about some of the nontraditional ways that people pursue spiritual needs. A very kind elderly lady approached me after the service and, with deep sincerity, laid out a case supporting the existence of intelligent extraterrestrial life. She wasn't simply arguing that aliens exist. She was advancing a very elaborate theory involving God-like celestial beings watching over humans with the goal of preparing us to be part of a much larger cosmic brotherhood. In due time, these aliens would reveal how all the world's religions can be unified under one super religion. She was thoughtful, calm, and otherwise looked like any other sweet elderly woman. And she is patiently waiting for aliens to save us from ourselves.

These examples are just a small sample of the many ways that people invoke the supernatural. Some of them might strike you as ridiculous.

Some of them might seem completely reasonable. But they all involve immeasurable forces that defy our scientific understanding of the world. That is, they all implicate something beyond the laws of nature as we understand them.

Supernatural thinking is so common we rarely notice it. Consider the following example. I was at a swim meet (I am always at swim meets these days) and because it was the same day that our university's football team was playing in a national championship game some of the men had set up a room in the school with a television. This way they could watch the game when their sons were not swimming.

So a group of people were in the room watching the game and our team was pretty far in the lead. This is where the story gets interesting. A girl who could not have been more than 9 or 10 years old said something to the effect of it being possible that our team could still lose. At that point, one of the men in the room became upset. He very firmly told the girl that she was going to have to leave the room and not return if she jinxed the game like that again. It wasn't just that she had raised the possibility that our team's fortunes could turn. She was tempting fate or creating some kind of negative energy that could alter the probable outcome of a commanding victory.

There must have been 15 to 20 men in the room (and a handful of women) and no one even flinched at the distraught man's concerns. I was carefully observing at this point and not a single person in that room gestured in any way that he was being silly. No eye rolls, laughter, whispers, or anything. Did people think his fears were reasonable? I don't know, but his suggestion did not appear to strike anyone as noteworthy. To think that a little girl could influence the outcome of a game simply by verbally recognizing that the tide could change is supernatural thinking. And people do this kind of thing every day, often without even realizing it.

Sometimes our supernatural thoughts and behaviors are relatively minor and inconsequential. Wearing a lucky pair of socks is not a big deal. Knocking on wood is not going to cause anyone any harm. In fact, as I discuss at length in Chapter 6, supernatural beliefs and related practices can have many physical and mental health benefits. But investments in the supernatural are not always minor events or healthy activities. Sometimes supernatural beliefs put both the believers and others in danger. In Chapter 7 I consider how supernatural thinking and beliefs can cause great harm.

For now, let my start by trying to tackle the basic question of how people are even able to think about the supernatural. What is it about our minds that allow us to speculate about and believe in things that violate natural laws?

It is a common idea that beliefs, whether they be supernatural or not, are learned. People are religious, for example, because they are raised in religious environments, right? This is partially true. Studies do show that one's religiosity can be at least partially explained by growing up in a religious household and having religious peers. But why are our parents religious, and why were their parents religious, and so on? In other words, though we learn specific religious doctrines and traditions from family and peers, why did humans ever start these doctrines and traditions? What is it about human nature that fosters these kinds of beliefs?

One proposal is that we are born believers, that supernatural thinking is just a natural part of how the human brain works. A number of researchers and writers have made some version of this claim. The basic idea is that supernatural thinking can be explained by innate cognitive processes and tendencies. Research based on this idea is often referred to as the cognitive science of religion. Throughout the book, when relevant, I touch on some of this work.

Central to my argument, however, is the notion that supernatural thinking and beliefs are not merely the result of natural cognitive processes, but that they are also motivated by basic existential questions about the meaning of life and inevitability of death. I take no issue with the cognitive perspective. In fact, my research connects to the cognitive science of religion. Critically, my motivational analysis builds on the cognitive approach because existential motives involve the cognitive processes implicated in supernatural beliefs.

The cognitive perspective is vital for understanding how humans are able to engage in supernatural thinking and why from a very early age we are compelled to believe in supernatural possibilities. However, this perspective does not fully explain why people maintain certain beliefs once they reach full cognitive development even though they abandon many others. Nor does it explain why people develop new supernatural beliefs as adults. Most importantly, it does not explain why people turn to supernatural beliefs in times of loss, pain, stress, and uncertainty or why such beliefs so effectively help people cope with these negative emotional states.

A cognitive account offers important insight but a motivational perspective is also vital. In this book, I describe an existential motivational approach to understanding the human proclivity to engage in supernatural thinking and to hold supernatural beliefs. I specifically focus on the unique motivational power of the human awareness of death and the desire to find and maintain a sense of meaning in life.

Like the cognitive approach, my own research and the case I put forward in this book treats supernatural beliefs as part of human nature. Humans are existential animals, beings driven to find enduring meaning in the face of an awareness of mortal finitude. And we are naturally drawn to supernatural ideas and beliefs in this pursuit. Socialization and enculturation influence what particular beliefs people tend to hold, but basic psychological needs and the cognitive processes involved in efforts to meet these needs underlie supernatural thoughts, curiosities, and beliefs.

Human psychology is extremely complex. There are undoubtedly a number of reasons that people turn to the supernatural. However, decades of research in psychology, which builds upon much older theorizing in fields such as theology, cultural anthropology, sociology, and philosophy, reveals that existential questions and concerns about death and meaning play a fundamental role in the supernatural lives of humans.

This book is not an attempt to say religion or any other supernatural belief is right or wrong. This book is about the psychology of supernatural thoughts and beliefs. What are the measurable variables that influence people's attraction to the supernatural and what are the measurable psychological and physical health implications of believing in the supernatural? These questions I can seek to answer using the tools of science. In fact, as a psychological scientist who studies human motivation, I have spent years seeking to answer these questions. And in this book, I try to at least partially explain what I have learned.

Supernatural

We Are All Going to Die—And We Know It

When I was a little boy I loved wearing my superhero pajamas. I was especially fond of the Superman set with the Velcro-attachable cape. I would run around the house pretending to fly through the air, liberated from the physical restrictions imposed by gravity. This is obviously not a unique childhood memory. Ever since the world was first introduced to superhero comics and Superman, the first comic book superhero, in 1938, we have collectively been enamored with the genre. In fact, in recent years, superhero movies have dominated the box office, grossing billions of dollars and creating an equally lucrative market for a wide range of toy, video game, food, and clothing products.

Of course, stories about mythical beings with magical powers were around long before modern-day comic books and movies. These types of media are just another manifestation of the human fascination with tales of those who can defy the laws of nature. But why are we so captivated by these stories and these characters?

Many have argued that one reason humans are attracted to stories featuring characters with superhuman abilities is because they provide an escape. But an escape from what? Entertainment in many forms allows a temporary respite from day-to-day stressors and hassles. But maybe stories of heroes with magical powers do more than provide a distraction from the challenges of life. Superman was introduced and popularized when the United States was licking its wounds from the Great Depression and being pulled into World War II. In times of economic uncertainty and war, people are reminded of just how vulnerable and fragile their lives are. Perhaps in such times we are drawn to narratives about superheroes because they allow us to imagine being strong and powerful, more than mere mortals.

A group of social psychologists tested this idea.[1] They focused specifically on the power of flight, arguing that humans are particularly attracted to this super power. Indeed, archaeological evidence suggests that our species has long fantasized about being able to soar through the air. Stories about human-like beings that can fly are found in many cultures and can be dated back to early human cave-paintings. Our ancestors had their own version of Superman. In fact, anthropologists have noted that many ancient civilizations around the world worshiped sky-gods or postulated human-like magical creatures or spiritual beings that had the power of flight. Dreams about flying are also very common. For example, researchers from the Central Institute of Mental Health Sleep Laboratory in Mannheim, Germany, found that over 60% of people report having dreamed of being able to fly or soar through the air.[2]

The research team proposed that humans around the world and throughout history have been and continue to be fascinated with the power of flight because this power symbolizes freedom from the confines of mortality. To fly is to defeat the laws of nature. Flight reflects transcendence. When people die, their bodies go down into the earth but their souls fly away. So flight fantasy is escapism, but escapism of a particular type. To fly is to symbolically escape death. Indeed, America's most iconic superhero, Superman, has the power of flight and is virtually immortal, kryptonite being his only real vulnerability.

The researchers put forward a simple hypothesis. If humans are attracted to the power of flight because it represents freedom from mortal limitations, then having people think about mortality should increase their attraction to flight fantasies. To test this, research participants were brought into a laboratory and asked to complete some personality questionnaires. In one of the personality questionnaires, half of the participants were presented with the following instructions: "Briefly describe the emotions that the thought of your own death arouses in you." They were then given a few minutes to articulate in writing their reflections on mortality. The other half of the participants were instead asked to describe their emotions associated with taking a future exam. I should note that the participants in this study were college students. So both tasks had the potential to generate some distress, but only one of them served as a reminder of the inevitability of death. The other task was more of a reminder of the inevitability of pulling a last-minute all-night cram session.

At a later point in the study, participants read a brief description of a flight fantasy and were asked questions concerned with the extent to which they like to imagine being able to fly.

The researchers proposed that flight fantasy is not merely a form of escape that people turn to any time they are confronted with something unpleasant. Instead, they argued that this fantasy is particularly about a longing to escape death. This is why they had some participants think about taking an exam. If flight fantasy equally serves as a form of escape anytime people are thinking about something unpleasant, something they would prefer to not think about in that moment, then the researchers would not find a difference between participants who thought about death and those who thought about taking an exam. But if flight fantasy is especially helpful when people are thinking about their mortal vulnerabilities, then those who were asked to ponder their mortality should express a greater desire to imagine being able to fly than those asked to think about taking an exam. And this is precisely what the researchers found. Thinking about death inspired flight fantasy. Imagining being able to fly may offer little assistance with a physics final, but it does help with the fear of death.

In other studies, this research team explored but found no evidence supporting the idea that contemplating mortality simply increases the desire to distract oneself with any imaginative activity. For example, they found that thinking about death did not increase people's interest in imagining having the ability to read other people's minds. When life experiences force us to face our existential reality, the fact that we are physical beings destined to die, the super powers that we are truly interested in are the ones that symbolize death transcendence. We want to fantasize about being able to fly because we know that we die.

And this is just the beginning. As humans, we go to great lengths to break free from our mortal chains, to feel like we are more than the sum of our biological parts. And these efforts are sometimes benign and sometimes humorous, but sometimes they also have rather serious social implications. Critically, these efforts to be more than mortal help explain why humans are and will likely always be supernatural thinkers.

AWARENESS OF DEATH CHANGED EVERYTHING

Like most parents, I remember when my children first became aware of their mortality. It was a particularly noteworthy awakening for my son. He must have been around 6 years old, and it started with a teary episode at bedtime. After I turned off his bedroom light, but before I could leave his room, he started to cry. He managed to get out the words, "Dad, I don't want you to die."

As part of normal psychological development, kids learn the implications of death. It may start with a difficult conversation in the wake of the death of a favorite pet or grandparent, or the recognition that their parents are aging and people who get old die. Eventually, they connect the dots and come to the full realization that they too share this fate. Inevitably, the questions follow, often in rapid-fire succession. Do we have to die? Why do we have to die? How long do people live? What is death like? Will it hurt? Will I be scared? What happens to us after we die? And so on. Understanding mortality is part of being human. But it is a great burden to shoulder. And it is a burden that has dramatically affected how we, as a species, organize our lives. The awareness of death created a unique psychological burden that demanded a solution. And our species found one: belief in the supernatural.

Most of us have wondered at some point: if I could get in a time machine and travel to any date, what would it be? Some people say they would prefer to go forward, to see what the future holds for our species. Will we finally get jetpacks and flying cars? Will we cure cancer or colonize Mars? Others want to go back in time to a particular era of interest. Maybe they would like to see what it was like for early European immigrants who traveled at great peril to the Americas. What was life like for these brave journeyers? Or perhaps they would like to get a glimpse of life in Ancient Rome or Egypt. Personally, if I could hop in a machine and travel to any point in time I would go back much further, to an era when our ancestors started to become the existential animals that we are today. Imagine when humans first started to stare up at the stars and ponder their place in cosmos. Or consider what it might have been like to begin to question the purpose of life and the implications of death. This is the world I would travel to. It is the world that truly sparked supernatural beliefs.

Though it is extremely difficult to pinpoint a specific period of time in which humans started to invest in supernatural ideas and beliefs, our ancestors left behind helpful clues. For example, ritualistic burial of the dead can be dated as far back as 100,000 years ago. But it was about 30,000 years ago that perhaps more compelling evidence for supernatural beliefs can be found, a time when our ancestors started to truly show signs of a species concerned about more than merely eking out an earthly existence. This is when archaeologists date the first religious-like cave paintings as well as the first elaborate examples of ceremonial burial that appeared to represent a belief that the person who died may be passing on to another realm of existence. The evidence suggests a concern with matters not just of the body but also of the soul.

But what is it about that time in human history that triggered our species' investment in supernatural ideas? It was around then that our ancestors most likely began to fully develop the advanced cognitive capacities that we have today, the properties that help distinguish us intellectually from other species: self-awareness, temporal consciousness, and abstract/imaginative thinking. It is crucial to understand just how much of an impact these abilities have had on our species and, ultimately, our inclination to believe in the supernatural. So let us consider each one of them in some detail.

We can focus our attention toward the self at a level of sophistication far beyond any other animal. And this high level of self-awareness has proven critical for us. It has allowed us to exercise a significant amount of control over our behavior. Instead of merely acting on impulse, we can regulate our behavior based on personal self-standards or goals (though we often struggle and fail to do so). We can empathize with others because by being able to reflect on our own feelings and goals we can imagine the feelings and goals of other people.

If you want to truly appreciate the value of this consciousness of self, spend some time with toddlers. Because their self-awareness has yet to fully take shape, they tend to act impulsively, focused on immediate desires and emotions. If they see a toy that looks interesting, they will just take it, even if another child is already happily playing with it. If they don't want to go to bed, and they usually don't, they will scream, often throwing themselves on the ground with reckless abandon. For toddlers, self-awareness is emerging but underdeveloped. They have a self that is selfish, a self that is not yet reflective or thoughtful. They have goals, but they are immediate and transient. They want mom to pick them up or fetch a favorite toy. And they want it now. They want a cookie, despite the fact they have not yet even had breakfast. And if the living room wall looks like it would make a fine canvas for some crayon art, they are going to use it for that purpose without a thought given to the fact that no one else in the house is expressing their artistic urges in that manner. Over time, through natural cognitive development and social learning, most young humans develop into beings that no longer throw temper tantrums or make decisions based on immediate hedonistic desires.

Of course, we can all bring to mind examples of fully grown adults who appear to have deficits in the self-reflection department. Likewise, we can see the many life problems these individuals experience as a result. And even highly self-regulated adults sometimes lose their power of self-awareness. Consider the example of mindless eating. Diet and nutrition experts often advise keeping a food journal and monitoring calorie consumption because people are often not consciously aware of their eating habits. They are surprised to find out they consume too many calories and are eating unhealthy amounts of certain kinds of food.

People also sometimes purposely shut down their awareness of self. Intoxication, for example, reduces self-awareness. And though this state can be quite desirable, allowing us, at least briefly, liberation from the insecurities, fears, and regrets that exist as a consequence of being highly self-aware, it also inclines us to behave like toddlers who lack self-control.

And, of course, this can easily become a problematic situation for adults. Toddlers don't need self-control because they can usually depend on the self-regulatory abilities of adult caregivers. Drunken adults are toddlers with car keys and access to firearms. In other words, self-awareness is functional. It helps keep us goal-oriented and conscious of our personal and social obligations, and it allows us to, for the most part, work with others in the service of a broader collective agenda.

In addition, our capacity to understand time is unparalleled and proves to be a critical partner of self-awareness. We are able to reflect on the past and ponder the future. So it isn't just that we are self-reflective, we can project the self in time. This capacity for temporal thought has proven vital for our ability to exercise self-control. Think again about toddlers: they exhibit little concern about the past or the future. They live in the moment. They don't want to go to bed because they are having fun right now. They lack the ability to reflect on a past self that did not get enough sleep and thus was cranky all day. And they cannot simulate the future self that will again be in this unfavorable predicament. My personal favorite was trying to strap my children into their car seats. They would arch their backs and often scream to resist being restrained by the safety straps. They simply were not capable of thinking about the potential future consequences of not being adequately secured inside the vehicle.

Until children fully mature as temporally conscious animals, they are unable to make optimal choices. Again, even adults sometimes fail to adaptively take advantage of their temporal consciousness powers. But most of us do use them when it really matters. As I type these sentences on a brutally cold and windy winter day in North Dakota, I look out my window and imagine the immigrants who settled in this part of the Upper Midwest. If they had not employed their temporal consciousness skills and planned accordingly for a long and harsh winter, the consequences would have been fatal.

Finally, humans are abstract and imaginative creatures. Thus, not only can we turn our attention toward the self and think in terms of time but also we can run all sorts of simulations in our minds and envision things we have never seen or experienced. We can imagine what it would be like to be a professional basketball player or win an Academy Award. We can imagine having super powers, surviving a zombie apocalypse, or traveling in a machine through time. And our imaginations don't exist simply so we can daydream about being rich, famous, and powerful. Our imaginative powers are functional. There was a period of time on this planet in which reptiles ruled. Dinosaurs were impressive creatures, but they were defenseless against the 6-mile-wide asteroid that slammed into the Earth and killed the party. The human imagination has provided our species with the tools to at least have a fighting chance against mass extinction threats, such as rogue comets and asteroids. For example, NASA maintains the Near Earth Object Program to monitor objects in space that may be on collision courses with Earth.

By being self-aware, temporally conscious, and imaginative animals, our ancestors were able to engage in long-term planning and complex problem solving. They were able to form and maintain increasingly sophisticated social groups and coalitions. They were able to suppress impulses and regulate their behavior in the service of future ambitions.

But, like all good things, the intellectual power our species possesses is not free. Because we can turn our attention toward the self, mentally time travel, and imagine pretty much anything we want to imagine, we are burdened with psychological vulnerabilities that no other animal shares.

Imagine another animal's response to threat. Take, for example, a rabbit. When a rabbit is pursued by a predator, it has a fight or flight response. At a physiological level, it experiences anxiety associated with this mortal threat. And, to save its own skin, it reacts. The arousal triggered by the threat mobilizes the rabbit to escape, to survive. And when the threat subsides, if the rabbit is lucky enough to escape, the fear ends. That is, the physiological arousal associated with threat, the stress of being on another animal's lunch menu, is temporary. It exists to help the rabbit survive. If a rabbit did not experience this arousal, it would be dead. There is no room in this cruel world for fearless rabbits. But the rabbit only needs to be aroused long enough to escape the threat. It does not ruminate about mortal dangers.

Humans, on the other hand, can think about the threat in a much deeper and enduring manner. What if the predator comes back? What if next time I cannot run fast enough? What if next time there are two of them? Am I safe? Will I ever be safe?

See the difference? Our intelligence is great, but it also creates a significant amount of distress, the type of anxiety that persists long after a threat subsides and often long before a threat ever materializes. Humans can play the "what if" game. Other animals cannot. And for some people, this type of anxiety can become so severe that it undermines the ability to live a productive and mentally healthy life. Even for the typical psychologically resilient adult, the intellectual enlightenment that comes with being human is accompanied by a certain amount of distress concerning possible threats to health and safety.

It gets worse. Not only do we worry about potential threats, such as being the victim of violence, car accidents, and cancer, but also we are able to fully contemplate the reality of our existence. Like all animals, humans are motivated to stay alive. However, unlike other animals, we are aware of our mortality. We realize that no matter how often we go to the gym, drink green tea, and wear our seatbelts in the car, eventually we will die.

Further, we recognize that death can strike at any time for reasons we can often neither predict nor control. Like the rabbit, we have a fight or flight response that mobilizes us to respond to proximal threat. However,

unlike the rabbit, all our fears do not disappear in the absence of immediate mortal dangers. We may be able to land a rover on Mars, split the
atom, and map the human genome, but at the end of the day, we are still
fragile biological organisms, and we are fully aware of this reality. In short,
humans face a unique and ever-present threat, an existential threat: the
awareness of inescapable death.

WE ARE NOT ANIMALS

The cultural anthropologist Ernest Becker wrote at great length about the
consequences of death-awareness in his 1973 Pulitzer Prize–winning book
The Denial of Death. Becker noted that, on the one hand, as humans we can
celebrate our unique intellect, our ability to think our way out of so many life
challenges and threats. But, regardless of our ability to solve many problems,
we cannot resolve the biggest one. We cannot change the fact that from the
moment we are born, we are on a journey to death. In life, there are many
paths to take, but they all have the same destination. Becker is not the only
or even first person to consider how the uniquely human awareness of death
influences us. A number of philosophers, anthropologists, sociologists, and
psychologists have written about the many ways that the knowledge and fear
of death have impacted our species. But I largely focus on Becker because it
was his work in particular that inspired the modern science on the consequences of people's ability to contemplate their own mortality.

Becker argued that though we cannot change our mortal fate, we can
do our best to deny and hide from it. As humans, we do not want to think
of ourselves as biological beings destined to the same finite fate as other
animals. We want to be special. We need to be special. Becker argued that
the awareness of mortality drove humans to strive to perceive themselves
as distinct from and superior to other animals because to be merely an
animal means to be born a purely physical being that disappears forever
when the physical body dies.

Inspired by the writing of Becker, in the mid-1980s three social psychologists, Jeff Greenberg, Sheldon Solomon, and Tom Pyszczynski, proposed

terror management theory, often referred to as TMT.[3] Throughout this book I refer to and elaborate on TMT as it is the theory that has generated the most scientific research on how death-awareness influences human thinking, including supernatural thinking. In fact, this was the theory that the research I discussed earlier on flight fantasy was based on. For now, let me just say that TMT was put forward as a way to test Becker's ideas. And one of these ideas is that humans want to deny their animal nature, to be more than mortal creatures.

For over 15 years now, a research team led by the social psychologist Jamie Goldenberg has been testing Becker's assertion that humans endeavor to deny similarities to other animals as a means to deny the reality of being mortal beings. Goldenberg's research is based on the TMT hypothesis that if people hold certain beliefs or engage in certain behaviors as a result of their awareness of mortality, then heightening this awareness of death should motivate those beliefs and behaviors.

In her first set of studies, published in 2001, Goldenberg and her research team wanted to test Becker's proposal that people deny their animality, in part, because of their awareness of death. Goldenberg thus hypothesized that experimentally heightening this awareness should in turn heighten people's disgust response to bodily products—the things that remind us of our animal nature—vomit, feces, and so forth. Likewise, experimentally heightening awareness of mortality should make people more sympathetic to the argument that humans are distinct from other animals and less sympathetic to the argument that humans have a lot in common with other animals. Said differently, if humans want to distinguish themselves from other mortal animals because we are aware of our mortality, then reminding people they are mortal should lead them to amp up their efforts to disassociate humanity from all things animal.

To begin to test these ideas, Goldenberg brought research participants into the lab and asked them to complete a set of questionnaires.[4] As is often the case in this kind of research, the participants were led to believe that they were taking part in a study about personality, but were not given any detailed information about the study. That is, in these types of studies, psychologists want to assess people's natural responses to stimuli, not the responses they think they should give, so researchers take careful steps to ensure that participants are not aware of the hypotheses being tested.

For half of the participants, the personality questionnaire packet included questions that required participants to reflect on and write about mortality (similar to the study I described on flight fantasy at the beginning of this chapter). The other half of the participants (the control condition) instead reflected on and wrote about experiencing dental pain, an unpleasant topic but one that is not typically associated with death. A lot of studies have used dental pain in particular as a control condition because it is something that many people report being very anxious about. Researchers doing these kinds of experiments have also used control conditions in which people think about anxiety-provoking subjects such as extreme physical pain, public speaking, and social exclusion. The point of using such control conditions is to test the potency of death-awareness, that it motivates beliefs and behaviors beyond those that might be caused by thinking about other, non-death-related sources of anxiety.

After writing about either death or dental pain, everyone responded to questions measuring disgust related to bodily products. For example, one item asked participants to indicate how disgusted they would be if they saw an unflushed bowel movement in a public toilet. Of course, most would probably find such an experience to be somewhat disgusting. And research on the psychology of disgust certainly suggests this is the case: bodily products such as blood, vomit, and feces trigger the disgust response. Goldenberg proposed though that reminding people of their mortal nature would serve to exacerbate this disgust response.

Goldenberg's hypothesis was supported. Research participants who were asked to briefly reflect on the topic of death became more disgusted when asked to imagine things such as seeing a bowel movement in an unflushed public toilet than participants in the control condition who were not asked to think about death. Being reminded of their mortality made people more easily repulsed by the creaturely aspects of human life. None of us like the surprise of entering a public toilet stall to discover that a previous occupant failed to exercise proper restroom etiquette or encountering a pool of vomit when we are walking down the street. Add thoughts of death to the equation and we find these encounters even more revolting.

Goldenberg then tested her second hypothesis, that experimentally heightening awareness of mortality should make people more sympathetic to the argument that humans are distinct from other animals and less sympathetic to the argument that humans have a lot in common with other animals. As in the first study, some of the research participants were assigned to an experimental condition that involved reflecting on death and the rest of them were assigned to a control condition. Participants were then told that the study was over and that they would now complete a second study related to attitudes. The study was, however, far from over. As part of this "second study," participants were asked to read and evaluate an essay written by an honors student from a local college. In actuality, there were two essays and they were written by the researchers, not college honors students.

One of the essays detailed many of the ways that humans are distinct from other animals. It highlighted, for example, how humans are more intelligent and less controlled by instinct and impulse. The other essay made the counterargument: humans are similar to other animals in many ways. In other words, one essay was written to showcase the continuity between humans and other biological organisms and the other essay was written to showcase all the ways humans are different from other biological organisms. Half of the research participants read one essay and half read the other. After reading one of the essays, all participants completed a questionnaire evaluating the essay (e.g., how much they like the essay and agree with it) and author (e.g., how intelligent they think they author is and how much they think they would like the author).

The results were striking. For people in the control condition who were not asked to think about death, there was no difference in evaluations of the essays. That is, people who read the "humans are similar to other animals" essay evaluated it and the author similarly to people who read the "humans are distinct from other animals" essay. Both groups generally liked the essays and authors. This outcome seems reasonable. After all, there are compelling arguments to be made for both positions. I recently read an article comparing teenage boys to wolves: both behave like pack animals. As a parent of a teenage boy and having once been one myself, this comparison made a lot of sense. But I can also easily think of the many ways that humans, even adolescent males, are distinct from other animals.

The results, however, were quite different for those who reflected on their mortal condition prior to reading one of these essays. For these folks, the "humans are similar to other animals" essay and author were evaluated significantly more negatively than the "humans are distinct from other animals" essay and author. Drawing comparisons between humans and other animal species may be an interesting and educational exercise, but it is not one people are inclined to engage in when their mortal vulnerabilities have been exposed. When people are reminded that they will die, they prefer information that suggests humans are unique beings.

Knowledge of death is a sensitive issue for our species. We see what happens when living things die—they appear to be completely extinguished. And we don't much care to share that fate. So what do we do? The same thing that we do anytime we want to deny vulnerability to a threat, we mentally distance ourselves from it. We do everything we can to hide our corporal nature, to push it far from consciousness. We are not animals. We are humans.

In subsequent work, Goldenberg proposed that though all people—both men and women—are motivated to deny their animal nature, women have to go to greater lengths to successfully deny their creatureliness because women are at greater risk of being associated with animality. That is, because of their pronounced role in reproduction, women serve as regular reminders of our species' animal nature. Women give birth, have breasts that produce milk for nursing babies, and, when they are not pregnant, get a monthly reminder of their corporality. In short, Goldenberg argues that it takes more effort for women to camouflage their animal nature.

In support of this argument, Goldenberg cites the many examples throughout history and across cultures in which societies craft rituals, customs, and products to disguise women's creaturely nature. Whether it is having women seclude themselves in special huts while they are menstruating, wear restrictive garments that reshape the natural form, or act "ladylike," the end goal is the same. Jonathan Swift humorously described the threat of perceiving women as physical beings in his poem *The Lady's Dressing Room*. The poem describe a man, Strephon, who sneaks into the dressing room of his lover Celia only to discover that the woman he had placed on a pedestal and viewed as a goddess is actually a flesh and blood mortal. He is repulsed by the discovery of dirty clothing and odor that evidences that Celia sweats. And worst of all, he finds her chamber pot.

> *Thus finishing his grand Survey,*
> *Disgusted Strephon stole away*
> *Repeating in his amorous Fits,*
> *Oh! Celia, Celia, Celia shits!*

And, if online polls and discussion boards offer any accurate insight, Celia would have been just as mortified to find out that Strephon had discovered her animal nature. For example, one recent poll on a popular British fashion website found that it takes woman on average 7.5 months of being in a relationship with a man to feel comfortable farting or burping in front of him.[5] This was a nonscientific poll and one that did not include males for comparison, but it does illustrate findings from the scientific literature. Teenage girls and women, more so than their male counterparts, spend a significant amount of time and money striving to mask their natural state.

Researchers have put Goldenberg's proposal to the test in the laboratory. In one set of experiments, a research team led by the social psychologist Cathy Cox and Jamie Goldenberg examined how increasing people's awareness of death affected reactions to breastfeeding women.[6] On the one hand, breastfeeding is generally socially valued, as it is viewed as the optimal way to nourish babies. On the other hand, many women report having negative experiences breastfeeding in public places, even if they are very discrete: receiving mean stares, rude comments, and even being asked to leave or breastfeed elsewhere.

In 2006, editors of *BabyTalk*, a freely distributed parenting magazine primarily read by mothers of infants, received an onslaught of negative letters because the cover of one of the magazine's issues depicted a woman breastfeeding a baby. Many of these letters were from women who described the cover as "gross." What gives? Evidently, for some people, breastfeeding is perceived as something good to do but something that is disgusting and to be done behind closed doors. Cox and Goldenberg proposed that one reason people do not want to see or think about women breastfeeding is because it is a behavior that reminds us that we are animals and, because we are aware of our mortality, we want to avoid anything that reminds us of our physical nature.

First, the researchers tested how thoughts of death affect people's general reaction to the idea of a woman breastfeeding in public. Specifically, as in research already described, participants were randomly assigned to a condition that involved reflecting on death or a control condition. Subsequently, participants were asked to read a story in which a woman was depicted breastfeeding in public. In this story, a woman brought her baby with her to meet her friend for lunch and during lunch breastfed the baby because the baby started to cry. After reading this story, participants answered questions about whether or not the breastfeeding woman's behavior was wrong.

Because, again, breastfeeding is widely considered to be the best way to nourish a baby, many of us would probably assume that we would have a relatively positive attitude about how this woman behaved. In public or not, she was simply trying to take care of her baby's basic needs. At a minimum, we would probably feel like we have no strong reason to harshly judge this woman. Indeed, polls show that the majority of American men and women believe that it is acceptable for women to breastfeed in public. But this is why scientists conduct experiments to assess actual attitudes and behaviors in response to particular stimuli instead of just asking people how they think they would feel or behave. Research has shown us time and time again that people are not always good at predicting their attitudes and behavior in response to varying life experiences.

In this case, the experience of having one's awareness of death elevated influenced reactions to a woman depicted breastfeeding in public. Participants in the heightened death-awareness condition evaluated the breastfeeding woman more harshly than participants in the control condition. Specifically, those who were reminded of their mortality were more inclined to assert that the woman was in the wrong for breastfeeding in public.

In another study, these researchers observed something even more powerful. Research participants were informed that, as part of the study, they would be interacting with another participant that is in the adjacent room—a sort of get to know you exercise. They were told that first they would complete a few personality questionnaires and then they would go to another room for the social interaction part of the study. As part of the personality questionnaires, some participants were given the death reflection task. Other participants—those in the control group—were not asked any questions about death. Subsequently, participants were informed that it was time for the social interaction task but that their interaction partner was not quite ready for the task.

Here is the important part. All participants were told that their partner brought her baby to the experiment. Some of the participants were told that their partner was in the other room breastfeeding her baby. And some of them were told that their partner was in the other room giving her baby a bottle. The experimenter then asked the participant for a favor. Specifically, she asked the participant to help her get the room ready for the social interaction part of the study. She pointed to two folding chairs in the corner and instructed the participant to set the chairs up so that the two participants could interact. Once the participant obliged, the experiment was over.

The truth is, there was no participant in the other room and there was not ever going to be a social interaction component to the study. What the researchers wanted to know is if participants would want to physically distance themselves from a woman who had just breastfed—as, the investigators argue, she would serve as a reminder that people are animals. More specifically, they wanted to know if participants whose awareness of death had been heightened would be the most inclined to want to distance themselves from the breastfeeding woman.

This is exactly what the researchers found. Once the experimental session was over, the experimenter measured the distance between the two folding chairs. If participants wanted to distance themselves from a reminder of human animality, then they might have been inclined to set the chairs further apart when the experimenter asked them to set the chairs up for the social interaction. Indeed, participants who had previously been asked questions about death set the chairs further apart than participants not asked anything about death. In addition, this effect of death-awareness on distancing only occurred for participants told that their interaction partner was in the other room breastfeeding. Death-awareness had no effect on how far apart participants set the chairs when they were told that their interaction partner was bottle-feeding a baby.

In other words, being reminded of mortality does not simply make people want to distance themselves from other people or from a woman who brought her baby to the experiment. It makes them want to distance themselves from those who highlight the fact that humans are physical creatures. Both women were feeding their babies, but only one of them was feeding her baby in the natural, animal way.

And it is not just breastfeeding. Studies show that other female behaviors and physical characteristics that highlight the creaturely nature of humanity also trigger negative and sometimes prejudicial reactions, particularly when the awareness of death has been elevated. For example, in one study, female participants who were asked to think about death judged a woman to be less competent if, while reaching into her purse, she dropped a tampon on the floor.[7] This effect did not occur if the woman dropped a hairclip.

Most of us would presumably not predict that we would hold negative attitudes toward a woman because she accidently dropped a tampon. But this is precisely what happened, at least among people who had first been reminded that they are mortal.

It is also worth noting that in this particular experiment all of the research participants were female. In other words, it is not the case that these negative responses to female creatureliness are observed only among men. Neither males nor females want to think about the biological nature of humanity, and both males and females want to avoid, as much possible, situations that remind them of it. And the research suggests that the reproductive qualities of women serve as potent reminders to males and females that humans are flesh and blood.

Of course, the problem is not women per se, but rather that through biology, women are more likely to publicly reveal human creatureliness. So, by this reasoning, any human behavior that suggests we are animals should trigger an adverse response. Indeed, research demonstrates that describing violence in animalistic terms decreases peoples' support for war.[8] Likewise, studies show that describing sex in animalistic terms can decrease its appeal, particularly when death-awareness has been elevated.[9] When people are reminded of their mortality, sex is viewed more positively when it is rebranded as "lovemaking," a far more elevated notion. And indeed, when people's sexual behavior is perceived as animal, or creaturely, they are often viewed as acting immorally. Many religious views on sex draw on this idea. Casual sex is often viewed as sinful, an animalistic impulse that humans should control. Sex within the parameters of a religiously sanctioned marriage is beautiful and celebrated. This analysis does not contradict other, evolutionary and social, explanations for cultural and religious views on sex. It simply reveals that existential motives can also play a role.

Other studies further showcase that death-awareness causes humans to reject their animal nature by demonstrating that having people think about mortality leads them to dislike animals.[10] Interestingly, researchers recently found that even among pet owners—people who presumably like having animal companions—thoughts of death increased negative attitudes toward pets, particularly if the research participants were presented with information highlighting how humans have a lot in common with animals.[11]

Of course, some people go the other direction. They don't distance humans from pets to feel special; they distance their pets from other animals, elevating them to a similar level of specialness as humans. They put their dogs in clothes and treat them like human children. My mother once told me that some friends of hers held a wedding ceremony for their two dogs. Evidently, when their child asked them why the family dogs were having intercourse outside of wedlock, their solution was to sanctify this relationship, to make an "honest woman" out of the female dog. The wedding was for fun and not a serious exercise; however, people attributing human-like thought processes and motives to dogs is not uncommon.

Curious to find out if this was an isolated event, after hearing this story I conducted a quick Google search on dog weddings. There are in fact a number of websites dedicated to this purpose. Some offer helpful advice for how to find two dogs that are a good match to "fall in love." Others provide tips on how to plan the ceremony. You can even purchase the appropriate wedding attire for the dog bride and groom from some of these websites. People have even gone so far as to create dog marriage certificates. Do they realize that dogs cannot read? Of course, the certificates aren't for the dogs. They are for the humans. Dogs are not aware of their mortality.

We gain some relief from convincing ourselves that we (and maybe our dogs) are distinct from other forms of biological life. But what does it really mean to believe we are not animals? We can disguise our natural odors with deodorants, lotions, and perfumes. We can shave unwanted and tame unruly body hair, wear clothing, and not fart in public. And we can pride ourselves in just how refined and civilized we are, looking down on those who fail to act with the proper etiquette. But what does all this really do for us? We still get injured and sick. We still feel pain. We still break. We still bleed. We still die.

With great effort, we can avoid being constantly reminded that we are in the same boat as other animals, and research indicates that this does give us some comfort. However, beneath the surface, the dread of knowing we are mortal is still there. We cannot fully suppress this knowledge. So what are we to do? What did our ancestors do? Our ancestors did not merely develop cultural practices, grooming rituals, clothing, and adornments that physically distinguished them from the "lower animals." They went much further. Humans, like other animals, have bodies. And bodies die. So simply having a body was not enough. Our ancestors needed to believe that they had some kind of essence that transcended death. They needed to believe that part of who they are would survive the expiration of the body. And so do we.

THE QUEST TO ESCAPE MORTALITY

Intelligence helped our ancestors become masters of their environment. But it also forced them to face questions about the nature of existence and the inescapable reality of death. Why were we born, only to die? What is the point of struggling to survive when death is the inevitable outcome? Does life have any meaning that death does not obliterate? As Becker and other scholars have argued, intelligence created the potential for existential terror. Ironically, the same intellectual abilities that rendered humans aware of their mortal predicament also provided them with the means to resolve it. That is, these abilities allowed humans to propose that maybe there is more to life than mere physical existence. Maybe there is a grander plan in motion. Maybe death is not the end.

When our ancestors reached a level of intellectual sophistication that allowed them to fully grasp their fate they became truly motivated to believe in the supernatural, to turn to worldviews that offered some hope of being more than mortal. And it was then, as many scholars have argued, that supernatural beliefs were truly born. These beliefs served a number of functions for our ancestors. They helped turn an often chaotic and unpredictable world into a world of design and order by offering creation stories that proclaim that everything happens for a reason. They provided explanations for otherwise seemingly unexplainable phenomena by invoking controlling supernatural agents. They helped regulate social behavior by outlining moral philosophies and rules that were associated with supernatural consequences (e.g., punishment or reward in the afterlife). However, at the core of supernatural thinking is the promise that there is more to existence than our brief time on this planet, and there is more to being human than being an animal.

The physical world is governed completely by natural laws. It is the world we understand through empirical observation, through science. Supernatural thinking allows for the belief or at least the hope that our existence does not boil down solely to the material. It unshackles the self from the confines of biology. Supernatural thinking allows humans to believe in an invisible world that is not constrained by the rules of nature.

Perceiving ourselves as distinct from other animals isn't simply about avoiding thinking about our part in the bloody and brutal drama that is biological life. It also involves denying our mortality entirely. In a recent set of published studies the psychologist Jessica Tracy and her research team observed that having people think about mortality increased their acceptance of intelligent design theory and decreased their acceptance of evolutionary theory.[12]

Despite the fact that there is an overwhelming amount of data in support of evolutionary theory, many still reject it. For example, a 2013 Pew Research Center Poll found that only 60% of Americans endorse the view that humans and other forms of life have evolved over time. Perhaps this is not surprising considering that evolutionary theory not only highlights our connection to other animals but also challenges the notion that we are special, that we are part of a supernatural order. To accept evolution is to admit or at least entertain the possibility that humans do not exist by supernatural design. In fact, of the 60% of people that endorsed evolution, almost half indicated believing that if evolution is true it is the result of God's work and not merely due to natural processes. So the ever-growing body of scientific literature in support of evolution may be winning people over, but many of these converts remain committed to the notion that life is special, the purposeful work of a creator.

Intelligent design theory, of course, quite explicitly advances the position that we are special. And thus this theory, despite being viewed as a pseudoscience by the scientific community, remains attractive to many people. The more we can convince ourselves that we are unique, that we are beings created with purpose, the easier it is for us to convince ourselves that we are meant for more than a mortal life. Perhaps Abraham Lincoln said it best: *"Surely God would not have created such a being as man, with an ability to grasp the infinite, to exist only for a day! No, no, man was made for immortality."*

Our ancestors arrived at the same conclusion as President Lincoln. When they realized that death is unavoidable, can happen without warning, and strikes without regard for age or social status, they needed to find a way to cope with the existential fear this knowledge provoked. They needed supernatural beliefs. They needed to know that death is not as bad as it sounds. In fact, some scholars have argued that God is the ultimate attachment figure.

According to attachment theory, a prominent theory in psychology, infants and children rely on the caregivers, typically their parents, for psychological security. Parents meet not only the physical needs of children—food and shelter—but also their psychological needs. Thus, children become "attached" to their caregivers, as these caregivers serve as anxiety regulators. When a baby cries and mom or dad picks her up and puts her at ease, these attachments are reinforced, causing the child to turn to these attachment figures when she feels threatened or distressed. But, as already discussed, children develop intellectually and eventually come to the realization that mom and dad can't protect them forever. In fact, mom and dad are just as physically vulnerable as they are. It is then that supernatural beliefs offer security. God (or another supernatural agent or set of agents) replaces the parents as an attachment figure because God is now the one that can offer comfort in the face of knowledge of the ultimate threat.

Ultimately then, supernatural ideas and beliefs are not about separating humans from other mortal beings—though they certainly help do this. Perceiving our species as distinct from other species, like fantasizing about having super powers such as the ability to fly, is just one strategy used to serve the broader goal of solving the problem of mortality. Supernatural beliefs are about separating what it means to be human from mortal existence. Supernatural beliefs offer a way to reconceptualize existence. They are about escaping death.

If supernatural beliefs exist, at least in part, to counter the awareness of death, then it would be reasonable to hypothesize that elevating people's awareness of death would increase their tendency to engage in supernatural thinking and endorse or show interest in related beliefs. In other words, if supernatural beliefs are the solution to the problem of death, then reminding people of the problem should incline them to turn to the solution. Psychological research supports this hypothesis. And in the coming chapters, I describe this research and how it can help us better understand the many ways that people invest in the supernatural. First, in the next chapter I discuss the important role that meaning in life plays in the relationship between an awareness of death and supernatural concepts and beliefs.

The Supernatural World Is a Meaningful World

The 2002 book *The Purpose Driven Life* was on the New York Times Bestseller List for 90 weeks and has now sold tens of million copies. It is a Christian devotional book intended as a guide to help modern-day believers understand their God-given purpose and how to live their lives in a way that gives them meaning.

If you don't like that particular brand of meaning, no worries. Go to your local bookstore and check out the self-help aisle. It is full of books offering you the secrets to a meaningful life. Or more relevant for the way most of us shop for books these days, get on Amazon.com and type in "meaning in life." The search will result in thousands of books. Some of these books are explicitly religious, helping people rediscover their faith or better understand how it fills their life with a grander purpose. Some of the books are more spiritual, abandoning traditional religious doctrines in exchange for a broader and less dogmatic approach to answering questions about life's meaning. And some of these books cleverly fuse philosophical ideas we would ascribe to religion and spirituality with more science-based guide-lines from contemporary psychology.

Why is there such a market for these kinds of books in all their variet-ies? Why do people appear to care so much about finding meaning and purpose in life? And does it even matter? Is feeling like your life is mean-ingful beneficial or is it just a personal indulgence like eating a cupcake or getting a massage at the spa, something that we might enjoy but is cer-tainly not necessary for living a productive life? And what does any of this have to do with the supernatural? That is, to what extent does supernatural thinking actually play an important role in our efforts to feel meaningful?

WHY MEANING MATTERS

Let's start with the question of whether meaning matters. Clearly people want to find it. It is not just the self-help book market that reveals this fact. People go to church, pick careers, and agitate for social causes all in the name of finding and fulfilling their purpose. But what do these pursuits do for them? The short answer: a lot. There is now a sizable and ever growing body of scientific research demonstrating that the perception that one is living a life full of purpose and meaning is a vital component of both men-tal and physical health.

Humans are constantly looking for the key to happiness. We're told that money won't make us happy, fame won't make us happy, physical beauty won't make us happy, and so on. All these things sound pretty awesome though, right? And many people clearly spend a lot of time, energy, and money trying get those sexy beach-ready abs and afford the consumer products that signal high social status. If these pursuits are not the key to the good life, what is?

According to the research, meaning in life will get you there faster than perfect skin or 15 minutes of fame. Feeling like one's life is meaningful is important for finding happiness and, critically, a more enduring sense of personal fulfillment.[1] Sometimes the things we do to attain meaning are challenging and they don't always immediately make us feel good. In fact, meaningful pursuits are often stressful and exhausting. I remember being pretty miserable at times when I was working on my PhD. My wife and I had small children and we were both attending graduate school. We were sleep deprived, totally stressed, and completely broke. However, we were pursuing personally meaningful goals.

Ask any new mother if she is happy and if she says yes she is probably lying or so sleep deprived that she has become delusional. Being a new parent is stressful and exhausting, but for most people parenthood eventually leads to a greater sense of purpose and meaning. In the end, the challenges and goals that give us meaning are what make us content, inspired, and optimistic. Meaning is an important part of being emotionally well adjusted.

Meaning does a lot more than make us happy. In fact, many psychologists who study mental health and well-being now argue that seeking meaning is more personally and socially valuable than seeking happiness. Meaning reduces the risk of mental illness and related problems. For example, people are less likely to develop depression if they see life as full of purpose and meaning.[2] They are also less likely to commit suicide[3] or struggle with drug and alcohol abuse as well other addictions.[4] When people do struggle with psychological problems and seek out professional help, perceptions of meaning may prove critical for recovery, as studies show that mental health treatments are more effective when the clients perceive life as meaningful.[5] It's quite simple. People who see their lives as having meaning or the potential for meaning are more motivated to get better: they have a *reason* to get mentally healthy.

The benefits of meaning don't stop there. A critical role of meaning is to help us navigate the harsh realities of life. Life is full of stressors: financial struggles, job headaches, health scares, relationship problems, and so on. And at some point everyone will have to face the hardship of losing loved ones. Plus, sometimes these experiences can be rather traumatic such as a cancer diagnosis or a horrible car accident. Studies indicate that meaning in life plays a crucial role in helping people cope with all sorts of life difficulties.[6] It is when people are able to find meaning in dark times that they are able to start to move forward with their lives.

I remember watching an interview with a mother whose son was an American Marine who died in combat in Afghanistan. Understandably, she was beside herself with grief. Losing a child is one of the worst fears of any parent. What made this death even more horrific for this mother was that her son was killed by friendly fire. To her, his death was meaningless. It served no purpose. He did not die saving a fellow soldier or in a critical battle that advanced the military objective. He died because of a mistake that unfortunately sometimes happens in the chaos of war.

How was she going to make sense of this and find meaning in his loss? To move forward and begin to heal she needed to make her son's death matter. In this particular case, the woman said she could not herself find meaning in the loss and was praying to God for guidance. She wanted to know why God took her son this way. Surely his death could not have been as meaningless as it appeared to be on the surface. There must be a grander plan, something she lacked the wisdom to see but desperately wanted revealed.

When a parent loses a child in such a horrible and seemingly senseless manner, how do they typically respond? Some fall into a pit of despair that they never fully come out of. In such cases, this despair is like a black hole: sucked in, the gravitational pull becomes inescapable. Others, though, manage to escape the black hole by seeking and finding meaning.

The death of a child is unfair. It violates our beliefs about how the world should work. Children should not die before their parents. They deserve a chance to have full lives. So when a child dies the belief that the world is meaningful is threatened. And any parent who has lost a child will tell you that the pain never fully disappears. But many parents are able to move forward because they find a way to restore a sense of purpose and meaning.

On a warm and sunny May day in 1980, 13-year-old Cari Lightner and a friend were walking down the street in their suburban neighborhood to the local church to spend their afternoon playing games and hanging out with friends at the church carnival. But they never made it to the carnival. At the same time the girls were giggling and talking while walking in the bike lane to the church, a 47-year-old man was behind the wheel of a moving car heading directly toward them. The man ran Cari over and drove off. She would soon die from the injuries that resulted from her body being hit so hard it was propelled 125 feet.

In addition to being totally devastated by the unexpected and tragic loss of her daughter, Cari's mother, Candace Lightner, soon found out that the man who killed her daughter was drunk when he hit her and already had several drunken driving arrests. This was a man who frequently got drunk and then got behind the wheel. Adding insult to injury, the police informed Candace that the man would likely not serve any time in prison for her daughter's death because the law did not offer stiff penalties for killing someone while driving under the influence of alcohol.

In the face of such a horrible and meaningless loss, Candace turned her despair and anger into a meaningful cause by founding MADD (Mothers Against Drunk Driving), now one of the largest activist organizations in America and one that has played an instrumental role in reducing drunk driving and related injuries and deaths through both public awareness and legislation.

We have all seen it time and time again. When parents lose a child to disease, gun violence, suicide, and numerous other seemingly meaningless events, they respond by channeling the loss into helping others. Grieving parents start charities to find cures for cancer. They go to Congress and advocate for stricter gun regulations. They lobby for more mental health funding. They create foundations in their child's name. They raise and donate large sums of money for charities relevant to their son or daughter's cause of death or life interests. Finding meaning isn't a luxury, it is a necessity. Meaning does not erase the pain, but it helps keep those grieving from loss mentally healthy. In fact, there is now a sizable scientific literature on the importance of meaning for general psychological health as well as coping with trauma and loss.

Meaning is not just about our mental well-being. Turns out, meaning has implications for physical health and longevity. Want to live a long life? Finding meaning may boost your odds, as studies indicate that people who perceive their lives as full of meaning and purpose are at lower risk of mortality. Regardless of age, adults who don't have a sense of meaning in life are at greater risk of death than those who perceive their lives as full of meaning.[7]

But why—and how—does this work? What does finding meaning have to do with actual physical health? For one, meaning motivates healthy behavior. Have you ever heard anyone say "My life is completely meaningless so I guess I should drink a green smoothie and go to the gym"? I doubt it. People who don't feel like they have a purpose or meaning are less inclined to make healthy choices. They feel like they have no reason to bother. We've already seen that meaning reduces the risk of addiction. More broadly, meaning provides a reason to live a healthy life.

The motivational power of meaning has also been found in studies looking at what leads people to use preventive healthcare. In one recent study, for instance, researchers found that the more men and women perceived their lives as having purpose, the more apt they were to have their cholesterol checked or get a colonoscopy.[8] Women were also more likely to get a mammogram and a pap smear, and men were more likely to get a prostate exam if they saw their lives as purposeful. Meaning mobilizes people to take the not-so-pleasant preventive steps that promote longevity. In addition, this research revealed that people who feel purposeful spend fewer days in the hospital. Meaning not only motivates people to take care of themselves but also helps them more quickly get back on the road to good health.

Meaning may even influence health at a more cellular level. In one study, researchers from UCLA followed for a 4-week period a group of women who had lost a close relative to breast cancer.[9] The researchers were interested in whether finding meaning after this loss would positively influence the women's immunity. Their findings showed that meaning did matter for health. Women who reported positive changes in meaning-related goals over the 4-week period also showed increases in natural killer cell cytotoxicity, or NKCC, which represents an important part of the immune system. Natural killer (or NK) cells attack virally infected and tumorigenic cells. In other words, NK cells are an innate biological line of defense, with high NKCC associated with high immune functioning. Thus, pursuing goals that provide meaning may contribute to a healthy biological profile.

This is an exciting area of research that I suspect will grow in the coming years as scientists begin to fully realize the power of meaning in life.

Clearly, meaning is important. It is vital for mental and physical health. But stepping back for a moment, why would humans need meaning to begin with? Why can't we just embrace the idea that we exist by chance and our lives have no real meaning or purpose? We could still enjoy having sex, drinking lattes, and anxiously awaiting the next Star Wars movie. Why is meaning so important for living a good and healthy life?

The answer to this question brings us back to the key issue of death-awareness and begins to reveal how all this is relevant to supernatural thinking and beliefs. Many psychologists have noted that humans are natural meaning makers. We seek order, structure, predictability, and certainty. The ability to make sense of our world is critical for navigating it. But these efforts are not really what distinguish our species from other animals.

At some basic level, all animals have to make sense of their world. Every morning my dog patiently waits for me to get up and let him outside, and upon his return to the house he heads straight to his food bowl in anticipation of me serving him breakfast. He is trained to expect this. He knows the morning ritual. In fact, if my wife or I do not feed him quickly enough, he will start nudging us with his nose. In his own way, he understands that we are his source of food and expects us to do our job of feeding him at a particular time each day.

And it is not just food. When I get home from work every evening my dog waits for me to play fetch with him. And if I do not act quickly enough, he brings the toy to me. This is the only time of day he does this. This is his play time with me and he expects it to happen. Patterns are very much a part of his existence. He has expectations about how the world works. But human meaning-making is on a whole other level. We are meaning makers on steroids. As we've discussed, humans are highly self-aware, and it is the awareness of self and death that makes finding meaning such a crucial and grand enterprise for us.

All the sex, lattes, and Star Wars movies in the world don't change the fact that life is fragile and temporary. A few years ago, my wife and I took our kids to New York City for a family vacation. One of my favorite parts of the trip was our visit to the American Museum of Natural History. The museum had this neat exhibit called the Harriet and Robert Heilbrunn Cosmic Pathway, a spiral that descended several floors of the museum and walked visitors through the 13-billion-year history of the universe. Each step you take down the path is accompanied by information about what was going on in the universe at that time. Once you get to the bottom of the Cosmic Pathway you see the era of humans represented on the time scale only to discover that across a 360-foot-long path our species only gets allocated about a human hair's width of space. Our species is but a tiny speck in the time scale of the universe.

To make matters worse, think about how temporally insignificant a single human life is. Like a lot of little kids in school, I got pretty excited thinking about the birth and death of stars and how one day our star would die and so would any life on Earth. This isn't a threatening thought for a child because in school we learn that we have billions of years before the Sun burns out. If people are still hanging around Earth in billions of years when the Sun swells into a red giant and consumes our planet prior to shrinking into a white dwarf, it's their problem, not ours. They should have gotten their act together and colonized other worlds. But what becomes more threatening for us as we get older is just how short our lives are in comparison to this cosmic timeline.

I'm not done. It gets even worse. When we think about the scale of the universe in terms of size, it only further reminds us of just how little we are. I will be absolutely ecstatic if in my lifetime humans successfully travel to Mars. It will be my generation's moon landing, an amazing feat of science and engineering. The moon is 238,900 miles away from Earth and Mars, at its closest distance, is 33.9 million miles away. The distance can grow to as much as 249 million miles when our planets are farthest apart, as each planet has its own orbital path around the Sun. Getting to Mars would be a pretty astounding accomplishment when you think about how much farther away it is than the moon.

But even a trip to Mars, as far away as it is, is a microscopic step into the cosmos. Just to get to the edge of our solar system is about 9 billion miles.

It gets even more ridiculous if you start thinking about traveling out of our solar system. Our galaxy has at least 100 billion stars. And astronomers estimate that there are over 100 billion galaxies in the universe. So getting to Mars is a big deal to us, but it is objectively hardly a meaningful distance when you think about the size of the universe. We are so tiny!

Hold on. I'm still not done. And it is not going to get any more uplifting. Not only are we tiny specks in the cosmos but also we are quite physically fragile. I will never forget that time as a teenage boy when I decided to jump my bicycle off of a launch ramp I had constructed with some neighborhood friends. It seemed like such an amazing idea at the time. We spent all afternoon building this ramp out of wood we had lying around because we thought it would be great to fly through the air on our bikes just like the pros.

The problem is we weren't pros. Far from it. We placed the ramp about half way down the block in an alley behind my house. I took my bike to the end of the block and got going as fast as I could toward the ramp. I wanted to hit that thing full speed to get the most air possible. It was going to be epic. I should note that, of course, I didn't take any appropriate safety steps. No helmet. No pads. Just shorts, a t-shirt, and the feeling of invincibility that seems to naturally accompany being an adolescent male without fully developed frontal lobes but a seemingly endless supply of testosterone.

But I wasn't invincible, nor was I a capable of pulling off such a stunt. And I found out both of those facts very quickly. I successfully launched off the ramp and got the air I was looking for. Everything was going great until the landing. Once my bike made contact with the ground I flew over the handle bars. You know that feeling of getting the wind knocked out of you? That came first. I couldn't breathe for what felt like an eternity. And once I caught my breath I began to notice how much everything hurt. My ribs, head, arm. I was in agonizing pain. I had all sorts of scrapes and cuts and was lucky to only have sprained my arm. It was epic, alright. An epic fail. If you want a good cringe (and a laugh) look up parkour fails on YouTube. You will see just how physically reckless young males can be.

Humans are not strong and powerful like the superheroes we like to read about in comics and watch in movies. A few minutes without oxygen can lead to brain damage, and it doesn't take much longer to die. Depending on what kind of surface you land on, a relatively short fall can be fatal. Get too hot and you die. Get too cold and you die. Get too thirsty and you die. And so on. Consider all the recent attention being paid to sports-related head trauma. As we begin to learn more and more about the neurological risks associated with concussions we are starting to truly appreciate the fragility of the human brain. Football players may seem like invincible gladiators in their protective pads and helmets, but now we know that their collisions can cause lasting damage.

So what? We're microscopic and fragile beings in the universe. Big deal. The problem isn't just that we are so small and so delicate. The problem is that we are *aware* of how small and vulnerable we are in every way. We are transient physical beings destined to die. If lucky, we can clock in almost a century. And all those years aren't going to be pretty.

As we noted before, our ancestors had to grapple with these insecurities and find solutions. Without modern astronomy, they had no idea just how little they were. But they must have looked at nature with awe and realized that they were just a small part of it. And they knew they couldn't be part of it forever. Indeed, research demonstrates that people tend to associate the wilderness with death.[10]

A couple summers back our family drove out to Yellowstone National Park. I wasn't prepared for the scale of it, so massive and chock-full of a diversity of natural wonders. It was absolutely awe-inspiring. As we were standing there gazing at what looked like an alien world of boiling geysers and fumaroles I was wondering how the first people who came across this site reacted. It must have been both beautiful and terrifying. Can you imagine stumbling across natural phenomena like the Grand Canyon or Yellowstone with no advance warning? They actually sell a book at the park called *Death in Yellowstone: Accidents and Foolhardiness in the First National Park*. Nature can be powerful and deadly.

Consider some recent research I collaborated on that was spearheaded by the social psychologist Matt Vess.[11] We were interested in how the experience of awe would influence perceptions of meaning in life. People often report experiencing awe when taking in nature's wonders. We enjoy this feeling. From this perspective, awe might promote meaning because we find it pleasant. But as I've noted, awe-inspiring natural phenomena can also remind us of just how small and fragile we are, which can in turn call into question our sense of meaning.

In one study, we had research participants watch one of two videos. One of the videos was used to induce a feeling of awe. This video featured a bunch of sweeping panoramic scenes of natural beauty—oceans, waterfalls, jungles, canyons. The other video was a segment of a person being interviewed by Mike Wallace in 1959. It did not contain any stimuli that would provoke awe.

After watching one of these videos, participants responded to questionnaires that assessed mood and perceptions of meaning. As one would expect, watching the awe-inspiring video increased positive mood. However, watching this video also decreased perceptions of meaning in life. The beauty of nature makes us happy but it also reminds us of our insignificance.

In a second study, we sought to determine whether it is, in fact, feelings of being little and insignificant that make awe-inspiring experiences a threat to meaning. We again had participants watch an awe-inspiring nature video or a video not related to awe. Then, in addition to assessing mood and meaning we also assessed the extent to which people felt insignificant in the grand scheme of things.

As before, watching the awe video increased positive mood but also decreased meaning and made people feel insignificant. And through statistical analyses we found evidence that it was these feelings of insignificance that compromised a sense of meaning in life when people were exposed to awe-inspiring natural scenery. No wonder the experience of awe is often associated with spirituality. As I will discuss in the next chapter, when a sense of meaning in life is threatened, people become more religious and more spiritual.

In Chapter 1, I discussed how humans separate themselves from nature. Through culture, our ancestors started the process of making humans distinct from other creatures in an effort to perceive themselves as more than mortal. Other animals are born and die as the natural circle of life. They have no meaning beyond death. Humans prefer to see ourselves differently. We were not born just to die. We have a purpose to serve. Our lives have grander meaning.

The question, then, is: how do we know our lives have meaning? What gives us any confidence that we are anything more than smart monkeys, primates clever enough to make spacecrafts that can help us make that trip to Mars I won't shut up about? As I discuss throughout this book, supernatural thinking can be detected in many of the endeavors that we pursue to find meaning and ultimately see ourselves as more than mortal. Sometimes this supernatural thinking is very easy to detect, and sometimes we have to look really hard to reveal it. But if we dig deep enough we often discover it, even in very unlikely places.

THE IMPORTANCE OF TELEOLOGICAL MEANING

From a scientific point of view, we were not created or designed but instead are the product of evolution. The natural events that shaped our world and our own existence were not purposeful. In other words, life is objectively meaningless. From this perspective, the only way to find meaning is to create your own, because the universe has no meaning or purpose. The universe just is. Though there are certainly a small percentage of people who appear to accept this notion, much of the world's population rejects it. For most humans, the idea that life is inherently meaningless simply will not do.

Instead, people latch onto what I call *teleological meaning*, which is derived from teleological thinking. Teleological thinking is when people perceive phenomena in terms of purpose. When applied to natural phenomena, this type of thinking is generally considered to be flawed because it imposes design where there is no evidence for it. To impose purpose and design where there is none is what researchers refer to as a teleological error.

For instance, the statement "The Sun exists to sustain life on Earth" is a teleological error because it proposes that the Sun has an intended purpose. The Sun certainly allows for life on Earth. Without it life could not exist. However, there is no evidence that this is the Sun's purpose or that it has any purpose at all. We are thankful for the Sun because it keeps us warm and nourishes life. But from a scientific perspective, this is not by design. It just happens to be that the Earth is in that sweet spot, making it not too hot and not too cold. Though viewed as scientifically invalid, teleological errors contribute to meaning.

For many, religion provides the foundation of teleological meaning. Religious narratives offer a teleological explanation of the world and human existence. Creation stories differ from religion to religion, but they all affirm the idea that life is purposeful, that our existence has grander meaning. And though more and more people, including religious leaders such as Pope Francis, embrace scientific theories that challenge traditional creation stories, many of them still hold onto the idea that there is a creator. They suggest, for instance, that God provided the critical spark for the existence of the universe and ultimately life.

But one need not directly invoke religion, or at least religion as we traditionally view it, to turn to teleological thinking. Have you ever heard someone utter the phrase "I guess it wasn't meant to be"? Have you said or thought it yourself? What about the phrase "Everything happens for a reason?" Or, ever heard anyone say, when referring to a romantic relationship, "We were meant to be together"? Even in the absence of religious faith or belief in a deity, people are attracted to teleological meaning. They treat the universe as if it has intentions or a plan. They treat nature is if it has a will or desires.

At a gut level, most of us treat the universe as if it is guided by invisible forces that impose purpose on the world. In fact, cognitive scientists have discovered that even trained physical scientists at some of the most prestigious universities in the world make teleological errors, especially when they have to make quick judgments and thus don't have time to override their gut level response.

In one of these studies,[12] a research team led by Dr. Deborah Kelemen recruited active scientists from the fields of chemistry, physics, and geosciences working at prestigious universities such as Harvard, MIT, and Yale. They also recruited undergraduate college students and members of the community to serve as comparison groups. All of these research participants were given the task of evaluating 100 statements as true or false. Some of these statements reflected teleological errors. For example, "The Sun radiates heat because warmth nurtures life" and "The Earth has an ozone layer in order to protect it from UV light." Again, these statements are considered errors because they infer design and purpose. Warmth does nurture life and the ozone layer does provide protection from UV light, but science does not treat these things as purposeful. So to believe such statements are true represents teleological thinking or, according to a scientific view, teleological judgment errors.

There was more to this study, though. Some of the participants were told to take their time when making their judgments, to really think about their answer. And some of the participants were given a time limit of just over three seconds to make each judgment, what the researchers referred to as a speeded condition. These participants had to give a more gut level response, since they did not have much time to deliberate on the answer. So what happened?

As one might expect, college students and community members judged more of the teleological statements as true (i.e., made more teleological errors) than trained physical scientists did. College students and members of the community, in fact, were quite similar in that both groups thought about 50% of the statements were true. Scientists, on average, indicated that about 22% of the statements were true. So being a trained scientist reduces teleological thinking, but it does not eliminate it.

In addition, the amount of time people were given to make their decision about the validity of teleological statements had a big impact. For all groups, including trained scientists, only being given three seconds significantly increased the likelihood of judging a teleological statement to be true. For example, scientists in this speeded condition judged 30% of the teleological statements to be true. Scientists given as much time as they needed to think the statement over only judged 15% of the statements to be true. Clearly, being given time to think about the answer reduced teleological thinking, but it did not completely prevent it.

Let's think about this a bit more. To be an active physical scientist at a top university such as Yale or Harvard means you have a considerable amount of education and experience conducting research. It also means you are a very accomplished scholar. It is not easy to get a job at any of these universities. So we are talking about highly intelligent and skilled scientists. The correct answer for all of the teleological statements, from a scientific perspective, was false. Think about this experiment as a test like the kind you take in school with a conventional grading scale of 90% and above being an A, 80% to 89% a B, and so on. Even when scientists at top-tier universities were given plenty of time to think through their answers, their average grade was a mid B (85%). And in the speeded condition, the average grade was barely a C (70%). When it comes to thinking like someone who does not see the world as a place of design and purpose, some of the best scientists in the world are B and C students.

What about religious beliefs? Being a scientist may not completely eradicate the tendency to think teleologically, but what about being an atheist? Atheists reject the supernatural. So is teleological thinking confined to believers? First, in their experiments, Kelemen and her research team assessed belief in God and found, not surprisingly, that physical scientists were less likely to believe in God than college students and adult participants from the community. But despite being a less religious group, scientists still made teleological errors. More recent research observed a similar pattern of teleological thinking among nonreligious adults in the United States and Finland.[13]

In another study, the cognitive scientists Bethany Heywood and Jesse Bering focused more directly on this issue of how religiosity or a lack of it might influence teleological thinking.[14] They recruited and interviewed believers and atheists. They specifically asked each person to describe important events from her or his personal life. The researchers were interested in the extent to which people would use teleological language in their descriptions of these events. As one would expect, believers were more likely than atheists to describe life events using teleological statements. It is common for religious people to believe that God has a plan for them, that they were created to serve a purpose, or that life events, even negative ones, are part of God's plan. Thus, it is not surprising that religious people talk about important life events as if they were destined to be.

However, it wasn't just the religious individuals that described life events this way. Half of the atheists provided at least one teleological explanation of an important life event, and three-fourths of the atheists either gave a teleological explanation or indicated having a difficult time not giving one. For example, one atheist participant described the experience of being fired from his job. He made it clear that he does not believe in fate, but at the same time when he lost he job he couldn't help but have the feeling that it was meant to be. In his time of distress and uncertainty, he felt the pull of teleological reasoning.

Atheists consciously reject teleological accounts of how life unfolds. They don't believe that they are the products of a creator or that they were born to serve a grander purpose. They typically don't believe that the universe has a plan for them. Atheists see themselves as logical beings, like Spock from Star Trek. They are not swayed by irrational emotions or wishful thinking. They believe in science and reason. And yet, when they are asked to describe defining events from their lives, atheists struggle to not think in terms of teleological meaning. At some gut level, even atheists are seduced by the idea that everything happens for some magical reason even if that reason is beyond their understanding. Religious people do not have a monopoly on the notion that things are "meant to be."

It is also important to emphasize that teleological thinking is a form of supernatural thinking, as it violates our scientific understanding of how the natural world works. Teleological explanations of natural phenomena and life events invoke supernatural agents and forces such as God and karma. To have a gut-level belief in fate or destiny is to endorse the supernatural. Of course, atheists are not consciously making such an endorsement, but, as I point out throughout this book, actions speak louder than words. And atheists' actions suggest that they too engage in this form of supernatural thinking.

As I said at the start of this chapter, finding meaning in life is a fundamental human endeavor. But do these supernatural beliefs—which are much more widespread than many of us realize—provide the meaning that we're looking for? That is, is there any scientific evidence that teleological thinking helps people meet the human need to perceive life as meaningful?

Studies indicate that teleological thinking does imbue life with meaning. Specifically, research reveals that the more teleological errors people make in the judgment task previously described, the higher they score on a questionnaire assessing belief that life is purposeful.[15] In other words, the more inclined you are to endorse teleological explanations of natural phenomena, the more inclined you are to believe that your life has some sense of purpose. Further, as I discuss in later chapters, many religious and spiritual supernatural beliefs that involve teleological thinking are positively associated with perceptions of meaning and help people cope with threats to meaning. So teleological judgments, though inaccurate from a scientific standpoint, appear to contribute to the general sense of life's purpose.

DEATH DRIVES THE NEED FOR PURPOSE

Let's return to the heart of this issue: why humans need meaning. The realization that we are transient and fragile beings destined to die inspires a longing for teleological meaning, which helps us feel like we are more than mortal.

However, does death-awareness influence the human tendency to engage in teleological thinking and beliefs? We conducted a series of studies in my lab to test this possibility.[16] In one experiment, we randomly assigned research participants to one of two conditions. In one condition, participants were instructed to spend a few minutes writing about their mortality, just like in the studies I described in chapter 1. Engaging in this writing exercise increases the awareness of death. Participants in the other condition wrote about the experience of physical pain. We chose pain as our control condition because we wanted both tasks to involve thinking about something unpleasant, something that would make participants feel anxious. However, our assumption was that thinking about pain would not increase death-awareness to the same level as actually thinking about death.

After completing the writing task portion of the study, all of the participants completed a teleological judgment task similar to the one previously described. Specifically, they were presented with teleological statements such as "Forest fires occur in order to clean up the forests" and "The function of rivers is to move water." Again, these statements are considered teleological errors because they impose purpose and design where there is none from a scientific perspective. Forests fires clean the forest, but that is not why they occur. Forest fires have no inherent purpose. Likewise, rivers move water, but nature did not magically create them to serve this function. They just do. After reading each statement, research participants indicated whether the statement was true or false.

If death-awareness inspires efforts to seek out teleological meaning, then experimentally heightening the awareness of death should increase the number of teleological errors people make. This is precisely what we observed.

In another study, instead of using the teleological judgment task, we administered a teleological meaning questionnaire that we created specifically for this research. For this questionnaire, participants read statements such as "The world has a grand purpose" and "There's a purpose for everything, even if we don't realize it" and indicated to what extent they believed each statement to be true. So in this study, we were not simply assessing teleological errors made when explaining natural phenomena. We were instead measuring people's broader belief in teleological meaning. And we found that the awareness of death increases this belief. Participants who wrote about death subsequently scored significantly higher on the belief in teleological meaning than participants who wrote about pain.

As part of this research project, we also approached this link between death-awareness and teleological thinking from the other direction. If people are attracted to teleological beliefs because it helps them cope with the awareness of death, then perhaps when people are encouraged to engage in teleological thinking, they will experience a decreased awareness of death. To test this, research participants were given the teleological judgment task. However, in this study, after making their judgments, we affirmed teleological thinking for one group of participants by giving them false feedback that each teleological statement was true.

For example, after responding to the statement "The Earth has an ozone layer in order to protect it from UV radiation," participants were told that the correct answer is TRUE. In addition, to make it seem more credible, we provided an explanation for the teleological assertion. For this example, participants were presented with the statement "The Earth's ozone layer is an effective shield from some kinds of UV radiation. Without the ozone layer, it would be very difficult for many kinds of life to live on the Earth's surface." This explanation does not actually provide any compelling evidence that the statement is true. There is no compelling evidence that the statement is true. That is why it is a teleological error. However, the information we provided appears to bolster the validity of the claim because it further explains the benefits of the ozone layer.

Essentially, for these participants, we pushed a teleological view of the natural world. But we had another condition as well. And in this condition, participants did the teleological judgment task but were provided no feedback. They read each statement and made their judgment but we did not give them any additional information as to whether or not these teleological statements were true or false. That is, in this control condition, we did not reinforce or encourage teleological thinking.

Next, we measured participants' level of death-awareness. Psychologists have developed what is often referred to as "cognitive accessibility measures" to detect the extent to which a concept is readily available or accessible in one's mind. There are a number of unique types of accessibility measures. The one we chose for this study was what is called a stem completion task. For this task, research participants are presented with a bunch of incomplete word stems one at a time on a computer screen. Their job is to complete the word stem using the first word that comes to mind. Since we were interested in death-awareness, we employed a version of the task that had incomplete words that could be completed to be death-related words. For instance, participants would see the stem COFF_ _, which could be completed to become the death-related word COFFIN or the non-death-related word COFFEE.

When doing this task, participants get dozens of stems that are purely neutral. They cannot be completed with any words related to death. These are what we call fillers, and they serve the purpose of reducing suspicion about the purpose of the task. That is, we don't want participants to figure out that the theme is death. But every now and then, the stem they see can be completed with a death-related word or a neutral word. And these are the word completions we are interested in.

The basic idea is that the more of these stems that participants complete to be death words, the more accessible death thoughts are in their minds. If death-awareness is high, then it should be easier and thus more likely that someone will generate a death-related word when trying to complete the word stem. For instance, if death-awareness is high, the word "coffin" should more readily come to mind when someone is presented with the stem COFF _ _. After the experimental session, we summed up the number of stems each participant completed to be a death word to create a total death thought accessibility score. The higher the score, the higher the level of death-awareness.

If teleological thinking helps people feel more than mortal, then facilitating this type of thinking might reduce the extent which death is easily accessible in one's mind. Based on this idea, we predicted that participants who were in the condition in which we encouraged teleological thinking would have lower death thought accessibility scores. They should complete fewer of the stems with death-related words.

Our prediction was supported. Participants who received the feedback promoting teleological thinking had significantly lower death thought accessibility scores than participants who did not receive such feedback. When the world looks like a place where everything exists or happens for a reason, the mind is better protected from the threat of death. No wonder religious narratives that offer teleological origins of the world are so pervasive across culture and time. They provide the perceptions of meaning in life that keep threatening thoughts of death at bay. Indeed, the social psychologist Jeff Schimel and his colleagues found that presenting people who believe in creationism with arguments challenging their teleological view of how humans and other animals came to exist increased death thought accessibility.[17]

MEANING IS FOUND IN THE HEART, NOT THE BRAIN

I want to return to this idea that even atheists who reject the supernatural and scientists who are trained to not rely on teleological explanations of the world do, in fact, engage in teleological thinking. If these types of people consciously reject supernatural explanations of the world and our existence, how could they get meaning from teleological thinking? Well, the short answer is meaning is found in the heart, not the brain.

Many people who reject the supernatural do so through thoughtful reasoning. They think hard about whether there is any compelling reason to believe in forces beyond the scope of our understanding of the laws of nature and then conclude that such beliefs are unwarranted. However, when these people are making teleological judgments, they are not fully deploying their rational thinking abilities.

Think back to the study I previously described in which physical scientists at prestigious universities were found to make teleological errors. Remember, one of the conditions in the study involved only giving the participants a few seconds to make their judgment concerning whether the teleological statement was true or false. In such a speeded condition, participants have to act quickly. They don't have sufficient time to reason through their choice. Under these circumstances involving more intuitive judgments, people, including trained scientists, are more prone to think teleologically. The scientists in the speeded condition made twice as many errors as the scientists in the condition with no time limit.

Teleological meaning comes more from an intuitive feeling than it does from a rational decision-making process. In the study examining teleological explanations for life events, many of the atheists struggled because their rational thought processes were at odds with their gut feelings. Their heads said such thinking was irrational, but their hearts said otherwise. Of course, I do not literally mean their hearts. All of our thought processes occur in the brain. But this is how we metaphorically represent this struggle. Our feelings and intuitions come from the heart, and our more calculative, empirical, and logical thoughts come from the head.

At some level, we all have this internal struggle between our intuitive feelings and our more rational thought processes. Our hearts and heads pull us in different directions. Anyone who is a parent knows exactly what I am talking about. Often, our hearts tell us to spoil our kids, to do everything we can to make them happy and comfortable. This comes from the feeling of love. At the same time, we also know that sometimes what is best for our children involves denying their wishes and impulses. Our rational parenting side drives us to create rules and consequences that will help keep our children healthy and safe and allow them to develop into responsible and hard-working adults. Most people would agree that good parents use both their hearts and their heads.

It might seem like thoughtful and rational thinking is always best, but intuition is also important. Many of our most fulfilling life experiences come from following our hearts. And studies indicate that meaning is often derived from intuition. That is, to find meaning, we often follow our hearts, not our heads. For instance, in my research lab we regularly administer an intuitive versus rational thinking measure created by personality researchers as a quick way to classify people as being more intuitive or more rational.[18] The measure is simple. Participants are asked whether their sense of self is located in the heart or the head. That is, what metaphoric identity best represents their personality? Are they a head person or a heart person? Interestingly, in our work and in research conducted in other labs, people tend to be pretty evenly divided on this question.

I should note that these labels also map onto more sophisticated personality measurements of analytical and intuitive thinking. Head people score higher on analytical thinking, and heart people score higher on intuition.

In the studies done in my lab, we also measure perceptions of meaning in life with different meaning in life questionnaires. And in these studies, we reliably find that people who classify themselves as heart people report significantly higher levels of perceived meaning in life than people who classify themselves as head people. More broadly, a number of studies using distinct measures of analytic and intuitive thinking reveal that meaning is found in intuition.[19] The more people embrace their intuitive side, the more they see life as full of meaning and purpose.

Not surprisingly, heart people, or intuitive thinkers, are more inclined to endorse the supernatural. For instance, heart people report being significantly more religious than head people and are also more likely to believe in supernatural phenomena such as miracles and the power of positive energy. Consider, for example, a recent project my lab took part in with a larger group of researchers in the United States and Europe. Across multiple studies including American and European participants, we observed that heart people score higher on a range of religious questionnaires and that this effect is the result of differences in intuitive thinking between heart and head people.[20] Participants who labeled themselves as heart people were more inclined to use intuitive thinking, which in turn inclined them to be more open to the existence of supernatural religious agents such as God. This work is consistent with a number of other studies showing that the less people tend to rely on intuition, the less likely they are to believe in God, identify as religious, and endorse a range of supernatural beliefs.[21]

Importantly, as we've noted, we all possess both sides. Sure, some will label themselves head people when forced to pick between the head and the heart, but this does not make them entirely heartless. Think about other personality traits that differ between people such as neuroticism. Neuroticism is a dimension of personality that represents a tendency to be anxious, to worry about things. Some people are highly neurotic. They worry about everything all of the time. Some people are extremely low in neuroticism. They seem to not have a care in the world. But even these folks have the capacity for anxiety. With the right pressures or stressors, they start freaking out just like everyone else.

I was acquainted with a guy in college who was one of the most happy-go-lucky guys I had ever met. He never worried about anything. Finals week, so what. He'll get through it. Rent is coming due and he hasn't been paid yet, no big deal. He'll work it out somehow. His Zen could not be broken, that is, until his girlfriend told him that she thought she might be pregnant (she wasn't). All of a sudden, he became quite intimately familiar with the feelings of worry and anxiety that people high in the trait of neuroticism commonly experience.

Likewise, even people who would largely consider themselves head people have felt the pull of the heart. And as I have discussed, researchers have exploited this fact with experimental designs that force people to use their more intuitive side. Have you ever felt emotionally moved by a movie or piece of music? Have you ever read an inspirational story of personal triumph that gave you that tingly feeling in your skin, making the hair on your arms stand up? In a religious context, people might refer to such feelings as spiritual.

Consider the following study. A group of researchers put people in an intuitive or rational mindset by having them write about an experience they had in which a positive outcome resulted from them following their instincts or intuitions (intuitive mindset condition) or from careful and reflective thought (rational mindset condition). They then administered a questionnaire assessing belief in God and found that participants in the intuitive mindset condition believed in God more than participants in the rational mindset condition.[22]

Intuitive thinking inspires faith. Christians don't say they have Jesus in their heads; they say they have Jesus in their hearts. More broadly, when people rely on their gut feeling, or act with their heart instead of their head, they think more teleologically and are more influenced by supernatural beliefs. And they are also better able to easily perceive life as meaningful.

When we think carefully and rationally about the world and our mortal predicament, we often feel small and insignificant. But when we trust our intuitions and follow our hearts, we feel more than mortal because we feel like we are here for a reason. We weren't just born to die and slowly disintegrate into cosmic dust, forgotten forever. We were born to serve a purpose.

Interestingly, at some implicit level people seem to understand this connection between the heart and supernatural beliefs. In the head versus heart research I previously mentioned, for one of the studies, participants were given the task of looking at a picture of a 44-year-old man wearing glasses and a sweatshirt. All of the participants looked at the same guy, but there was one critical difference. For half of the participants, the man was pointing at his head. For the other half, the man was pointing at his heart. While looking at this picture, the participants were asked to rate the man on a number of different traits. One of the traits was belief in God.

The prediction was that the man pointing to his heart would be more likely to be perceived as a believer than the man pointing to his head. And this prediction was supported by the data. The research participants knew nothing about this man and had no real reason to perceive him as a believer or atheist. Yet, the subtle gesture of pointing to his heart moved participants to perceive him as more religious.

Earlier in the chapter, I talked about the many ways that people seek to find meaning in an experience or loss that seems meaningless, such as the loss of a child. Certainly, one could argue that when people are advocating for social policies or starting nonprofit organizations they are not necessarily seeking teleological meaning. Often, these parents are trying to make their loss meaningful by working to make sure no other parent has to go through such a horrible experience.

However, in most of these cases, the positive real changes they are trying to make in order to help others do invoke some level of teleological meaning derived from supernatural beliefs. For instance, parents will often say that God must have taken their child for a reason. God was having them experience such a loss so that they would be inspired to go out and make a difference in the lives of others.

In other words, the death of their child was not random. God has a plan. Their child's death was intended to serve a larger purpose. Psychologists have documented a diverse range of coping mechanisms that people rely on and have found that when individuals are dealing with the loss of a loved one they are especially likely to turn to faith and a belief in fate.[23] Fate is about teleological meaning. It advances the notion that everything that happens is part of a grand plan.

Over the next few chapters I discuss the growing body of research revealing the many ways that people, believers and nonbelievers alike, engage in supernatural thinking and turn to supernatural beliefs in order to allay their deepest existential fears and find or maintain perceptions of transcendent meaning.

Religion

The Most Powerful Form of Supernatural Belief

I was working on this book when the news broke that former First Lady Nancy Reagan had died. The media coverage that followed her death was quite touching. Some of the stories focused on her contributions to society as First Lady. A lot of the coverage put the spotlight on the very dedicated and loving relationship she had with her husband, former President Ronald Reagan. She was one of her husband's most trusted advisors and an extremely supportive and protective wife. They were virtually inseparable.

Her husband, President Reagan, had of course died years before from Alzheimer's disease, a loss that would be difficult for any spouse and must have been especially hard for a woman who had dedicated herself completely to her husband. Part of what was so touching about the tributes paid to Mrs. Reagan was the acknowledgment made by every news outlet I watched that she is now reunited with her loving husband. Whether you believe in life after death or not, the sentiment is heartwarming. How can one not be moved by the idea that two people who loved each other dearly for over 50 years are once again together?

Many atheists will tell you that that hardest part of disbelief is accepting the idea that when your loved ones die you will never see them again. Our connection to others is powerful. Humans are inherently social animals. We need relationships to thrive. The close bonds we have with romantic partners, family, and our dearest friends are vital for our psychological and physical health. In fact, studies show that loneliness is as deadly as abusing alcohol, smoking, and obesity.[1] Not surprisingly then, a good portion of our time and energy is spent seeking and maintaining close relationships.

In chapter 2, I talked about how hard it is for a parent to lose a child. It is arguably the worst kind of loss. Losing any loved one is extremely difficult, though. And, for many, one of the only sources of emotional reprieve when relationships are severed by death is the hope of being reunited for eternity in the afterlife. Indeed, research indicates that one way people cope with the loss of loved ones is by believing they can still talk to them even though they have died, what scholars have termed "after death communications."[2]

There are many reasons people are attracted to religion. It offers structure to our lives, a set of rules and moral guidelines. Religion offers cultural continuity—the idea that we are part of a group that has been around for some time and will continue after we are gone. Religion connects us to others. Most people who worship do not do so alone. They congregate with other people. Religion is a way to be part of a group and form close relationships. Religion also often facilitates social clout and standing in the community. Some people go to church, in part, because it is a good business decision.

In short, religion yields a number of returns that have little or nothing to do with the supernatural. Even some atheists attend church because they recognize the social and cultural benefits of doing so. One study found that about 20% of atheist scientists from elite universities attend church to expose their children to religion, appease a spouse, or connect to a broader community.[3]

However, at the core of religion is the supernatural. More than anything else, religion offers a way for people to feel like they and the ones they love can, in some way, be more than mortal. All of the more practical social and cultural benefits of religion could perhaps be reproduced with secular belief systems. But clearly our ancestors didn't find such secular group identities sufficient. They wanted immortality and meaning that transcends the death of the body. And so do modern humans. Sure, participation in traditional religious organizations is on the decline in many parts of the world, including the United States. And this might be, in part, because people are finding more and more opportunities to find structure, meet social needs, and secure important business contacts in more secular venues. But, as I discuss later in the chapter, there is plenty of evidence that religion is thriving. For now, I want to dig a little deeper into this assertion that religion is ultimately about offering a supernatural solution to the problem of death.

IS A MIND AWARE OF DEATH A RELIGIOUS MIND?

My dad was very much a man of God. He dedicated his entire adult life to his religious faith as a missionary, pastor, and chaplain. In these roles, my father helped many people come to terms with their own approaching mortality as well as the death of their loved ones. He reassured people suffering from terminal illness that upon death they would enter a new and eternal phase of existence, and one that would be pain and sorrow free. He comforted those who had lost children, spouses, parents, siblings, and dear friends by sharing with them his faith in the hereafter, his belief that their loved ones were no longer suffering but were now waiting for them in a better place.

On a few occasions my father and I had some pretty heavy conversations about the validity of religious belief. As young people often do, I was questioning his traditional views. How could he hold such beliefs? There was no compelling scientific evidence supporting the claims made in the Bible. And he would respond by sharing these experiences he had with people in their most vulnerable and hopeless states. Faith wasn't about evidence. It was about hope. As I discussed in the last chapter, faith is a matter of the heart, not the head.

A number of years ago my dad was diagnosed with multiple systems atrophy, or MSA. It is a very rare and horrific neurological disease. There is no cure or effective treatment, and there is no real understanding of what causes it. Essentially, once a person develops this disease he or she has around 5 or so years to live. These remaining years of life are accompanied by a gradual decline in the ability to walk, talk, and do basic self-care. A distinct characteristic of the disease is a diminished ability of the brain to regulate blood pressure, making sufferers vulnerable to frequent falls caused by loss of consciousness.

When my father was diagnosed with MSA he was told to start making preparations for his decline and death. Life would get harder and harder as he started to lose his mobility and eventually his ability to talk and swallow, and the actual dying process would likely not be a peaceful experience. These forecasts were all correct. From the time of diagnosis to his death, my dad would experience being confined to a chair, not being able to feed or bathe himself, having a difficult time talking, occasionally passing out, which would often result in injury from falling over, and so on. He slowly lost almost everything that made him the physically strong and independent man I grew up with. But he never lost his faith. And this faith helped him make this final journey to death honorably.

One day my dad said something to me I will never forget. At this point, his disease was fairly advanced. He was not able to leave the house or be left home alone. We (me, my wife, and our two kids) were in town visiting him, and I volunteered to stay at the house and watch him so other family members could take my mother to a movie. At this point, my mom rarely got out and had definitely earned a little respite. So it was just me and my dad hanging out and watching television. My dad was not much of a talker. I think he preferred to let his actions speak for him. It was common to have long periods of silence when the two of us were together. And at this point talking was a bit difficult for him. He could still vocalize his thoughts, but his words were labored.

However, without prompting, he began talking about his feelings concerning his condition. He made a joke about how physically helpless he had become. To the end, my dad never lost his humor. But he was worried about being a burden on my mother. He very dispassionately suggested that he might need to be put in a nursing home to make my mom's life easier, something my mom was definitely not going to consent to. He wasn't complaining; he was being practical.

He then shifted his attention to more substantive thoughts on his prognosis. He was not sad. Instead, he expressed a feeling of gratitude and optimism. He said that facing this terminal illness was his final earthly test, the last leg of a journey. He did not feel sorry for himself. He felt thankful for the good life that he believed God gave him. And he noted that it would be ridiculous to feel sorry for himself when there is so much suffering in the world. He was given so much more than so many others and would not indulge in self-pity. Through his faith, my father was able to take perspective, to appreciate the 74 years of life he experienced.

Having recently lost my father to this degenerative neurological disease, I saw the power of the promise of life after death firsthand. My father's faith allowed him to counsel so many others facing loss and death. Ultimately, his faith helped him face his own mortality with a level of strength and courage that was truly inspiring. My dad had what I described in chapter 2 as teleological meaning. He believed that God had a purpose for his life and death. And he hoped he was fulfilling that purpose. More than anything, he felt the security of the promise of eternal salvation offered by his Christian faith. His body was dying, but his soul was going home. And despite how bad things got, he never lost that faith. If he had any doubts, he did not share them with me.

Every day people are facing death and drawing on their supernatural religious beliefs for strength and comfort, just as my father did. There is now a sizable scientific literature on religion as a coping resource for dealing with terminal illness. For example, in one early study, in a sample of patients receiving cancer treatment, higher levels of religiosity were associated both with greater perceptions of meaning in life and lower levels of despair.[4] In another study of patients with advanced cancer, researchers similarly found that the more patients turned to religion to cope with their diagnosis the better psychologically adjusted they appeared to be.[5]

As one review of the literature summed it up, people all over the world facing a range of illnesses from heart disease to AIDS turn to their religious beliefs to find a sense of meaning and face their diagnoses without falling into a state of hopelessness.[6] And using religion to cope can actually reduce symptoms and improve health. I discuss this research in detail in chapter 6.

It is not at all surprising that people who are already deeply religious turn to their faith to cope with issues related to death and dying. After all, what would be the point of having a religion if you couldn't lean on it during your darkest times? The real question then is: does the awareness of death actually inspire people to become religious?

The idea that the awareness and resulting fear of death sparked religion is an old one. Lots of smart people, including a number of philosophers, anthropologists, sociologists, and psychologists, have made this claim. Larry King, famed broadcaster and longtime host of CNN's Larry King Live, succinctly summed up this idea in a recent interview when he stated, "I think the only reason for religion is death. If you didn't die, there would be no religion."

In chapter 1, I discussed the work of the cultural anthropologist Ernest Becker. Becker, like many other existential thinkers, believed that religion is ultimately about fighting back against the existential threat of death. I focus on Becker in particular because his work was the primary inspiration for terror management theory (TMT), which is the theory that has generated the most scientific research linking death-awareness to religious and other forms of supernatural belief.

Becker actually viewed all cultural belief systems, religious and secular alike, as serving a death-denial function. He proposed that people know that the body dies and thus they attach their symbolic sense of self (their identity) to religion because religious beliefs offer two types of death-transcendence. First, religion offers symbolic death-transcendence— the feeling that part of one's self will live on through a cultural group or in the memories of others. Other group identities also offer symbolic immortality. For instance, Becker pointed out that nationalism is akin to religion in that it offers a way to feel part of something bigger and longer lasting than oneself. Consistent with this reasoning, many studies have shown that people become more patriotic and willing to make personal sacrifices for their nation after thinking about death.[7]

Critically, religion offers literal immortality—the feeling that the self will actually survive physical death in some form. Secular identities and belief systems do not so directly offer a means to escape the finality of death. This is why many scholars have argued that secular beliefs will never fully replace religion.

Becker and many others have framed religion as a response to the threat of death, but what does the scientific research reveal? Psychologists have been examining the relationship between the fear of death and religiosity for decades and the results have been somewhat mixed. There have certainly been a number of studies showing that higher fear of death is associated with greater religiosity. For instance, one recent study looking at thousands of people across three nations (Malaysia, Turkey, and the United States) found that high anxiety about death is associated with greater religiosity and that this relationship is similar across the three countries.[8] But there have also been studies showing the opposite pattern: high religiosity is associated with low fear of death. And there have also been studies that find no relationship between these variables as well as studies that suggest that the relationship is rather complex.

For instance, some surveys suggest that it is people who are anxiously uncertain about their faith that have the greatest fear of death.[9] The idea is that people who do not know what to believe may have the most to worry about. Hardcore believers aren't so worried, because they are confident that they will be rewarded in the afterlife. Why fear mortality if death is merely a doorway to another realm of existence? Likewise, perhaps those who are confident that there is no God aren't particularly excited about mortality but at least feel they don't have to worry about being eternally punished for their lack of faith. As a result, they can invest in other symbolic structures that make them feel that they have some kind of meaning that will survive physical death. But those who are uncertain may be vulnerable to greater anxiety about what death means and what may or may not happen afterward.

The problem with all of these studies is that, because they are correlational in nature, it is impossible to know which variable is the cause and which is the effect. Does the awareness and ultimately fear of death motivate people to become religious? Or might religious belief lead to a fear of death? Correlation studies also often make it difficult to determine whether two variables even have a cause and effect relationship. Perhaps another unmeasured variable increases both a fear of death and religion.

Even if it is the case that fear of death instigates religion, it remains unclear as to what kind of relationship to expect between death anxiety and religious belief. A positive correlation between these two variables would be consistent with the idea that fear leads to religion. However, one could use that same explanation to predict the opposite relationship. If people turn to religion to cope with the fear of death, then higher religiosity might be associated with a lower fear of death. As people find comfort in the promise of death-transcendence offered by religion, they should be less worried about their mortality. It is no wonder the literature on this issue is all over the place. This is where good old experimental science comes in.

If is true that religion is ultimately about supernatural beliefs that allow us to feel immortal, then we would expect that experimentally heightening the awareness of death would increase religious beliefs. The psychologists Ara Norenzayan and Ian Hansen at the University of British Columbia conducted a series of experiments to test this idea.[10] In the first study of this series, similar to other studies examining TMT, research participants completed a questionnaire in which they were asked to briefly write about death or a control topic not related to death. Next, the participants were asked to indicate their level of religiosity and the extent to which they believe in God.

The researchers found that participants asked to write about death reported being significantly more religious than participants who did not write about death. An identical pattern was found on the belief in God. Simply thinking about death increases religious identification and belief in God. These findings are especially powerful considering that religious identification and belief in God are fairly stable attitudes and the researchers were able to influence them, even if only slightly and temporarily, with the pretty nonthreatening task of spending a few minutes thinking and writing about death. Imagine what could happen with a far more impactful reminder of mortality such as an actual threat of death.

After finding evidence that the awareness of death triggers religious inclinations, Norenzayan and Hansen conducted additional studies to further probe how knowledge of mortality impacts supernatural thought processes. In one of these studies, they considered whether or not death-awareness increases people's tendency to accept supernatural explanations for the effectiveness of prayer. People often pray for others who are sick or in need. And sometimes these people get better or their situations improve. But there are reasons to be skeptical that prayer had anything to do with these improvements.

A local woman in the town I grew up in loved to tell a story about how God answered her prayers. When she was struggling financially, unable to afford groceries, she prayed to God for help. Soon after she started praying, a bag of groceries mysteriously appeared on her doorstep. God had answered her prayers. Of course there are other possible explanations. Perhaps neighbors, friends, or fellow congregants from her church knew of her need and wanted to anonymously offer help. One of the more practical benefits of being part of a religious congregation is that the church functions as a social safety net. Good churches help out their members when they are in need. In this way, churches serve a vital role in the community.

But that is not how this woman saw it. It wasn't her fellow churchgoers that came to the rescue. It was divine intervention. These kinds of anecdotes are common. According to a 2010 USA Today/Gallup poll, 83% of Americans believe God answers prayers.[11] But why are people so quick to attribute positive life outcomes to God? Does death-awareness make people more inclined to believe in the power of prayer? Norenzayan and Hansen tested this possibility.

In this study, to elevate awareness of death, some participants read a story that involved someone dying. Participants in the control condition read a similar story; however, this story did not contain any death-related themes. In other words, some participants were exposed to material reminding them of mortality and some were not. Subsequently, participants read an article about women at a Korean fertility clinic being significantly more likely to get pregnant if they had been prayed for. After reading this article, participants completed questions assessing the extent to which the article provides evidence that God exists and can answer prayers.

Does death-awareness make people more likely to believe in a higher power that answers prayers? It seems that the answer is yes. Participants who read the story that contained death themes were more likely to believe that the article about the Korean fertility clinic provided good reason to believe in God and the ability of God to answer prayers. Experiences that remind people of the finite nature of life make them more open to the possibility that God uses supernatural powers to intervene in the lives of humans.

Interestingly, in a subsequent study, the researchers found a similar effect when the word "God" was replaced with the word "Buddha," even among Christian participants. In this study, participants read a similar story about the power of prayer—women in fertility treatment were more likely to get pregnant if they were prayed for. However, this time, the article made it clear that these were Buddhist prayers. Therefore, the effectiveness of prayer in this case suggested specifically that Buddha is a supernatural agent that can answer prayers. Critically, the participants in this study were North Americans, many of them Christian. One might assume that most American Christians would not be inclined to grant Buddha any supernatural power since most American Christians are monotheistic (i.e., believe in one God, a Christian God) and thus do not acknowledge deities from other religions. But this is why we conduct experiments. We want to know how people actually behave, not how they think they would behave.

The researchers suspected that heightened death-awareness would motivate belief in the power of prayer, regardless of which deity it was attributed to. That is, they hypothesized that death-awareness would generally make any kind of supernatural religious idea attractive. And they were right. Participants who read about death exhibited a heightened belief that Buddha is a higher power who can answer prayers. And this effect held even when the researchers only analyzed the results of Christian participants. This is just one study, but it suggests that death-awareness can motivate people to affirm any evidence for a higher power, even if this evidence does not conform to their particular religious faith.

Certainly there are many religious people who would not take such a flexible position on the power of different gods. It is important to note, however, that this research was not focused on identifying differences within religious groups on how flexible their beliefs are. Such research does exist. For instance, surveys demonstrate that a small percentage of believers could be classified as religious fundamentalists and these folks have a very rigid and narrow theological worldview. Christian fundamentalists would not be so open to the idea that Buddha exists and can answer prayers. I consider in more detail the nature and consequences of religious fundamentalism in chapter 7.

Not only do thoughts of death promote religion but also religion helps keep people from thinking about death. In chapter 2, I discussed research connecting teleological thinking to the awareness of death and briefly mentioned a study by Jeff Schimel and his research team showing that challenging creationist teleological beliefs increased death-related thoughts.[12] In their experiment, participants were recruited based on their response to a series of questions regarding creation beliefs. Specifically, in a large survey potential participants indicated their belief in the Judeo-Christian account of creation as well as their belief in the theory of evolution.

The researchers identified and recruited two groups based on responses to these questions: those who held Christian creationist views and rejected evolution and those who accepted evolution and rejected creationism. Importantly, participants did not know that was the reason they were being recruited. All they knew was that they had qualified for an experiment based on some characteristic determined by a large survey.

Upon arriving at the laboratory, research participants were informed that the experiment was a test of how people read and process information and that they would be reading an article and then completing some other tasks. In reality, the researchers were interested in whether challenging the validity of creationism would increase the awareness of death among those who hold creationist beliefs. To test this, some of the participants were given an article to read that described scientific findings inconsistent with the idea of creationism, such as fossil record evidence in support of evolutionary processes.

Participants in a control condition read a more neutral article about the history of measuring people's attitudes. Next, participants completed the word fragment task described in chapter 2. As a reminder, this task involves presenting participants with word stems and having them complete the stem. Some of the words could be completed to be death or non-death-related words (e.g., COFF_ _ could be COFFEE or COFFIN). Higher death-awareness is reflected by a greater number of words being completed as death-related. The more death is on people's mind, the more likely the death-related word completions will pop into their thoughts.

The researchers hypothesized that if religious beliefs help people manage concerns about death then undermining these beliefs would increase the awareness of death. Thus, for those who believe in the Christian narrative of creation, being presented with evidence that is inconsistent with that narrative should elevate thoughts related to mortality. Results supported this hypothesis. Reading the article supporting evolution increased the number of stems completed as death words, but only among strict creationists—those who rejected evolution.

This finding complements research I discussed in chapter 1 showing that thinking about death increased people's acceptance of intelligent design theory and decreased their acceptance of evolutionary theory. Of course it is not the case that belief in creationism and evolution are inherently at odds. To make the experiment as clean as possible, the researchers specifically recruited those who exclusively hold a creationist or evolutionary viewpoint. In reality, many people take a more hybrid perspective. They accept the overwhelming evidence in support of evolutionary processes, but they hold onto the idea that there is a supernatural creator, that God put evolution in motion.

The appeal of this belief makes sense. If religious beliefs help people cope with insecurities about being mortal beings destined to die, then holding on to some aspect of these beliefs will be desirable. Scientific evidence may challenge the specific views of when and how life emerged on this planet. But science may never be able to eliminate the idea that a supernatural being provided the spark.

SUPERNATURAL RELIGIOUS BELIEFS OFFER TELEOLOGICAL MEANING

Supernatural religious beliefs do more than offer a direct path to surviving mortality. In fact, some religious traditions have very little explicit focus on the afterlife. However, all religions offer teleological meaning, which, as discussed in chapter 2, is a key component of feeling more than mortal. In particular, religious narratives offer humans an explanation for their existence. Thus, supernatural religious beliefs should be linked not only to death-related thoughts but also to perceptions of meaning.

Many studies connect religiosity to meaning in life. The more religious people report being, the more they also report that their lives are full of meaning and purpose. In fact, this positive relationship between religiosity and meaning is one of the most reliable effects I find in my own research. Almost without fail, I observe that measures of religiosity are positively correlated with measures of meaning. In addition, I almost always find that believers report higher levels of meaning than atheists. This does not mean that atheists are walking around in existential despair with no sense of meaning or purpose. In general, people, believers and nonbelievers alike, find life to be pretty meaningful. The data simply indicates that believers experience the highest levels of perceived meaning.

Most of the research linking religiosity to meaning is correlational. And as I have noted already, these types of studies have serious limitations. In addition, most of these correlational studies do not focus specifically on supernatural religious beliefs but instead simply ask people to indicate the importance of religion in their lives. Remember, religion does a

lot for people, and many of the benefits of being part of a religious community may have little to do with the supernatural. Thus, to truly test the
potential for supernatural religious beliefs to help people feel meaningful,
experimental research specifically focused on the supernatural aspects of
religiosity is required.

Over the last few years my lab has been doing this kind of experimental work. For instance, in one study we focused on people's willingness
to believe that religious supernatural agents such as God and guardian
angels influence the lives of humans.[13] We were particularly interested
in the idea that people might believe in miracles as part of their effort to
gain a sense of teleological meaning. To test this, we randomly assigned
Christian participants to one of two conditions. Half the participants
read an existential essay that challenges meaning. It focuses on how min-
iscule our world is in the universe, how short our time has been as a species on the cosmic timescale, and how brief the lifespan of a human being
is. Research shows that reading this kind of existential essay increases a
sense of meaninglessness and motivates efforts to restore perceptions of
meaning.[14]

Participants in the control condition did not read the essay reminding
people of their cosmic insignificance. Instead, they read another philosophical essay that has no real meaning-relevant implications for humans.
It was an essay regarding the limitation of computers. This essay gave the
participants something stimulating to read, but was not something that
would prompt them to contemplate the meaninglessness of their existence.

Then, all of the participants read testimonials involving miraculous
events and responded to questions concerning the extent to which they
believed these testimonials to be true and compelling evidence for the
existence of miracles.

One of the testimonials concerned a man reporting an out-of-body
experience after being shot by a mugger. He described his feeling of float-
ing up into the sky only to hear a voice telling him to go back, that it was
not yet his time to die and he had more work to do on Earth. This testimonial suggested that God had spared this man's life so that he could fulfill
his purpose.

Another testimonial we used was about a man who was in a terrible car accident. His car flipped over and he was trapped. He could smell gas and feared that he would be burned to death as he was unable to escape. But then he saw a light and the car door suddenly opened. An arm reached in and pulled him out of the vehicle. But when he collected himself and got up off the ground there was no one there. The Good Samaritan who saved his life had vanished. When the EMTs arrived they told the man he should not have survived such a horrible accident. The man proclaimed that it must have been a guardian angel that saved him.

The final testimonial we had participants read concerned a female drug addict who had overdosed. She had hit rock bottom and should have died. In fact, the emergency room doctor told her that he thought she was dead for sure, that she should not have survived her overdose. The woman believed that God had given her a second chance. And as a result, she never used drugs again.

After reading each of these miraculous testimonials, the research participants answered a number of questions about the testimonial. Did they believe the miraculous account provided by the person? How convinced were they that each of these stories was true? Did these people actually experience a miracle or divine intervention of some kind? Are the people telling these stories credible? In other words, we assessed participants' inclinations to believe these miraculous tales.

On average, participants in the control condition (the people who did not first read an existential essay about the cosmic insignificance of human life) were slightly convinced. They were just above the midpoint of the scale on how much they believed the testimonials. In other words, even though our participants did not know the people claiming to have experienced the miracles and had no real reason to believe their astonishing accounts of events, they tended to be open to them. This makes sense considering all of these participants were Christians and were thus likely to be generally open to the possibility of miracles.

Importantly, participants in the existential threat condition felt significantly more confident. That is, the participants who first read an essay about the cosmic insignificance of humanity were more inclined to accept these testimonials as true and the people who gave them as credible than the participants who did read the meaning-threatening essay. When people are reminded of how small and insignificant human existence is, they are motivated to believe in the power of religious supernatural agents such as God and guardian angels. Miracles imbue the world with teleological meaning.

In a twist on this idea, my lab also considered the potential for supernatural religious beliefs involving evil spirits to provide teleological meaning.[15] At first this seems like an odd idea. Why would people gain meaning in life from believing in things like demons, the devil, and evil curses? Such an idea not only seems intuitively strange, it also goes against much of what we know from the field of psychology. The general consensus from the scientific literature is that people gain meaning from positive emotional experiences. Religion provides meaning, but religious experiences are typically positive in nature. People feel loved and protected by God, and that helps make them feel meaningful.

This is precisely why we wanted to test if meaning could also be derived from thinking about malevolent supernatural religious forces. Maybe religion is a source of meaning simply because it makes people feel good and when people feel good they also feel meaningful. Similarly, maybe an experience that threatens meaning drives Christians to increase their belief in miracles because miracles are emotionally positive. It is a comforting feeling to believe that God and guardian angels have your back. This would suggest that it is the positive feelings generated by religion, not its supernatural nature, that is important for meaning. In other words, religion may not be special in its ability to generate meaning. Any positive thoughts would work just as well.

However, if it is the supernatural component of religious beliefs that is providing meaning and not just the positive nature of these beliefs, then believers should show an increased belief in evil supernatural religious forces when their sense of meaning in life is threatened. Most people don't want to think about Satan, demons, and other evil forces, but their existence would support a broader religious narrative that offers teleological meaning. For example, the possibility of demons existing is scary, but if demons exist that would suggest angels exist. If Satan exists, then God must exist. And so on. In short, people may invest in unpleasant supernatural religious beliefs because even though such beliefs are frightening, they also reinforce the idea that there is grander meaning in the world.

To test this idea, we used the same meaning manipulation previously described. Half of the participants read the philosophical essay about how small and insignificant humans are, and the other half read the philosophical essay about computers. After reading one of these essays, all of the participants completed a questionnaire assessing supernatural evil beliefs such as the belief in the power of dark magic and the idea that evil forces are constantly tempting people.

Our results supported the idea of meaning-motivated belief in evil supernatural religious agents. People in our study who reported being highly religious were more likely to believe in supernatural evil forces if they had read the existential threatening essay than if they had read the essay about computers. In other words, a threat to teleological meaning increased belief in the more terrifying aspects of the supernatural. We did not find this effect among those low in religiosity. People who do not strongly identify as religious are less likely to turn to the more frightening religious-related supernatural beliefs in order to reaffirm a sense of meaning in life.

In another study, we found a similar pattern of results but using a different approach. In this study, instead of experimentally manipulating meaning we measured it with a meaning in life questionnaire. In other words, we allowed participants to tell us whether they currently feel like their life has meaning or not. Next, we had participants complete a task that allowed us to assess their motivation to believe in evil supernatural forces. Specifically, we presented them with a written profile of an 18-year-old male named Owen who was convicted of murdering his sister. The profile described Owen as having a history of antisocial violent behavior and coming from a dysfunctional home with an abusive father.

After reading the profile, participants responded to a series of questions regarding the causes of Owen's horrible crime. Some of these questions concerned the extent to which participants thought his crime was the result of nonsupernatural causes such as growing up in an abusive household. Some of the questions concerned the extent to which participants thought his crime could be attributed to supernatural evil forces such as having a dark soul or evil spirit.

How did participants respond? Did they think Owen's behavior could be explained by natural causes such as a history of abuse or did they favor a more supernatural explanation, one that would support the existence of malevolent spirits? How people responded depended on their level of religiosity and perceived meaning in life. People scoring high on perceived meaning or low on religiosity were not inclined to invoke supernatural evil forces as a causal factor. However, people who were both high in religiosity and low in perceived meaning did believe that Owen's crime could be at least partially attributed to his evil soul.

In a follow-up study, we found an identical pattern with an experimental manipulation of meaning. Highly religious people exposed to the idea that life is meaningless were especially inclined to view Owen's behavior as caused by supernatural evil forces.

Now remember, people high in religiosity typically score high in meaning in life. Therefore, what this pattern of results suggests is that when highly religious people are in a meaning funk and thus need to restore a sense of meaning, they are more likely to invoke the supernatural, even if this involves unpleasant thoughts about people having dark souls or being influenced by evil spirits.

Does this mean Christians want to watch movies about demon possession and satanic cults when they are feeling down? I doubt this would be their first choice. But what these studies suggest is that when meaning is under threat people will seek it out wherever they can find it. Pizza might be your favorite food but if you get hungry enough I suspect you would settle for a burrito, or anything else that would meet your caloric needs. Quick parenting tip: if you want your kids to be open to trying a new food to eat, wait until they are really hungry. When kids are desperate for food they are more likely to eat something they may normally find unappealing. Similarly, when people need meaning they will turn to emotionally unpleasant beliefs if those beliefs help affirm a broader meaning narrative and thus serve to help restore meaning.

Religion isn't just about making people happy. The darker side of religious supernatural beliefs may be scary, but it also it also plays a role in helping people reject the notion that the world is a meaningless place. The epic struggle between religious supernatural forces for good, such as God and angels, and forces for evil, such as Satan and demons, makes people feel like they are part of a meaningful cosmic drama. Whether it makes you happy or afraid, the supernatural world is a meaningful world.

In fact, supernatural religious beliefs may be so well suited to provide meaning that people automatically turn to such beliefs in response to meaning threats that they are not even aware exist. Consider an experiment conducted by the psychologists Daryl Van Tongeren and Jeffrey Green showing that subconscious cues about meaninglessness can inspire religiosity.[16] In this study, research participants thought they were taking part in a study on memory. As part of the memory task they would be asked to fixate on a dot in the center of the computer screen and wait for a series of words to appear on the screen. Later in the study they were to be tested on their memory of this list of words. However, unbeknownst to the participants, on the periphery of the computer screen they were being presented with a different set of words. But these words were presented so fast that they were not consciously aware of it, what researchers call subliminal priming. The words were only on the screen for 50 milliseconds. Here is the important part. For half of the participants, the subliminal words were related to meaninglessness (e.g., chaos, empty, futile). For the other half of participants, the words were neutral (e.g., curved, echoes, furnace).

After this part of the study, participants completed questionnaires measuring perceptions of meaning in life and religiosity. The researchers proposed that even a subliminal threat to meaning would be sufficient to decrease conscious perceptions of meaning and increase religiosity. And this is exactly what they observed. The participants who were subliminally exposed to words about meaninglessness were less likely to endorse the idea that life is full of meaning and purpose than the participants who were subliminally exposed to neutral words.

Participants in the subliminal meaning threat conditions also reported higher religiosity than those in the neutral condition. The researchers also asked participants after the study if they saw any of the subliminal words. Not a single participant could correctly identify any of the subliminal words. At best, some participants reported seeing a quick flash on the screen but had no idea what it was. A fraction of a second of exposure to words related to existential meaninglessness such as chaos and futile was sufficient to move people's self-reported levels of religiosity. Again, imagine what happens in situations that more powerfully challenge people's perceptions of meaning in life.

These are just a handful of the studies connecting supernatural religious beliefs to the human quest for meaning. But I think you get the idea. When people are facing situations that make them feel insignificant and meaningless, they are often attracted to the teleological meaning afforded by religious narratives. And the more people believe in supernatural religious agents such as God and angels as well as the validity of supernatural religious phenomenon such as miracles, the more they see the world as a meaningful place where everything happens for a reason.

THE SO-CALLED DECLINE OF RELIGION

A quick look at any major public poll regarding the beliefs of Americans paints a pretty bleak picture for religion. Virtually all surveys indicate that religiosity is on the decline in the United States. The number of atheists and agnostics is growing. Most Americans still believe in God, but far fewer are actively engaged in religion.

Religious identification and church attendance has been steadily declining for decades. Even the most optimistic estimates suggest that only about 50% of Americans regularly attend church. Some surveys suggest the number is closer to 15%–20%. Just a couples of decades ago, about

95% of Americans reported belonging to a religious group. Now, polls suggest that this number is closer to 75%. This is what many observers have referred to as the rise of the "nones." In chapter 5, I interrogate these and related numbers more thoroughly.

For now, the question I want to consider is: does the rise of "nones" represent a decline of the religious mind? Are people rejecting religion wholesale, or are they rejecting a specific brand of traditional religion? Based on research I and others are conducting, some of which I discuss in the next two chapters, it appears that many people remain hungry for ways to pursue their spiritual journeys and connect with fellow travelers. However, a lot of these folks simply don't identify with what most churches have on offer. Maybe it is because we are a more globally connected society, have more access to information than we ever have before, or are more scientifically educated. Or perhaps large, hierarchical religious organizations aren't sufficiently nimble to keep up with rapid social and cultural changes. Some have argued that the problem isn't that churches don't change but that they have changed too much, that they have lost their way. Whatever the cause, many Americans, particularly young adults, have lost interest in the traditional church.

Religion in America is not unlike many other products in the free market. If a church does not meet the needs of its congregants, it risks losing them to other churches or organizations that offer meaning-making opportunities. I don't say this to demean religion by treating it like a consumer product. My point simply is that if people are looking for a spiritual home, a place to worship, meditate, and connect with others, and they have options, they will be attracted to the one that best fits them, or perhaps just one that provides a different approach.

When our ancestors developed an awareness of self and death, they started turning to the religious belief systems that are still evolving to this day. Over time, like anything in the marketplace of ideas, some religions have fallen out of favor. Some have completely gone extinct. Some have been recycled and subsequently enjoyed a renaissance period of growth and prosperity. And, believe it or not, new religions are still being formed in the present day.

For instance, one of the newest relatively large religions is Falun Gong, which was founded in China in 1992. Though Falun Gong has been described as being a practice and not a religion, it certainly has the characteristics of a religion. It has a spiritual leader, includes religious texts that invoke the supernatural, deals with metaphysical issues, and boasts millions of followers all over the world. This religion borrows from other beliefs ranging from Buddhism to New Age religion, but focuses specifically on a set of physical exercises involving meditation and movement.

Though it may sound like this religion is more of a Tai Chi class than a faith, its founder, Li Hongzhi, has made its supernatural components very clear. For one, he claimed that the growth of the religion has prevented the occurrence of a number catastrophes and that demonic beings from outer space are manipulating many of the world's leaders and scientists as part of an effort to annihilate humankind. Falun Gong's description of positive and negative energy in the body is also of a supernatural nature, as it does not reference measurable physiological processes.

Falun Gong is not the only religion that has emerged in recent decades. A number of New Age religious movements emerged during the 1970s. And as I discuss in chapter 5, the world is full of religious-like supernatural beliefs that lack the organizational structure to qualify as religions. I am not a religious studies scholar and certainly do not have the expertise to chime in on the debate of whether these new religious movements should be treated as similar to the more historically established faith traditions that most of us are familiar with.

I am, however, a psychologist who studies why people believe the things they believe. For the questions I focus on, whether different spiritual movements are technically classified as religions or not is often irrelevant. What is important is that regardless of the particular belief system that people attach themselves to, the motives appear to be similar. Supernatural religious beliefs of all varieties represent people's efforts to feel more than mortal.

Of course, most people do not run off and join one of these new religious movements. Instead, they make a more modest change. They leave the traditional church their parents attended and shop around for a place of worship that offers a familiar approach to faith with a modern touch.

Some have argued that this approach may be the key to the survival of religion in America. For instance, the fastest growing category of Christians in the United States is nondenominational evangelist. Public polls indicate that while denominations such as Southern Baptist have been facing declining membership for years, Christian churches that are not formally associated with a denomination are enjoying year after year growth.[17] It is not entirely clear why this is the case, but something about these churches is attracting new members.

Throughout history, rulers and governments have tried to squash religion, sometimes by force, and different secular movements have also sought to challenge the validity and social value of religious doctrines. In addition, some of the most prominent religious narratives about the creation of the universe and the origin of biological life have not stood up well to scientific discovery. Yet, religion remains one of the most powerful cultural systems of belief in the world. Just when it appears that religion is on the ropes, it makes a comeback.

We might currently be in what some scholars have referred to as "The Great Decline" of religiosity, but a closer inspection of the religious lives of Americans suggests that this decline may be more a period of transformation than extinction. Fewer and fewer people are going to church, but, as I discuss in chapter 6, religious identity and faith have many mental and physical health benefits. Is the growth of the nondenominational evangelical movement a sign of a religious revival in America and beyond? Time will tell.

But what about those secular Europeans we are always hearing about? Or the hardcore atheists who want nothing to do with any kind of religious faith? They seem to be legitimately abandoning religion. Perhaps, but perhaps not. In the next two chapters I consider other, subtler and more cloaked ways that people turn to the supernatural to grapple with existential questions related to death and meaning. Some might believe they have thrown off the shackles of religion, but have they truly abandoned the supernatural world?

The Secret Supernatural Lives
of Atheists

I conduct research on the psychology of belief and disbelief. As a result, I have talked to and collected data from many atheists. What I have discovered is that "atheist" is a more complex self-identification than many realize. For one, atheists vary in the extent to which they are confident about their disbelief. Some feel absolutely certain that there is no God, whereas others are unsure but still generally come down on the side of not believing. The idea of an uncertain atheist may come as a surprise to some because it is usually the confident ones who are vocal about their disbelief.

People also sometimes change their minds or fluctuate in how confident they feel. Getting older, becoming more self-reflective, reading arguments for or against religion, losing a loved one, or having a profound life experience can move the needle toward belief or disbelief depending on a number of variables.

Since I study the psychology of religion and do a lot of writing on this topic, when I am out in public I often violate the social custom of not talking about religion. If I am talking to someone I don't know well, after an initial feeling-out process, and if the moment feels right, I will ask them about their beliefs. I know, some think it's kind of rude and certainly can be awkward. But I am doing field research, seeking to understand the nuances of people's thoughts on God, the afterlife, and other issues of faith and spirituality. So I embrace the awkwardness and probe away.

One day I was sitting up at the bar at one of my favorite local pubs. The place was pretty dead and I was having a nice conversation with the bartender on a range of harmless topics. The conversation moved close enough in the direction of more philosophical questions and I had reached a sufficient level of Dutch courage to ask the young man pouring my beer what his thoughts were on religion and God.

His response, which is not an uncommon one, especially for a young adult, was that he doesn't know. Some days he thinks no way. In a modern world in which many beliefs can be derived from data, how could he put his faith in something beyond the testable. Science has taken down so many old assumptions about the world, revealing that it is not flat, not the center of the solar system or universe, is much older than a biblical time-line would suggest, and so on. Why believe at all? Maybe our ancestors needed faith and superstition as a way to make sense of their existence, but modern humans know a lot more about the world and how it works.

In addition, he wonders, as many do, whether religion and a faith in God does more harm than good. He sees plenty of people completely disengaged from faith and they seem happy, thoughtful, generous, and successful. And religious tribalism seems to be a source of intolerance and conflict. Why allocate any mental energy to questions that he may never get a satisfactory answer to? What can he expect to get out of having a spiritual life?

But on other days his skepticism wavers. Sure, science has challenged specific traditional religious narratives, but does that necessarily leave no room for the divine? Does he have to abandon his openness to the idea that there may be something beyond the material just because he considers himself a modern man? Is it not possible to be both empirical and spiritual, to leave some space for the possibility of the supernatural while being grounded in a scientific understanding of the natural world?

And aren't there some benefits to being connected to others who share a faith? Sure, some folks seem perfectly fine without religion, but many appear to be reaping a number of benefits from exploring spiritual questions with others. Will he be missing an important aspect of the human collective experience if he doesn't join in? Will he one day look back with regret?

This thoughtful young bartender expressed a sense of ambiguity about religion and spirituality. At times, he feels the pull of spiritual and religious ideas. Other times he doesn't. He is not alone. For many, belief is not a black and white issue or a simple yes or no question. It is a journey that involves skepticism, doubt, uncertainty, and fear, but also openness, curiosity, exploration, inspiration, and hope.

Moreover, survey data suggests that there is some uncertainty about what constitutes atheism. According to the Pew Research Center,[1] in 2015 only about 3% of Americans self-identified as atheists, though another 4% referred to themselves as agnostic. Of course, 3% is a small number, but it is one that has doubled since 2007.

Interestingly, in this survey, 8% of self-proclaimed atheists also indicated that they believe in God or universal spirit; 2% indicated being absolutely certain of the existence of God or a universal spirit. What? How can they believe in a God or universal spirit if they identify as atheist, since atheism means disbelief in a deity? Making things more confusing, on a separate question, about 9% of all people in the survey said they do not believe in a God or universal spirit. How could this be if only 3% self-identified as atheists? Why aren't these different numbers matching up? A small percentage of people who identify as atheist actually believe in a God and about three times the number of people who call themselves atheists do not believe in a God. What gives?

There are a number of factors that may help explain these seemingly conflicting numbers. One possibility is that many people who don't believe in God do not want to call themselves atheists. After all, there is a considerable amount of prejudice against atheists, a topic I address in chapter 8. Atheists are one of the most distrusted and disliked groups in America. People perceive them as lacking a moral code.

Another possibility is that there is disagreement about what it means to be an atheist. Some of the more vocal public proponents of atheism have taken a fairly aggressive stance against religion, referring to it as foolish, a social ill, even a mental illness. Maybe some nonbelievers associate atheism with that kind of thinking and don't want to be connected to what appears to them to be a mean-spirited social agenda. This might partially explain why there are so few female atheists. Nearly all surveys show that women are more likely to identify as religious than men and are certainly more religiously active (e.g., pray more, attend and volunteer at church more), but even women who don't believe in God may be less interested in the atheist label if it is perceived as hostile toward religion and those who practice it. This would be consistent with the large body of research showing that women tend to be more agreeable and empathetic than men. There are also social cognitive factors that help explain why women are less likely to be atheists, a topic I return to later.

In addition, returning to the confidence issue, perhaps some people generally think they don't believe in a God but don't feel certain enough to declare themselves full-blown atheists. A friend once told me that he generally sees himself as conservative and almost always votes along conservative lines but doesn't feel sure enough to label himself a Republican, the major party most aligned with conservatism. He feels that such a simple act of taking on a categorical label would lock him into a group identity and close his mind to alternative ways of thinking and thus prefers to remain unattached to a particular political party. Might some nonbelievers similarly not want to close the door on religion or spirituality by the symbolic act of self-identifying as atheist?

As far as those few who do call themselves atheists but also say they believe in a God or universal spirit, perhaps they view atheism as a rejection of the church or a formal religious doctrine. Maybe they don't entirely reject the idea of a supernatural being or other nonmaterial forces, they just don't like to think of themselves as religious or perhaps even agnostic. This possibility would suggest that, to some, the atheist label might represent a more free-thinking approach to spiritual questions. Yes, atheism by definition means disbelief or lack of belief in a deity, but lay conceptions of an idea do not always align with the dictionary. Clearly, more research is needed to better understand the complexities of people's disbelief and their views on what it means to be associated with atheism, and how these views may differ from culture to culture or among people of different age and social groups.

My main point here is that even when we are talking about what on the surface seems to be a group of people unified by a single idea—disbelief in a deity—things can get messy. And I am going to make things even messier as I discuss in this chapter research indicating that atheists are sometimes attracted to religious ideas and influenced by supernatural concepts, even if they don't realize it.

PROFILING THE ATHEIST

Before tackling the supernatural lives of atheists, it is important to consider what we actually know about this group. Who are these rare folks who reject the religious beliefs that so many hold dear? As noted before, there is much still to learn about the nuances of disbelief, but surveys have revealed certain characteristics of atheists as a group. According to Pew, atheists tend to be relatively young (mean age = 34), male (68%), and white (78%). Atheists also tend to lean left politically and show high levels of support for socially liberal positions such as abortion rights and legalized gay marriage.

Though atheists are disinclined toward religion, they are not totally devoid of interest in existential and spiritual issues. According to Pew, about one-third of atheists report frequently feeling a deep sense of spiritual peace and well-being and 35% say they often wonder about the meaning and purpose of life. Further, 54% of atheists indicate that they often feel a sense of wonder about the universe, a sentiment only 45% of American Christians reported having. Though there has been very little research on the spiritual lives of atheists, social scientists are beginning to explore this topic. For instance, surveys of scientists suggest that some atheist scientists embrace the idea of a spiritual atheism, a way to approach deep existential questions in less traditional ways.[2] I return to this topic in chapter 8 when discussing common but often incorrect beliefs about believers and atheists.

Of course, there are plenty of atheists who do not identify as spiritual at all. Are these folks completely unmoved by the supernatural? Do they have no interest in or gain no benefit from ideas and beliefs we tend to associate with religiosity and faith? Perhaps. Based on research concerning the cognitive characteristics that dispose people to religiosity and supernatural beliefs, there might be a small minority of individuals who simply have little or no religious inclination and no interest in spirituality.

For instance, some cognitive scientists have proposed that supernatural beliefs require a certain level of "theory of mind," which is the ability to put oneself in another person's head and imagine their thoughts, feelings, and intentions. Some folks are very good at this. They easily and frequently take the perspective of others. Others are less inclined to engage in this kind of mind-reading. Offering some support for this social cognitive view, researchers found that autistic individuals were less likely to believe in God than neurotypical individuals.[3] The researchers also found evidence suggesting that this difference between autistic and neurotypical individuals on belief in God was the result of autistic individuals expressing lower theory of mind. Other studies similarly link trait differences in theory of mind with levels of supernatural belief: people who are not inclined to think about the thoughts and feelings of others are less likely to believe in God and other supernatural agents.[4] This research also helps explain why women tend to be more religious and spiritual than men.

Women score higher on empathizing with others, which is also reflected in career choices. They are more likely than men to gravitate to fields that involve people. Even within science, women tend to prefer life and social sciences over physical sciences. For instance, my field of psychology is quickly becoming dominated by women. The majority of undergraduate and graduate students in the field are female. Disciplines that do not focus so directly on people such as engineering, computer science, and physics remain largely dominated by men. And these career interest differences are also predicted by theory of mind. In other words, there are social and cognitive factors that influence a range of interests, including interest in the supernatural.

More recent research, however, offers a somewhat different perspective. Across a series of studies, researchers found evidence suggesting that it is not simply the tendency or desire to think about the thoughts and feelings of others but more specifically a moral concern for others that orients people toward belief in God.[5] Belief in God and other supernatural agents might be more about social emotions than social cognitive inclinations. Of course, the proclivity to think about others' thoughts and feelings and the extent to which one has moral concern for others are likely related. More research is needed to fully investigate how both social cognition and emotion influence religious and spiritual inclinations.

The researchers did observe the typical gender difference in belief in God; women were more likely to be believers than men. However, they found evidence that this gender difference is accounted for by women scoring higher on moral concern. This finding is also consistent with the broader literature previously mentioned that women are more empathetic and interested in roles and careers that involve people. Women might be more attracted to such roles and careers because they are more concerned about the health and well-being of others.

However, all of the work discussed thus far focused on people's self-reported supernatural beliefs. There may also be people who say they are not religious and have no belief or interest in the supernatural but are unaware of and thus unable to self-report their supernatural proclivities. Might atheists, or at least some of them, be wrong about their own lack of investment in the supernatural?

FOXHOLE ATHEISM

As discussed in previous chapters, the awareness of death is a powerful motivator of religious belief. People want to be more than mere mortal beings destined for complete annihilation. And religious supernatural beliefs are quite useful in this campaign to transcend mortality. Believers often marvel at and, quite frankly, doubt, atheists' ability to maintain their lack of faith when faced with the reality of death. Can people really hold fast to their disbelief? Certainly, there are committed atheists who do not turn to faith when facing death. However, a large survey of adults of all ages and from countries all over the world suggests that as people approach old age, they become more inclined to believe in God, a trend that is found even in largely secular European countries.[6] The increased awareness of mortality that occurs as a function of aging and many other life experiences may not turn most atheists into dedicated believers, but do they crack the supernatural door, even just a bit?

A team of researchers led by Dr. Jonathan Jong experimentally explored this idea that even atheists may be attracted to belief in God when grappling with concerns about mortality.[7] Obviously, in an experimental setting you cannot randomly assign people to face a real threat of mortality in order to determine if there are any foxhole atheists. However, based on the proposal from TMT that heightened awareness of death heightens people's efforts to affirm some kind of meaning and death-transcendence, the researchers proposed that having atheists think about death might attract them to religious ideas.

You might be skeptical, thinking that there is no way that simply thinking about death for a few minutes is going to make atheists believe in God. If it were that easy, there would be no atheists. After all, everyone is confronted with death thoughts on a regular basis. Like you, the researchers didn't expect death thoughts to lead to religious conversion. Instead, they proposed that the relatively minor provocation of thinking about mortality would influence religious cognition in a subtler way. They didn't expect atheists to change their explicit attitudes, but when thinking about the existential threat of mortality, might atheists feel the pull of religion at a more intuitive level of cognition?

In this experiment, believers and atheists were asked to briefly write about their mortality or a topic unrelated to death, just as in terror management experiments I discussed in previous chapters. Subsequently, participants completed a cognitive association task in which they categorized words related to the concepts of "real" and "imaginary" on a number of practice trials. Specifically, they were told to hit one key if the word that popped up on the screen was associated with "real" and a different key if the word was associated with "imaginary."

In later trials, words related to religion, such as "God," "soul," and "Hell," were added to the mix and participants were instructed in some trials to use the same key to categorize religious words that they would use to categorize words related to "real." In other trials, they were told to use the same key to categorize religious words that they would use to categorize words related to "imaginary." The goal of this task is to determine how quickly people can correctly strike the key if the word falls within *either* appropriate category.

On some trials participants have to strike the same key for words related to the concepts of "real" and "religion," whereas in other trials they have to strike the same key for words related to the concepts of "imaginary" and "religion." Being able to more quickly hit the appropriate key on trials in which words related to "real" are matched with religious words suggests that the research participants are finding it relatively easy to associate the concept of "real" with the concept of religion. Again, these responses are happening in milliseconds, so the participants do not have time to deliberate about these associations. They are just providing intuitive-level responses.

What do you think happened? First, I should note that in a previous study in which the authors assessed explicit religious beliefs with a self-report questionnaire after having participants write about mortality or a control topic, only self-declared believers exhibited higher religiosity as a function of thinking about their inevitable death. Contemplating the reality of mortal finitude did not inspire atheists to consciously endorse religious faith.

However, in the experiment using the cognitive association task, a different story emerged. Thinking about mortality made atheists quicker at associating the concepts of "real" and religion and slower at associating the concepts of "imaginary" and religion. Atheists may not consciously believe that God is real, but when reminded of their corporal nature, it became a little easier to couple God with the concept of "real."

It is worth noting that this type of cognitive association task is not without controversy. Notably, similar tasks used to measure what social scientists call implicit attitudes (i.e., attitudes outside of conscious awareness) have received a considerable amount of criticism recently, in part, because scholars and social activists had argued that these kinds of cognitive measures can be used to assess racism and sexism that people are unwilling or unable to self-report. The idea is that if people are, for example, faster at associating negative words with pictures of African Americans than pictures of Caucasian Americans, then they are implicitly or unconsciously racist.

The problem with that argument is that scores on these types of measures are not stable across time, making it impossible to treat them as diagnostic of a racist or sexist disposition. Also, these measures often do not predict self-reported attitudes or, importantly, actual behavior. Thus, it is difficult to know exactly what such measures are telling us about human psychology. Researchers and activists should not be suggesting that cognitive associations mean anything more than, well, associations. And they certainly should not be using these measures as tools that can accurately reveal people's level of racism or sexism. They appear to have little or no impact on actual beliefs or behaviors.

That being said, there might be something to learn from the finding that thinking about death makes atheists faster at associating the concept of "real" with religious concepts. For instance, it might suggest that at a more intuitive level, atheists, even if only very briefly, feel the pull of the supernatural when thinking about existential questions related to death and meaning. When they more deeply or rationally contemplate religious beliefs such as the belief in God, they consciously reject the idea. They override their intuition. This would be consistent with the idea that meaning-making tends to involve intuition more than rational deliberation. Thinking about death provokes the pursuit of meaning, which in turn may privilege intuitive cognitive processes. Only through further analytical thinking might atheists override gut-level associations.

RELIGION BENEATH THE SKIN

I had a colleague who, despite being a very confident atheist, was afraid to write the word "God" down on paper. He was raised in the Jewish faith and was taught that that sacred scripture forbade writing the word. Though there is some disagreement among Jewish scholars and rabbis as when or if it is ever permissible to write the word "God," he was raised to believe it was never acceptable. Interestingly, despite abandoning any faith in a deity, he remained unable to engage in this simple behavior. In fact, he had tried on numerous occasions. He would sit at his desk with paper and pen in hand telling himself that as an educated man who does not believe in the supernatural it was completely irrational to follow this custom. It should not be a problem to write the word "God" if there is no God. And his parents or other family members would never know, so there was nobody to offend in the privacy of his office. Yet, he found himself paralyzed, unable to do the deed. It was as if his rational mind was telling him to do it but his body was too afraid to follow through. How does this work?

Research using cognitive association measures offer one way of probing intuitive religiosity among atheists. But this is not the only method scientists have used. Other research has also considered whether atheists exhibit any signs of religiosity by focusing on physiological processes instead of cognitive processes.

Physiological processes are influenced by psychological variables. For instance, when people experience emotions such as fear or anxiety there are accompanying, and measurable, changes in the body such as fluctuations in heart rate or cortisol (a hormonal indicator of stress). Therefore, if researchers want to know whether religious ideas are influencing people but don't want to rely on self-reported feelings, they can measure the physiological correlates of the psychological states they are interested in assessing.

Take, for example, two recent studies conducted by psychologists in Finland.[8] In these studies, the researchers sought to determine the physiological effects of daring God to do harmful things. The idea is simple. If atheists do not in any way believe in God, then challenging God to hurt them and others should not cause physical distress. Believers, on the other hand, should be distressed by provoking the deity.

In the first experiment, atheist and theist participants were instructed to read aloud a number of statements. Some of these statements concerned asking God to do awful things. For example, one statement was "I wish God would turn my friends against me." Some of these statements were offensive but did not involve God, and the remaining statements were neutral.

While participants read these statements aloud, the researchers measured physiological arousal via skin conductance with a small device attached to each participant's finger. Skin conductance is a measure of electrical conductance of the skin. When people become more physiologically aroused (more anxious) their skin conductance increases. That is, moisture increases electrical conductance, and when people are anxious or stressed they sweat, so the moisture on their skin increases. Critically, this is an automated process—it is not consciously controlled. The sweat glands are controlled by the sympathetic nervous system so if a person is anxious, even if they do not consciously realize it, the moisture level of their skin is elevated.

After the research participants read all of the statements, the researchers asked them how uncomfortable making these statements made them feel. As one might predict, when asked, atheists stated that daring God to do harmful things did not really bother them. They did not believe in God so asking him to be hurtful was like asking Santa Clause to call off Christmas or the Easter Bunny to forgo delivering candy baskets this year.

Believers, of course, reported being very uncomfortable challenging God in this way, even though they were merely doing what the researchers instructed them to do. They did not want to agitate God by reading aloud these types of provocations, and thus doing so was quite distressing. In fact, it is pretty impressive that these researchers were able to get believers to cooperate with this task. In short, results from the self-report measure of anxiety painted a predictable picture. Atheists said they weren't both-ered by the task and believers reported high levels of discomfort.

The skin conductance results, however, painted a very different picture. When distress was assessed with skin conductance instead of self-report, believers and atheists were equally distressed by provoking God. For both groups, daring God to cause harm increased physiological stress to similar levels. In other words, for atheists, the conscious feelings as assessed with self-report questions did not match the unconscious, physiological expe-rience as assessed with skin conductance. Atheists may not consciously believe that challenging God upsets them, but the body tells a different story. Physiologically, atheists and believers were indistinguishable. Both groups were unnerved by inciting God to do harm.

In the second study, the researchers wanted to rule out the possibil-ity that the physiological effects observed were due to the task involving wishing negative events to occur. Maybe atheists were physiologically aroused because they were making statements that involved negative out-comes. Even if you do not believe in God, daring God to turn your friends against you makes you think about your friends turning against you, and this could trigger a stress response. Who wouldn't feel distress after making these kinds of unpleasant statements? Therefore, the researchers asked participants in the second study to read additional statements that involved harmful outcomes but did not invoke God, such as, "I wish my friends would turn against me."

The results were striking. Atheists had higher skin conductance when reading aloud the harmful statements that involved God than when read-ing aloud the harmful statements that did not involve God. It was the reli-gious aspect of these negative statements that affected atheists, not the fact that the statements were inherently unpleasant. Atheists may not con-sciously believe in God or consciously be emotionally aroused by daring God to be hurtful, but they exhibit a bodily stress response similar to that of believers who provoked God.

Have you ever had to stand up in front of a group to give a presentation and convinced yourself that it is not that big of a deal, that you are not that anxious only to realize that you are sweating? Of course, we are often well aware of our insecurities and the physical symptoms associated with them. But sometimes people are not so good at appreciating their physiological responses to certain stimuli. How we want to feel about something is not always reflective of how our bodies are behaving. Just like people who think they are more socially confident, funny, or generous than they really are, atheists may think they are more immune to the influence of supernatural religious ideas than they really are. Maybe my colleague who could not force himself to write the word "God" simply doesn't realize that religion still impacts on his life.

SOMETIMES YOU NEED TO BE A CLEVER SOCIAL SCIENTIST: ASSESSING ATTITUDES INDIRECTLY

Cognitive association tests and physiological measures sometimes reveal different results than self-report. Does this mean researchers should never employ self-report measures when they are seeking to reveal the extent to which religious and spiritual concepts impact people? Can we not trust people to be able or willing to consciously describe their own attitudes, opinions, or beliefs? What about all the public polling data that people collect or the fact that for some attitudes, self-report is the best and most efficient method we have available to us? Is self-report data hopelessly flawed in the study of topics related to religiosity and spirituality?

Of course not. There is no need to call for the abandonment of one of the oldest and most common ways of assessing attitudes. For many attitudes, people are willing and able to report what they think. Lots of attitudes are fairly innocuous. In addition, most pollsters and attitudes researchers guarantee confidentiality and anonymity, so people can feel free to express their honest beliefs without fear of social repercussions. And, this probably won't come as a surprise, but many people like sharing their opinions. Moreover, as already noted, scholars have actually learned quite a bit about how religiosity and spirituality influence people simply by having people complete self-report questionnaires.

That being said, sometimes you can't just outright ask people to report or describe their own psychological states or processes. But this does not necessarily rule out a self-report approach. Researchers just need to be especially clever at isolating and measuring influential variables. And this is a skill that social and behavioral scientists have been honing for decades.

The basic idea is that if you want to find out how someone is being influenced by a concept or belief you cannot always simply ask them directly. They may not know the extent to which different variables are acting on them or may not want to tell you. Instead, you create a research paradigm that experimentally manipulates a variable of interest and then you assess attitudes or behaviors that you as the researcher would expect to be influenced by that variable. Critically, you design the paradigm so that the research participants do not detect the link between the variable you are manipulating and the attitude or behavior you are measuring.

Much of the research I discussed in previous chapters relies on this approach. For example, hundreds of experiments derived from TMT have shown that when people think about death they respond by displaying elevated support for prominent cultural belief systems that provide perceptions of meaning in life and a feeling of symbolic immortality—that part of who they are will live on through their broader and more enduring cultural identity.

In one study,[9] for instance, participants in the experimental conditions were asked to spend a few minutes writing about mortality and participants in the control condition were asked to spend a few minutes writing about a topic not related to death. For both conditions, participants were told that the task was a newly developed personality measure, that what they wrote would be content-analyzed and provide information about their personality. This is what psychologists call a cover story. It helps disguise the true purpose of the task. The participants are unaware of the fact that they have actually been randomly assigned to different conditions. They assume they are all completing the same personality task. In reality, some are being reminded of their mortality and others are not. And the researchers were not particularly interested in what they wrote. The intent of the task is to manipulate the extent to which people are thinking about death.

Next, participants completed a couple of unrelated questionnaires, such as a measure of mood, and then they were given the critical self-report questions. This is where being clever comes into play. The researchers wanted to measure whether being reminded of mortality motivated people to cling to the cultural belief systems and identities that give them meaning and perceptions of symbolic immortality. So what did they do? Did they ask people directly to what extent they are invested in their cultural belief systems in the service of finding meaning and immortality? Nope. Not at all.

Psychologists tend not to directly ask such questions because of the concerns associated with self-report that we've previously discussed. Most notably, sometimes people simply do not realize why they believe the things they do and therefore are not particularly good at reporting the underlying motives for their attitudes and beliefs.

Instead, researchers provide participants an opportunity to exhibit their commitment to an attitude or belief. Going back to our example, in this study, participants were told they were going to read an essay written by a foreign university student and that after reading the essay they would be given the opportunity to evaluate the essay and the essayist.

The essay was, in fact, written by the researchers and was created to affirm a pro-American worldview. It discussed how America is such a great place of opportunity, that anyone who worked hard could find success and happiness through hard work. The essay essentially reinforced the American dream narrative. After reading the essay, participants responded to the evaluative questions. They indicated the extent to which they agreed with the essay and found the author to be knowledgeable and intelligent.

The researchers reasoned that if national identity provides a defense against the threat of death-awareness, then participants who were reminded of the mortality in the previous personality task should respond to this pro-American essay and its author more favorably. That is, experimentally heightened death-awareness should inspire an increased desire to affirm an important cultural identity.

This is precisely what happened. Participants who had previously written about their mortality—and it is worth noting that all participants were

Americans—evaluated the essay and its author more positively than participants in the control condition who did not write about death.

The researchers argued that this pattern of results supports the idea that people invest in and defend cultural belief systems and identities as a way of coping with the awareness of death. The experiment relied on self-report measures. That is, participants reported their attitudes about the essay and essay author. However, the experiment did not require that the participants understand their attitudes were a response to concerns about mortality. Participants were never asked to connect the dots between death-awareness and cultural beliefs themselves or to introspect about how knowledge of mortality influences these beliefs. Instead, the experiment was designed to test whether increasing death-awareness would increase the extent to which people turn to the cultural worldviews that provide meaning and symbolic death-transcendence.

This approach is distinct from the types of self-report methods people may be familiar with from public polling or simple survey research. And this approach is the cornerstone of much of experimental social psychological research. Social psychologists and other behavioral scientists realize that they often have to approach self-report research cleverly, using more indirect means of finding out what people believe and why.

Being a good behavioral scientist is often like be being a good detective. Good detectives can't always just ask their suspects direct questions. They often have to use more indirect approaches to trick the suspect into revealing the truth. Or they have to look for clues and make connections not revealed by direct questioning. Similarly, behavioral scientists often have to be tricky, taking a less direct approach at determining what people think and know. And, as I discuss next, this approach has helped reveal how even atheists are influenced by religious ideas.

EVEN ATHEISTS LIKE IMMORTALITY

As we discussed in chapter 3, one of the distinguishing and powerful aspects of religion is that it offers perceptions of literal immortality: the promise of life after death. This is why some scholars have argued that religion is the most effective weapon against existential fears related to death and meaninglessness.[10] Building on this idea, the social psychologists Nathan Heflick and Jamie Goldenberg tested the possibility that even atheists would gain some psychological comfort from the possibility of an afterlife.[11]

For the reasons we've already discussed, these researchers did not expect atheists to self-report that they believe in an afterlife or find the idea of an afterlife to be comforting. Atheists aren't likely to think that the prospect of an afterlife offers them anything. So to determine whether atheists do gain any benefits from afterlife beliefs, the researchers had to take a less direct approach.

In this study, participants were informed that they would be reading a randomly selected newspaper article for a memory task that they would complete later in the study. There was no memory task. In actuality, this was the first critical experimental variable in the study. Some participants read an article arguing that near-death experiences provide evidence for a blissful afterlife. The article did not take a religious approach but instead was written to describe the potential for an afterlife in more medical or scientific terms.

To bolster the scientific credibility of the article, participants were led to believe that it was written by a Harvard Medical School professor. Anyone can propose that near-death experiences are evidence for life after death, but such a claim appears more worthy of consideration when the person making it is a medical expert at one of the most prestigious medical schools.

The other participants did not read this article but instead read an article arguing that near-death experiences do not provide evidence for an afterlife, that they are merely the natural consequence of oxygen deprivation and stress. These participants were given scientific reasons to doubt that near-death experiences provide any evidence for life after death.

Next, as in previous research, participants were randomly assigned to write about death or another topic, after which they read and evaluated an essay criticizing American culture.

So what, exactly, were the researchers trying to test? Numerous experiments demonstrate that when people think about death they more negatively evaluate those who challenge an important cultural identity or worldview. As we know, cultural identities and worldviews offer meaning and perceptions of symbolic continuance beyond death, so when people are reminded of their mortality they more tightly cling to and defend their cultural identities and worldviews.

However, other studies have also observed that the need to engage in this kind of existential defense following a reminder of mortality can be eliminated by bolstering perceptions of meaning or some form of immortality prior to the mortality reminder. For instance, and most relevant to the current discussion, in one study, participants who read the article arguing that there is scientific reason to believe in life after death did not respond to being reminded of mortality with the typical pattern of increased efforts to affirm meaning and symbolic death-transcendence.[12] This study, however, did not specifically focus on atheists.

Think of this as a shield or armor. If people are provided some kind of psychological shield that offers a defense against the threat of death-awareness, then when that threat appears (by having people think and write about death), shielded individuals shouldn't need further efforts to affirm a sense of meaning and immortality. Their existential security is already in place.

Based on this idea, Heflick and Goldenberg reasoned that if atheists gain existential security from the idea that near-death experiences provide evidence for life after death then they should not need to respond to thoughts of death by defending their American cultural identity. In support of this idea, they found that for participants who first read the article asserting that near-death experience can be explained by biological processes (i.e., no evidence for life after death), a death reminder increased negative evaluations of the article criticizing American culture. This was the case for atheists and believers alike. Thinking about death triggered the existential defense system. It made people cling to their American cultural identity. This is the same effect that has been observed in dozens of previous experiments.

However, this effect was eliminated among participants who first read the article proposing that near-death experiences cannot be explained scientifically (i.e., evidence for existence beyond death). Critically, this was even the case among atheists.

Atheists generally do not believe in the afterlife. And most atheists would probably not report believing in an afterlife even after thinking about death, because they generally do not consciously think that there is reason to believe in an afterlife. However, when provided with information offering some hope for life after death, especially when this information was presented more in medical terms than in religious terms, atheists appeared to gain some existential benefits. That is, they did not need to further engage psychological defenses against the threat of death-awareness.

Studies such as these demonstrate that self-report can be a valuable tool even when researchers do not expect participants to fully understand their own motives. Atheist participants were not asked whether they believed the case for the existence of life after death was strong or convincing. Instead, they were given an unrelated and secular opportunity (i.e., nationalistic defense) to respond to the threat of increased death awareness. Atheists who were presented with the argument for immortality did not use the secular opportunity to counter death thoughts. But those who were presented with the counterargument that there is no reason to believe in life after death did employ the secular defense against death. Atheists may gain some comfort from the prospect of an afterlife whether they realize it or not.

WHY DON'T ATHEISTS JUST JOIN IN?

If atheists show some cognitive and physiological signs of religiosity and can gain some psychological benefits from concepts associated with religion, why don't they just join in and consciously embrace their spiritual nature? First, it is important to remember that atheists probably don't realize they get any benefit for religious or spiritual ideas. Before reading this chapter had you ever heard of any of these studies I just described?

I assume that most people are unaware of this research and would be surprised to find out that atheists more quickly associate God with the concept of "real" after thinking about death, show physiological signs of anxiety when challenging God to do harm, or receive psychological protection similar to believers when given hope (in more scientific sounding terms) that there may be a blissful existence beyond physical death. It is hard to see the value of religious concepts if one does not realize that he or she is benefiting from them.

Think about a different example. You could not believe that you are benefiting in any way from having a police force in your city. You may even have very negative attitudes about the police and see them as causing more harm than good. Some folks hold such beliefs. However, this does not mean you are not receiving any benefits from the police. Police serve a number of important functions whether you believe it or not. People who don't value the police still reap the benefits of local law enforcement. In other words, the police do not need you to believe in them in order to serve the community. Nonreligious folks may be similar in their inability to see what they are getting out of religious ideas and concepts. Might the mere existence of religion be beneficial, even to those who don't perceive it as valid or important?

In addition, most of us, religious or not, are pretty defensive of our beliefs. We don't like the idea that we may have aspects of our personality or self-concept that we don't fully appreciate or even want. Do you know someone who has a horrible diet but thinks he is living a healthy lifestyle? Thinks he is athletic but never exercises? Is a good guitar player but actually is pretty mediocre? Thinks he can dance like Michael Jackson but looks more like he is having a seizure on the dance floor? You get the idea. Our self-views can be biased because they partially reflect how we want to see ourselves. Many atheists may not want to see themselves as being influenced by religious and spiritual ideas and so they struggle to accept the possibility.

I once had a pretty heated discussion with a fellow social psychologist about this issue. I was describing some of the findings I just discussed as well as some other related research we are currently conducting in my lab and he became very defensive. He was quick to dismiss the data, claiming that the experiments must be fundamentally flawed in some way. Maybe the participants really weren't atheists. Maybe the researchers were biased. And so on. Interestingly, he did not have a specific or particularly compelling alternative explanation of these findings or any evidence of systematic bias in the studies. The findings simply did not sit well with him. Of course, as scientists and consumers of science we have to be critical of all research. Studies have flaws and limitations. And many do not replicate. But we also need to be mindful of our own biases. Just because we don't like a finding does not mean it is wrong.

The Secular Supernatural

et's talk about the "nones." Public polls identify a growing group of Americans often referred to as religious nones—individuals who do not identify with a specific religious group or tradition. According to a Pew Research Center poll, as of 2014, nones make up about a quarter of the US population.[1] Nones don't feel as if they belong to a religion, but this does not mean they are atheists or have no spiritual inclination. For instance, about 60% of nones believe in God or a universal spirit, according to Pew.[2] And even those who do claim to be atheist may feel uncertain about what they do and do not believe and what they are and are not open to exploring spiritually. As we discussed in the last chapter, there is only a very small percentage of people who are extremely confident in their rejection of all things supernatural.

Young adults in particular are abandoning what they perceive as culturally outdated religious organizations and instead opting for a more individualized approach to spiritual matters. Indeed, Pew data indicates that over one-third of American millennials are unaffiliated with a religion.[3] Some of them are atheist, but many simply do not feel aligned with any particular traditional faith. They are people who grew up in one faith but do not agree with all of its teachings. Or they are people with parents from different faiths and thus don't see themselves as having a single religious identity. They are people who were not raised in church-attending families or people who simply cannot settle on a single religious identity. And some of these people just feel that organized religion is not welcoming.

Some young people reject formal religion simply because they find it boring. They are seeking experiences that feel fresh and exciting, and religion isn't something that checks that box. They see religion as being about the past, a tradition maintained by old people. Churches are clearly aware of this issue and scrambling to entice a younger crowd. As we discussed in chapter 3, new nondenominational churches appear to be thriving. They are attracting young adults and families looking for a spiritual home, but one distinct from the church they grew up in. Still, the numbers don't lie. Many young people are walking away from religious affiliations and practices.

The "nones" may be leading an exodus from religion on a scale never seen before in American history, but their abandonment of the pews does not mean they are abandoning their desire to explore the supernatural. There are, in fact, many clues suggesting that as people turn away from religion they more heavily invest in alternative endeavors to access the supernatural. Consider, for instance, the growth of publishing in spirituality. HarperOne, an imprint of HarperCollins and one of the largest publishers of spiritual books, has a new line of books they are calling the HarperElixer series. Here is the description of this line of books taken directly from the HarperElixer webpage:[4]

> HarperElixir books, handpicked with purpose and intent, are selected specially for you—those who are spiritual, magical, compassionate, and curious, those who want to find truth, meaning, miracles, discover the mysteries, and answer the call to go deeper and to find

answers to fundamental questions: What is my purpose? Where am I going? How can I have more meaning in my life and relationships?

Sound familiar? These are the types of questions people are trying to answer through religious faith and the types of questions that result, in part, from an awareness of self and death. As religion loses its grip on them, people are becoming more and more interested in new and less restrictive ways of thinking about spiritual questions involving the supernatural.

And as we've seen, like other forms of business in the United States, the supernatural business is part of a free market. Ideas have to compete against one another to gain traction. And as large bureaucratic religious organizations struggle to adapt to rapidly changing social and cultural views and challenges, a new and nimbler option may be emerging. Books, magazines, television, and especially the Internet have allowed people to access a range of supernatural ideas and customize their own religious-like identity.

In chapter 3, I discussed more contemporary religious movements. These movements offer new ways for younger adults and families to worship and connect. However, they are still tied to particular religious traditions. In this chapter, I focus on supernatural ideas, beliefs, or possibilities that are not associated with specific religious traditions. They represent a more à la carte approach to existential questions and concerns about death and meaning. People can entertain any supernatural idea they want to without approval from a religious hierarchy or institution, and this freedom allows them to pursue existential needs in a range of unique ways.

As was made clear in the last chapter on cognitive, physiological, and indirect measures of religiosity, just because people say they are not religious does not mean that they are not influenced by supernatural thoughts and beliefs. But that was more about intuitive associations and cognitions. These were not beliefs that people were knowingly endorsing. Now let's consider some of the conscious beliefs that people who reject formal religion turn to in order to meet existential needs, the types of beliefs that attract people like the religious nones.

NEW AGE SPIRITUALITY

Ever heard the phrase "spiritual but not religious"? What do people actually mean when they say that? When I ask people about this distinction a common answer is that being spiritual but not religious means to not identify with any one particular religious system of belief but to acknowledge that humans have a spiritual essence beyond the material. In other words, spirituality implies dualism, the existence of nonphysical forces or energy. From this perspective, the religious idea of a soul might be correct or at least is in line with the notion of spiritual energy.

Some of the people I have talked to who refer to themselves as spiritual but not religious say they believe in reincarnation. They don't necessarily have a specific belief about how people come back but generally favor the idea that a person's self or essence has more than one go at life. Others do not use the term "reincarnation" but say they believe that humans have some kind of spiritual energy that is left behind when their body dies. Perhaps this energy returns to the Earth or the universe in some way the human brain cannot comprehend, but, critically, it is not extinguished. And some say they don't really know what they believe but they just have a strong feeling that there is something to the human condition beyond what science can or will ever be able to explain.

Many popular activities such as yoga, martial arts, and meditation involve these types of spiritual ideas. As someone who has participated in a number of yoga and martial arts classes throughout my life, I cannot begin to list the number times I have experienced the call to channel, focus, or calm my spiritual energy.

Some of the most popular concepts related to this type of spirituality fall under the category of new age or alternative healing. New age healing methods prominently feature the type of dualistic supernatural thinking referenced here. They assume a spiritual energy, something not understood by traditional Western materialist medicine. And though these methods are widely criticized as being pseudoscientific, they are thriving.

Reiki is one such popular spiritual healing method. It involves the use of human touch to redirect life force energy in the body in order to treat symptoms associated with a range of diseases such as cancer and depression. With the endorsement of some celebrities, Reiki is also becoming a popular tool for weight loss. The basic idea is that stress is a barrier to weight loss and Reiki, by moving energy around in your body, reduces stress, ultimately making it easier to shed those pounds.

Despite the fact that there is no evidence supporting the existence of the type of energy in the body that Reiki and other alternative healing practices propose, hundreds of hospitals in the United States offer Reiki as part of their treatment services. And some health insurance companies cover the cost of Reiki. More and more healthcare professionals are taking Reiki training courses so they can add this form of therapy to their arsenal of treatment options. Relatively secular countries such as the United Kingdom offer Reiki as a treatment option in many hospitals. This is particularly noteworthy considering that the United Kingdom has nationalized healthcare. Thus UK tax dollars are being used to fund a treatment that is not based on any reputable scientific evidence but instead is based on a belief in supernatural energy.

If Reiki and other alternative healing methods, and there are lots of them, are pseudoscientific, why are they so popular? I propose that these spiritual healing methods are attractive because they contribute to existential security. They speak to peoples' need for meaning. Indeed, research indicates that people are attracted to alternative medicine and healing practices not because they have rejected conventional medicine but because these more spiritual practices affirm a meaning-providing worldview focused on holistic health.[5]

And by affirming meaning, these healing practices may actually have therapeutic value. Meaning promotes health. People who feel like their lives are meaningful are more motivated, recover more quickly, and live longer. (I discuss the many mental and physical health benefits of supernatural beliefs in detail in chapter 6.) As fewer people seek spiritual counseling from traditional religious sources, they may increasingly turn to these new age healing practices.

THE POWER OF THE PARANORMAL

Do a little late night channel surfing and you will likely come across some kind of television program about ghost hunting, haunted houses, communicating with the dead or spirits, and other amazing supposed real-life stories involving the type of supernatural phenomena typically associated with horror movies. For instance, one of the most popular television programs on the cable channel SyFy is a reality program called Ghost Hunters. The show focuses on a team of ghost hunters who investigate reports of haunted places and has been aired for over 10 seasons now.

The paranormal reality television genre more broadly has been quite popular with viewers based on the dozens of shows across network, cable, and Internet channels that have aired over the last couple of decades. And this does not include the many books and other forms of media concerning supernatural paranormal activity.

Though we tend not to associate these kinds of interests with religiosity, there are noteworthy similarities between beliefs about God and other religious phenomena and beliefs and curiosities regarding paranormal supernatural forces such as ghosts. First, there is reason to believe that for some people, paranormal supernatural beliefs may reflect efforts to fill the existential void potentially created by abandoning more traditional religious beliefs. Consider, for example, survey data indicating that as religiosity declines in America, belief in ghosts and other supernatural spiritual forces is increasing.

In one 2009 Pew survey, nearly 30% of respondents reported having felt in contact with someone who has died and nearly 20% reported believing that they have been in the presence of a ghost.[6] A 2012 poll similarly found that 28% of respondents believed they had been in the presence of a ghost, 32% believed that ghosts could interact with and even harm humans, and 45% believed in the existence of ghosts or that spirits could come back from the dead.[7]

These numbers are much higher than those of decades past, when more people were religious. In fact, in the 2009 Pew survey, people who did not frequently attend church were twice as likely to believe in ghosts as those who were regular churchgoers.[8] The less plugged in someone is to a specific religious faith, the more likely they are to believe in other types of supernatural forces such as ghosts.

This pattern of less religiosity being associated with greater belief in nonreligious supernatural phenomena is found cross-culturally. We always hear about secular Scandinavia. Countries like Sweden are increasingly nonreligious. However, it turns out, according to polling data, as religion is on the decline in Sweden, paranormal beliefs such as belief in ghosts are on the rise.[9] In this survey, 37% of respondents indicated believing in paranormal phenomena that cannot be explained by science, but only 21% reported believing in God. Many so-called secular cultures contain myths and superstitions related to supernatural spirits and forces. And, just as in the United States, as traditional religiosity declines, paranormal media is becoming increasingly popular in secular Europe.

Looking more broadly at the full range of these kinds of beliefs, according to the 2009 Pew survey, about 65% of Americans report holding supernatural paranormal beliefs of some kind. In addition to belief in ghosts, these include belief in reincarnation, spiritual energy, and psychic powers. Contrary to what some modern atheists may claim, it does not appear to be the case that decreasing levels of religiosity reflect a move toward an exclusive reliance on rational and empirically based beliefs.

It is certainly true that as science reveals more and more about the human condition, people are increasingly invested in consuming science and basing decisions on data. However, this does not mean they are completely shutting down their interest in the supernatural. To many, science and the supernatural are not at odds. It might be more accurate, then, to say that as people move away from one type of supernatural belief system such as a religious faith or become less dogmatic about that belief system they have more spiritual bandwidth available for exploring other supernatural ideas such as those related to the paranormal.

To compare nonreligious supernatural beliefs to religion suggests that these beliefs are motivated by the same existential needs that inspire religious faith. That is, they help people grapple with concerns about death and meaning. Is this true?

Over the last couple of years my lab has been conducting research to answer this question, and we have found preliminary evidence supporting the idea that belief in supernatural phenomena such as ghosts serves an existential function.[10]

In one experiment, for example, we sought to undermine belief in ghosts to determine whether doing so would decrease people's perceptions of meaning in life. If the idea that ghosts are real provides meaning in life, then discrediting evidence supporting the existence of ghosts should lower people's sense of meaning.

In this experiment we presented participants with a famous picture of a British soldier (Freddy Jackson) from World War I whose image was supposedly captured in a group photo taken after he was confirmed dead. In other words, the image appears to have been Freddy Jackson's ghost. Participants also read a brief paragraph explaining why this photo is evidence of a ghost. As the story goes, Freddy Jackson had been killed a couple of days before a picture of his squadron was taken. In fact, it was reported that his funeral was the same day as the photo shoot.

Here comes the critical part. Half of the participants were presented with additional information debunking the ghost story. For example, the photo, which was supposedly taken in 1919, did not appear until 1975. Furthermore, the person who revealed this photo in 1975 also had told other interesting stories involving topics such as UFOs and time travel: he might not have been the most reliable source. Plus, by the time the photo was publicly released in the 1970s, conveniently, none of the other individuals in the picture were alive to testify to its authenticity. In fact, no evidence could be found that there was even a man in the squadron named Freddy Jackson. Combined, this evidence casts considerable doubt on the validity of the Freddy Jackson ghost story.

To ensure that our efforts to debunk the ghost story worked, we had all of the participants in this study answer questions concerning their belief that the photo was a real ghost caught on camera. Not surprisingly, participants who were presented with the additional information discrediting the legitimacy of the photo were less likely to believe the photo was a real ghost than participants who were not provided with this information. We effectively debunked the ghost story for half of the participants.

After answering questions about whether they believed the picture to be of a real ghost, participants completed the critical measure of interest, a questionnaire assessing the extent to which they perceive life as meaningful. Did revealing the picture to be a hoax decrease participants' perceptions of meaning in life?

Yes. Participants who received the additional information debunking the ghost story reported lower levels of meaning in life than participants who did not receive this information. The possibility of ghosts affirms meaning, so when a famous ghost story is debunked meaning takes a hit. No wonder people like paranormal television programs that offer some hope for the existence of ghosts.

But why? What about the ghosts makes one's life feel more meaningful? It makes sense that losing one's faith in God could jeopardize the feeling that life is meaningful, but why would losing faith in the possibility of ghosts have a similar psychological impact? Remember, part of what gives humans a sense of meaning is the idea that we are more than purely physical beings destined to die and turn to dust. We want to feel immortal in some way. The possibility of ghosts offers hope that there is some kind of nonphysical energy not extinguished by physical death. Ghosts open the door to an existence beyond what science has taught us. And if there is some kind of nonphysical realm, some form of energy that mortality cannot totally snuff out, perhaps we are more meaningful than we realize.

If nothing else, the idea of ghosts offers the hope of uncertainty about what physical death means. A purely materialist view of existence suggests that a human being is nothing special, just another physical organism. From this perspective, humans are born and die and that is it. In other words, a materialist view does not leave a lot of room for imagining something grander. But if ghosts are real, it means we don't really fully understand our essence. Maybe our earthly lives only represent one phase of the existence of our minds. Maybe the physical body dies but the mind continues on in some form of energy beyond what science can measure.

Psychologists typically treat the feeling of uncertainty as a threat to meaning. After all, uncertainty is often an unpleasant feeling and typically associated with a lack of confidence in what one believes and how one is living. But uncertainty can be psychologically beneficial to the extent that it offers hope. In other words, sometimes meaning comes from mystery. Many agnostics will say that though they do not see any compelling reason to believe in a God, they do not call themselves atheists because they don't believe science can provide any certainty that God does not exist. The uncertainty leaves open the possibility of a deity and, whether people realize it or not, this possibility, as slight as it may seem, can be a source of meaning. If ghosts are potentially real then just maybe there is something more to existence than the physical.

Our research on the connection between existential motives and belief in ghosts is preliminary at this point. However, more generally, research indicates that supernatural paranormal beliefs are related to the need for meaning. For instance, people who report having experienced encounters with supernatural forces report a greater sense of meaning in life than those who have not had such experiences.[11] Research also finds that meaning in life is positively correlated with a broad range of paranormal beliefs such as belief in psychic energy, the predictive power of astrology, and the existence of dark magic.[12] And as I discussed in chapter 3, many studies, including experimental research from my lab, demonstrate that the need for meaning motivates supernatural religious beliefs such as belief in miracles[13] and evil supernatural forces.[14]

I suspect many people merely find paranormal supernatural ideas and possibilities fun to think about and not something they spend a lot of time pondering or investing in. But isn't this similar to religion? Many people who self-identify as religious are really only casual believers. In surveys, far more people will say they are religious and believe in God than actually attend religious services. And even fewer give money to the church, volunteer for church activities, and take on positions of leadership. Most religious people are not living like monks, completely dedicated to a holy lifestyle. Their day-to-day lives are largely secular, but they set a little space aside for their faith. They like the existential comfort they get from the sense of meaning and immortality that religion provides but they are not so dedicated that they will prioritize their faith over other goals and interests.

Said differently, even though most people like to spend a little time thinking about and hoping for something beyond the material, the demands of daily existence keep them largely focused on the physical world, not the supernatural one. This isn't to say people aren't truly committed to their beliefs. It is more accurate to say that a little faith can go a long way.

Paranormal supernatural beliefs about ghosts and other forces may similarly require minimal commitment to reap existential benefits. Like religion, there will be a small minority of hardcore believers, the ghost hunters and avid followers who faithfully consume all related media and make pilgrimages to famous haunted locales. When I started writing this book I actually looked into staying in a haunted house just for the experience of having done it. In my research I discovered that the closest place for me to stay is the Villisca Ax Murderer House in Iowa. In 1912, an attacker or group of attackers murdered an entire family and two family guests in their beds. The perpetrators were never caught. The current owners of the house claim that paranormal investigators have documented evidence of paranormal activity in the house and numerous guests have offered further testimonials of ghostly encounters including hearing children's voices and seeing objects move and fly around the house. Psychics have also claimed to have successfully communicated with the spirits haunting the house. When I looked at the availability calendar on the booking website I was impressed that it was booked pretty full, especially considering the minimum cost is over $400.

According to the *Wall Street Journal*,[15] paranormal tourism is on the rise and may generate over $500 million in revenue in the United States each year. As more and more people become fascinated with paranormal activity, the paranormal industry in all its forms continues to grow to meet this new level of demand.

Most people who entertain ghost beliefs will not go so far as to take a cross-country road trip to visit a haunted house. But you don't have to physically visit a haunted house to gain existential comfort just as you don't have to make a trip to holy Christian sites to gain comfort from a belief in God and Jesus Christ. The very possibility that there may be forces and energy beyond the material world is enough to offer hope that we are more than decaying biological matter.

SUPERNATURAL LITE: EXTRATERRESTRIAL INTELLIGENCE

For some who reject the idea of a God or other supernatural religious agents, the idea of ghosts might be a hard sell. Paranormal investigators do their best to make the hunt for ghosts appear more scientific and less religious by using technological equipment and methods that, on the surface, appear to be documenting measurable paranormal activity. However, they are still ultimately making a case for the supernatural, forces beyond established scientific understanding of the physical world.

Though it does appear to generally be the case that as people move away from more traditional religious beliefs they become more open to other supernatural ideas such as ghosts, there are also those who reject all things supernatural. So what about these folks? As we discussed in the previous chapter, they may be intuitively benefiting from supernatural concepts such as God and life after death. But do these individuals consciously hold any beliefs that touch on the supernatural?

I think they do, or at least some of them do. And based on my research and the work of other scholars, it appears that belief in extraterrestrial intelligence (ETI) is one such belief. First, on the surface, belief in ETI does not invoke the supernatural. The idea that there is other intelligent life in the universe is not necessarily inconsistent with our understanding of the physical world. In fact, a number of scientists and scholars have argued that it is quite reasonable to predict that intelligent life would have evolved somewhere else.

Therefore, it seems sensible to treat ETI beliefs as something quite distinct from belief in ghosts or other supernatural agents and forces. In fact, there are legitimate scientific endeavors to search for life on other worlds such as SETI (the search for extraterrestrial intelligence). These efforts employ established methods and instruments and enjoy the support of many respected scientists. So we can certainly think of interest in ETI as being unrelated to the supernatural.

That being said, one need only dig a little deeper into specific ETI beliefs to realize that there is a big distinction between dispassionately searching for life on other worlds and some of the conspiracy-like beliefs many hold. In a 2012 *National Geographic* poll,[16] only 17% of American respondents indicated that they don't believe that UFOs are real. In that poll, 36% were confident that UFOs are indeed real and the remaining 48% were unsure.

So, despite there being no compelling evidence that UFOs exist, there are over twice as many believers as nonbelievers. More surprisingly perhaps was that in the same poll, 79% of respondents reported believing that the government is keeping secrets about UFOs from the public and 55% indicated that they believe the government threatens those who witness a UFO.

A different poll found that around 50% of Americans believe that intelligent aliens are monitoring human activity on Earth.[17] In other words, many of the beliefs about ETI do not simply represent an openness to and interest in searching for alien life on other planets. Instead, they reflect more specific beliefs that aliens have traveled to Earth, are covertly monitoring human behavior, and are being hidden from us by the government.

A closer look at some of the specific beliefs people hold about UFOs and alien visitors reveals a number of similarities between these beliefs and supernatural religious beliefs. Alien visitors are often depicted as having God-like powers such as telepathy and mind control. Sometimes these powers are viewed as benevolent. These enlightened beings are here to watch over humans and help us reach our full potential. Aliens may even be concealing themselves from humans because we have not yet reached a point of species maturity to join a broader cosmic community. Once we get our act together these cosmic guardian angels will reveal themselves and help us reach that next level of enlightenment.

Sometimes aliens are viewed as more malevolent agents who are here to exploit and potentially even destroy our species. Hollywood clearly likes this view, judging from the number of movies made involving sinister intelligent alien beings attacking Earth. Fortunately, according to the movies, people, particularly Americans, seem well equipped to defeat alien invaders and save the world.

Beliefs about ETI are particularly attractive to many religious skeptics because they can be described in ways that do not invoke the supernatural. However, there is also no compelling evidence that the God-like aliens people often envision exist. Just because intelligent life *could* exist somewhere else in the vast universe does not mean that an intellectually superior and technologically advanced alien species has found its way to Earth and is watching over us (or plotting to destroy us so they can take all our natural resources).

These particular ETI beliefs sound a lot like belief in gods and other supernatural agents. This is why I refer to them as "supernatural-lite." They often don't explicitly involve the supernatural, but they do involve a certain level of faith and a willingness to believe in powerful agents without compelling evidence of their existence.

As with supernatural belief in ghosts, ETI beliefs appear to be on the rise as religion is on the decline. According to the National UFO Reporting Center, the number of reported UFO sightings has been steadily increasing over the last 20 years. In the modern world fewer and fewer people look at nature and see the work of God. However, more and more people are evidently seeing flying saucers.

In countries like the United Kingdom, where there are relatively large numbers of atheists, belief in UFOs is quite common. For example, one 2014 poll found that 42% of UK citizens believe in UFOs but only 25% believe in God.[18] Other surveys suggest the number of people in the United Kingdom who believe in God is actually higher than 25%, but all studies that have asked questions about God and UFOs have found that more people believe that aliens have visited Earth than believe in the existence of a deity.

Not only are ETI beliefs generally increasing as religion's influence decreases but also psychologists have observed an inverse correlation between an individual's personal religiosity and belief in ETI.[19] And I'm not talking about the scientific pursuit to find life in the universe: I mean the more religious-like ETI beliefs such as the belief that a superior alien species is watching over humans and even the belief that aliens have greatly influenced human culture (e.g., aliens built the pyramids in Egypt).

My lab has been conducting studies on this particular topic and, like other researchers, we have discovered a reliable relationship between low religiosity and high belief in ETI.[20] We also find more specifically that atheists and agnostics are significantly more likely to hold ETI beliefs than those who identify as religious. In most of the studies my lab conducts we include questions about religiosity and belief in UFOs and intelligent aliens visiting Earth and we reliably find the same pattern of results. Those who do not identify as religious (religious nones, agnostics, and atheists) are more inclined to believe that UFOs are real and aliens are among us than those who do identify as religious. The author Michael Shermer asserted that ETIs are "secular gods—deities for atheists."[21] His assertion appears to be correct. Despite there being no compelling data to support these kind of ETI beliefs, many atheists hold them.

These ETI beliefs seem particularly attractive to people who reject supernatural ideas and beliefs related to religion. But do these beliefs, like religion or belief in ghosts, reflect efforts to find existential security? I thought they might—and thus set out to test this possibility.[22]

In our first study, we used a meaning threat manipulation to see whether people are more likely to endorse ETI beliefs when their sense of life as meaningful has been undermined. Half of the participants read the life-is-objectively-meaningless philosophical essay described in previous chapters. The other half read the control essay. Next, all of the participants completed a questionnaire assessing ETI beliefs such as the beliefs that UFOs are real, intelligent aliens have visited Earth, and the American government is hiding UFO evidence from the public.

Results confirmed that people use ETI beliefs to affirm meaning. Participants who read the life-is-objectively-meaningless essay reported significantly higher levels of ETI beliefs than those in the control condition. In other studies we observed similar relationships between scores on meaning measures and ETI beliefs. The less people perceived their lives as meaningful and the more they were searching for meaning in life, the more they believed in ETI. When meaning is compromised and people are scrambling to restore existential security, they are more attracted to the idea that intelligent aliens are among us.

In this research, our team also sought to connect the link between meaning-seeking and ETI beliefs to a lack of religiosity. As noted before, studies generally find that ETI beliefs are more common among the nonreligious. And in chapter 3 we saw that research indicates that religion is a powerful source of meaning: higher religiosity is associated with higher levels of perceived meaning. Thus, we proposed that one reason nonreligious people are more inclined to hold ETI beliefs is because they have deficits in meaning.

Michael Shermer, as we saw, claimed that ETIs are deities for atheists. But are atheists interested in ETI beliefs because they are searching for meaning? To test this, in two different samples we administered questionnaires assessing religiosity, perceptions of meaning, the desire to search for meaning, and ETI beliefs. We then tested a statistical model linking these different variables. First, we observed all the correlations that would be expected. Low religiosity was associated with low perceived meaning and a higher level of search for meaning. Low religiosity was also associated with greater belief in ETI. And low perceived meaning and high search for meaning corresponded with high ETI beliefs.

Critically, using statistical modeling techniques we found support for a model linking low religiosity to high ETI beliefs via a lack of meaning and a desire to find it. That is, nonreligious folks were less inclined to view life as meaningful and thus more motivated to search for meaning than religious folks. And this existential vulnerability appeared to make these nonreligious individuals more attracted to belief in alien visitors. We found an identical pattern when we specifically compared atheists to theists. Atheists are less likely to perceive life as meaningful than theists and thus more inclined to be searching for meaning. And this search for meaning leads atheists to believe in UFOs and alien visitors.

What is it about these ETI beliefs that potentially offer meaning? If they are not explicitly supernatural in nature, how do they make humans feel more than mortal?

There are a number of possible explanations. As noted, intelligent aliens are often viewed as intellectually and technologically superior to humans. In this way, some believe that these beings will ultimately provide humans with the keys to longer life, perhaps even immortality. Many narratives about ETI involve aliens having developed cures to human diseases and medical interventions that can reverse the damage of severe trauma and disability and even stop the aging process altogether.

Beyond the medical innovations that these beings could potentially offer, the idea that there is an advanced species watching over humankind can provide a sense of existential value, that humans have been deemed important enough to observe and protect. Some even believe that alien beings are responsible for human existence, that they are our creators. Such a belief makes the world seem less random and unpredictable. We were created with greater purpose in mind.

More generally, the existence of other life in the universe makes people feel less cosmically alone. If other intelligent beings exist, perhaps we are not merely accidents of nature.

Thus, ETI beliefs show just how powerful the pull of the supernatural is for humans. Interest in the search for alien life does not need to implicate the supernatural, but it often does involve some kind of supernatural-lite belief. For many, it is not enough to simply be curious about the possibility of other intelligent beings in the universe. They want to imagine that god-like aliens are among us. In addition, because many ETI believers are atheists or agnostics and do not see any connection between their beliefs about alien visitors and supernatural religious beliefs, they often become quite defensive when a connection is suggested. I have had a number of interesting encounters with irritated atheists when presenting my research on the existential motives for ETI beliefs among atheists. And, after publishing an op-ed in the *New York Times*[23] on this research, I received a number of e-mails and letters from ETI advocates insulted that I would suggest their beliefs are motivated, like religion, by existential questions about meaning.

I remember one very smart psychologist giving me a very baffled look when I described beliefs about UFOs, alien abductions, and government cover-ups as being similar to other paranormal beliefs because they defy an accepted scientific understanding of the world. He challenged the idea and suggested that these beliefs are, in fact, quite reasonable and that it was ridiculous to compare them to beliefs related to ghosts, psychic powers, and deities. And yet, he could not generate a shred of evidence for such beliefs.

TRANSHUMANISM AS TECHNO-SPIRITUALITY

Let's consider another way people may be doing supernatural-lite. I proposed that one of the reasons ETI beliefs are attractive to those who reject the supernatural is because these beliefs can be cloaked by scientific and technological jargon and thus seem pretty far removed from concepts such as ghosts and spirits. Paranormal investigators seeking evidence for the existence of ghosts are, of course, similarly trying to distinguish themselves from religion in their own way by using tools and methods that they consider to be more scientific than spiritual. But there are other movements that go even further to pursue existential needs in ways that make their members feel completely divorced from all things supernatural.

One of these movements is transhumanism. The general goal of transhumanism is to improve and enhance the lives of humans using science and technology. The specific feature of this movement that is most relevant for this book is the pursuit of immortality. Transhumanism, like religion, seeks to solve the problem of death. However, unlike religion, transhumanism does not necessarily invoke supernatural beliefs to make people feel more than mortal. Its adherents put their faith in science, not religion.

How do transhumanists think science will provide eternal life? There are a number of possibilities. Scientific and medical innovations have already allowed us to live longer and healthier lives than our ancestors. Future breakthroughs could cure diseases, stop the aging process, or provide us a way to escape our fragile and mortal bodies altogether. Perhaps we will be able to one day transfer a person's consciousness to a machine or computer. A lot of these ideas sound more like science fiction than actual science, but the common theme is that humans can create their own salvation. God won't save us, our own intelligence and ingenuity will.

This definitely sounds pretty far removed from supernatural beliefs, right? After all, the whole idea is based on the assumption that we are on our own. There is no soul or afterlife, no God to rescue us. We have to think our way out of death. Not surprisingly then, the transhumanism movement is populated largely by atheists. It gives people with no faith in the supernatural their own way to actively combat the existential threat of mortality. To the extent that the fundamental concern of religion is mortality, transhumanism could be thought of as a secular religious movement.

Indeed, social psychologists recently explored the potential for transhumanist ideas to offer religious-like protection against the existential threat of mortality.[24] In this research, participants read articles supporting one of two positions. One article made the claim that medical and technological advances being made right now are making it possible and even likely that people will be able to live much longer lives in the near future and that it is even conceivable that by the middle of this century we will have the ability to extend human life indefinitely. In other words, scientists are getting closer and closer to solving the problem of biological death.

The other article described the idea of science being used to indefinitely extend human life but took a more critical approach, arguing that there is little scientific evidence to support the claim that we are on the verge of stopping or reversing the aging process. This article described indefinite life extension ideas as nothing more than pseudoscience. So one article made it appear that the idea of indefinite life is reasonable, whereas the other article made it appear that such an idea is nothing more than wishful thinking.

In this study, the researchers also had some participants think about their mortality and some think about a non-death-related topic. This feature was added to determine whether the existential threat of heightened death awareness influenced transhumanist attitudes about the possibility of indefinite life extension. The final component of the study was a questionnaire measuring transhumanist attitudes. It specifically assessed the extent to which participants supported the goal of indefinite life extension, thought the goal was achievable, and wanted to have their own lives extended.

The study produced two interesting patterns of findings. First, providing people with reasons to be optimistic or pessimistic about indefinite life extension affected participants' level of support for this goal. However, people's level of religiosity greatly influenced this effect.

For those who identified as highly religious, being presented with a case for or against indefinite life extension did not influence attitudes. Highly religious people have already found a solution to the problem of death through their faith in eternal salvation. It was only for nonreligious participants that reading one of these articles had any impact on attitudes. Specifically, nonreligious individuals were significantly more likely to support the idea of scientists pursuing indefinite life extension if they had read the article suggesting that it is a legitimate and achievable goal that could be reached in the coming decades. Nonreligious participants who were not given such hope had attitudes indistinguishable from their highly religious counterparts.

In short, providing those who do not have a religious path to immortality with hope for immortality through scientific innovation inspired support for transhumanist ideas and goals. Atheists don't want to die and disappear forever any more than anyone else. The problem of mortality is a problem all humans face, regardless of their religious beliefs.

The other pattern of findings involved the heightened death-awareness manipulation. Having people think about death influenced their support for the goal of indefinite life extension. But again, religious identification played a critical role. For highly religious people, thinking about death actually decreased support for indefinite life extension. These people believe in life after death based on religious faith. Therefore, the existential threat of death-awareness pushed them toward their religious path to immortality, thus decreasing their support for trying to use science to solve the problem of death.

To some highly religious people, transhumanist goals might be perceived as humans trying to play God, a potential threat to their religious worldview. Indeed, other research shows that people who strongly believe they have an eternal soul are not particularly concerned about the possibility of the world ending.[25] They have a religious path to immortality.

The results were the opposite for nonreligious participants. Thinking about death inspired these participants to exhibit greater support for the scientific pursuit of indefinite life extension. Nonreligious individuals are less inclined to believe in an afterlife. Therefore, when they are grappling with existential fears they become more hopeful about finding immortality on Earth through medical innovations. This finding is consistent with the idea advanced by some scholars that scientific efforts to replicate or upload people's brain patterns are rooted in existential fears about death.[26]

In the last chapter I discussed research showing that even atheists can gain some existential comfort from the hope of consciousness beyond death, even if they do not realize it. Transhumanism, however, offers them a more palatable belief system, something they can thoughtfully endorse because it is consistent with an atheist worldview that humans are on their own. But it turns out even the transhumanism movement that, in many ways, represents an antisupernatural belief system is influenced by the existential power of supernatural thinking.

In 2006, a small group of transhumanists founded the Mormon Transhumanist Association based on the belief that Mormonism and transhumanism share a number of similar ideas. Notably, both perspectives advance the idea of improving human life and seeking some form of transcendence. Of course, this similarity could be made between transhumanism and many religions. The Mormon Transhumanist Association offers a venue for members to discuss the relation between technology and spirituality, share information and educational materials regarding transhumanist ideas, and work together to advance the causes of curing diseases and extending human life.

Despite transhumanism being a movement that tends to attract atheists, the majority of the members of the Mormon Transhumanist Association believe in God (60%) and are members of the Church of Latter Day Saints (62%).[27] They are people who see supernatural beliefs and the pursuit of immortality through science as going hand in hand.

Transhumanists even have their own church now. The Church of Perpetual Life[28] offers anyone of any faith (or no faith) a way to have fellowship with others interested in the pursuit of eternal life on Earth through scientific and technological innovation.

Though not all transhumanists are happy about the mixing of spirituality and transhumanism, a number of enthusiasts have argued that there are many similarities between both traditional and new alternative religious movements and the ideas being advanced in transhumanism. Religion and transhumanism both promote self-improvement, efforts to make the world a better place, community involvement, and finding meaning through some form of death-transcendence.

As more people become interested in transhumanist ideas and possibilities we will likely see even more efforts to bridge the gap between scientific and spiritual approaches to existential questions. Some of the individuals who consider themselves spiritual transhumanists discuss ideas that sound quite similar to the ETI beliefs previously considered, such as the possibility that God-like intelligent beings exist in the universe. Some spiritual transhumanists have proposed that humans can themselves endeavor to be God-like. We can solve the problem of death and even create new life through innovations in artificial intelligence. If there is a God and he created us in his image, then perhaps it is our destiny to become more like him. Maybe God wants us to engineer our own salvation.

Like other new religious, spiritual, and supernatural movements, there is no single unifying set of beliefs or tenets for spiritual transhumanism. It represents a more open and explorative way of approaching existential questions about life, death, and meaning. Clearly though, transhumanism cannot escape our species' supernatural nature. Even when people purposely set out to create an approach to resolving existential concerns that does not involve supernatural ideas, these ideas eventually begin to creep in.

HOW DO ALTERNATIVE SUPERNATURAL AND SUPERNATURAL-LITE INTERESTS COMPARE TO RELIGION?

An important remaining question is how well nontraditional supernatural and supernatural-lite beliefs meet existential needs and help people cope with the many life challenges that can undermine meaning and, ultimately, mental and physical health. Lab studies linking these beliefs to meaning offer a nice theoretical test. But do these nontraditional beliefs actually work in the real world? The short answer is we don't know.

Research linking death-awareness and the pursuit of meaning to these nontraditional ideas and beliefs is relatively new, especially compared to the decades of research linking traditional religiosity to perceptions of meaning and self-transcendence. In the next chapter, I discuss at length research showing that supernatural beliefs have many real-world positive and enduring health benefits. Most of this work, though certainly not all of it, focuses on traditional religious beliefs and identities. So we know a lot about how traditional religion provides existential comfort and improves the quality of life for many. We simply do not know, in a real-world setting and in the long run, how well less traditional supernatural beliefs work in terms of helping people find and maintain a sense of transcendent meaning, the type of meaning that contributes to a happy and healthy life.

What we do know, as discussed in this book, is that people are attracted to supernatural ideas and beliefs when grappling with existential questions about death and meaning. Many, perhaps most, turn to more conventional beliefs. But a growing number of individuals are turning away from traditional beliefs and seeking meaning in other supernatural beliefs. Unlike the traditional religions, many of these beliefs are not associated with a well-formed institutional identity or historical and culturally binding narrative.

This raises the question, even if people are able to satiate the need for meaning in the short term by believing in ghosts or aliens, or going to a transhumanist church, will this approach work in the long term? And will it work when the threat to meaning is substantial? Are the beliefs ultimately little more than a poor substitute for religion, never really providing people with a deep sense of fulfillment about the meaning of their lives? There is simply not enough existing research to answer the question of whether or not these beliefs sufficiently restore or provide meaning.

That being said, the research my lab conducted on the need for meaning and ETI beliefs offers reasons to doubt the ability of at least some atypical beliefs to provide a strong sense of meaning. Remember, in that research we found that nonreligious individuals had lower levels of meaning and greater belief in ETI than religious individuals. This supported the idea that a lack of meaning among nonreligious people motivated belief in ETI. Indeed, we also found nonreligious people were more motivated to search for meaning and this was associated with greater ETI beliefs. These findings suggest that a lack of meaning and the resulting desire to acquire it inspires belief in UFOs and alien visitors. However, if ETI beliefs were providing meaning similar to more traditional religious beliefs, then why did the nonreligious ETI believers score lower on meaning than religious people in the first place?

Other research also suggests that people who do not turn to conventional supernatural beliefs are more vulnerable to experiencing deficits in meaning. The social psychologists Ken Vail and Melissa Soenke observed that reminders of mortality did not decrease perceptions of meaning for Christians, but did compromise meaning for atheists.[29] They reasoned that Christians have an established supernatural belief system they can turn to when grappling with concerns about mortality but that atheists do not, and thus are left vulnerable. They did not, however, measure other supernatural or related beliefs, so it is impossible to know whether these atheist participants held other, less traditional, supernatural or supernatural-lite beliefs.

Again, more work is needed, but what little research exists is consistent with the idea that searching for meaning does not always equal finding meaning. The need for meaning motivates a range of supernatural interests. This is clear. The question then is, which supernatural interests and beliefs actually provide meaning?

ARE THERE ANY TRUE NONBELIEVERS?

The research discussed in this and previous chapters poses another interesting question: Are there any true nonbelievers? If atheists are moved by religious concepts at the physiological and intuitive level, are attracted to nonreligious supernatural and supernatural-lite beliefs, and struggle to keep spirituality out of secular movements such as transhumanism, is there any reason to believe that there are people who are not in some way influenced by supernatural beliefs?

This is also a difficult question. Certainly, people vary in the extent to which supernatural concepts and beliefs guide their actions. Some people are extremely spiritually inclined. They embrace the idea of the supernatural and feel comfortable turning to supernatural beliefs when making life decisions. On the other end of the continuum are people who consciously reject all things supernatural and are influenced by these concepts less directly. From this perspective, there might be some people for whom supernatural thinking has an inconsequential impact on their lives. But it is also worth noting that this would probably be a very small group. Atheists already make up a small percentage of the world's population and, as discussed, some atheists endorse a range of ideas and beliefs that are essentially supernatural in nature. I suspect if there are any people who are truly not personally affected by supernatural thoughts and beliefs, they are an extremely rare breed.

In addition, it would likely take a considerable amount of training and vigilance to avoid the influence of supernatural ideas. Many of the most hardcore atheists and skeptics are scientists or people with a considerable amount of education in fields such as philosophy. These people have the benefit of training on how to spot illogical arguments and identify pseudoscientific claims. Many have also have spent a considerable amount of time thinking critically about the arguments against religion and other supernatural beliefs and so they are less inclined to be influenced by such beliefs.

And, remember, even some of the most educated scientists at some of the most prestigious universities engage in supernatural thinking (teleological errors) and especially so when they are relying on intuitive processes to make judgments. Vigilance matters, and we know from decades of research in psychology that people cannot be vigilant all of the time. We get distracted, try to engage in multiple tasks simultaneously, and experience fatigue. And all of us, regardless of background or education, have to grapple with existential questions about death and meaning.

Perhaps there are those with the preparation and discipline to live a life nearly free of supernatural inclinations, but I doubt there are many. And, based on the research, many of the people who think that supernatural ideas and beliefs do not affect their attitudes and behaviors are simply wrong. In the final chapter, I discuss this issue more and how atheists and believers ultimately share a common humanity.

In the next chapter, however, I turn my attention to the many physical and mental health benefits of supernatural beliefs. An ever-growing body of research reveals that supernatural beliefs help people in many ways. This raises the question: Even if people could, through training and great vigilance, completely cut out all forms of supernatural thinking and belief in their lives, should they?

The Many Benefits
of Supernatural Beliefs

As a result of advances in information technology, Americans are constantly bombarded with updates about the endless danger of terrorist organizations, the instability of the global financial market, new viral epidemics threatening to spread across the world, another mass shooting, the latest natural disaster, and so on and so on. Regardless of our efforts to limit our exposure to unpleasant information, we can't ever truly escape the constant reminders of just how violent, chaotic, and uncertain the world is and, as a result, how fragile our own existence is.

I used to live in England, and my wife and I would walk to work together every morning after escorting our children to school. I always looked forward to this routine. It was a pleasant stroll, a chance to stretch our legs and chat a bit before the workday. But one morning what was normally a relaxing commute became a frightening reminder of how one little misstep or stroke of bad luck can end the whole party.

If you have ever been to Europe you know that the streets and side-walks are pretty narrow and often crowded. One morning when we were walking around a particularly tight curve in the road near the university we worked at I felt the slightest brush across my shoulder and quickly turned my head to see that a large double-decker bus moving at a pretty high speed was inches from my face. Evidentially, I was walking closer to the edge of the sidewalk than I realized and the bus coming around the curve was right up to the edge of the street, nearly hitting the curb. I was of course startled to turn and realize I was inches away from being splat-tered like a bug by this large vehicle. A single step off of the sidewalk at that particular moment would have been disastrous.

Most people can probably think of a situation involving a close call with death. That certainly wasn't the first or last time I was acutely reminded of how easily I could be badly hurt or completely annihilated with little warn-ing. I have read many testimonials from people who had very powerful brushes with death. For example, a number of people were saved from cer-tain death during the 9/11 terrorist attacks because they missed their train or flight, were taking a smoke break, or were simply late to or absent from work that day. Some of these people struggled with making sense of their good fortune. They were of course happy to be alive, but so many others died. In some cases, the same actions that saved their lives took someone else's.

One story that really stuck with me is about United Airlines flight attendant Elise O'Kane. Elise made a mistake when selecting her work schedule using the airline's scheduling software and as a result was not scheduled to work her normal flight from Boston to Los Angeles on September 11. Instead, she was assigned a flight to Denver at the same time. She was not happy about this change, but the way the scheduling system worked she could not do anything about it.

On that day when she was taking the employee shuttle from the parking lot to the airport before her flight she overheard another flight attendant talking about how excited he was that he got called in to work the flight to Los Angeles, the flight Elise normally worked and preferred. He was look-ing forward to arriving in LA and drinking a Bloody Mary on the beach. The fact that this young flight attendant was so excited made Elise less annoyed about having her normal flight schedule altered over a simple error. She even briefly chatted with her replacement. At least her mistake was making someone else very happy.

But the story did not have a happy ending for Elise's replacement. He would never get to drink that Bloody Mary because he was on Flight 175, the plane terrorists used as a missile on the South Tower of the World Trade Center. Elise's life was spared because of a simple slipup she made punching her work preferences into a computer, a mistake that set into motion the death of another flight attendant.

Many people told Elise that God had saved her, that what had happened was meant to be. But as you can imagine, this was a difficult explanation for her to process. She lived, but someone else died. She did not cause the death. Terrorists did. But normally that would have been her flight. Elise said that this experience caused her to reevaluate her life and think deeply about what she wanted to do and how she could give back. She eventually decided to go to nursing school and now works as a nurse, though she did continue to serve as a flight attendant and eventually worked that flight from Boston to Los Angeles so that she could go to that beach bar her replacement mentioned and drink a Bloody Mary in his honor.

As I have said before, humans are in a precarious situation. Our intelligence advantages us in so many ways. But it also allows us to understand the realities of mortal existence. An honest appraisal of our situation can be quite debilitating. Any decision could put us on the path to death.

A well-liked local athlete in my community was recently hit by a car and killed while cycling on a country road. This was a man who was engaged in an activity normally associated with good health. He was relatively young and in great physical shape. He had a job and a family. And just like that, he was killed by a distracted driver.

Despite knowing that daily life is fraught with danger, most people are able to get up every morning and go about their lives. People still drive cars and ride on trains and planes even though they know an accident could kill them. They still travel to big cities, tourist attractions, and destinations abroad despite the fact they realize that these are potential terrorist targets. And these are just regular folk. Think about the firefighters, police officers, and soldiers whose jobs often mean purposely approaching mortal danger. They don't let the ever-present threat of death paralyze them.

Throughout this book I have argued that supernatural thoughts and beliefs are partially responsible for people's ability to manage existential concerns, as they help humans feel like they exist for a reason, are living meaningful lives, and have some kind of nonmaterial essence that transcends the mortal confines of their physical bodies. Now let's take a more direct look at the health benefits of supernatural thinking.

Supernatural ideas and beliefs may help us feel meaningful, but does this translate into actual health outcomes? Do these beliefs allow people to adaptively navigate the difficulties, challenges, and dangers of life? Feelings of meaning and self-transcendence are pretty abstract concepts that do not inherently reflect biological functioning and healthy behaviors. In other words, just because a person believes that she has an essence that endures beyond death does not mean she is actually healthy or living a healthy life. Supernatural beliefs could be nothing more than a form of self-delusion, something that makes humans feel safe from death but does not actually help us thrive as a species. Let's consider the science.

First, it is worth noting that much of the research connecting supernatural beliefs to health has focused on religion. This is not surprising, considering that religion is the most common form of supernatural belief. Most of the people in the world describe themselves as religious and report believing in a deity. This was historically the case and still is, even though, as discussed in previous chapters, traditional religiosity is on the decline in many places. For billions of people around the world, religious faith is an important part of life. Naturally, a lot of the research I discuss in this chapter focuses on religious supernatural beliefs. However, I also touch on other forms of spirituality and less traditional supernatural beliefs when possible.

USING SUPERNATURAL BELIEFS TO COPE WITH STRESS

My health insurance plan pays for a good part of my gym membership each month if I meet two conditions. First, I have to go to the gym 12 times a month. If you are a penny pincher like me, this is actually a pretty good incentive to hit the gym. It drives me nuts if I don't get enough gym visits in to get that reimbursement. The second condition is I have to complete a yearly online health survey. The survey contains typical questions regarding actual body statistics such as height, weight, numbers from my most recent medical exams such as blood pressure, cholesterol, and so forth. It also assesses lifestyle variables such as the amount of fruit, vegetables, sugar, and alcohol I consume.

In addition to these types of questions that are obviously associated with health, the survey also measures stress-related factors. In fact, a considerable amount of the survey is dedicated to stress: How stressed out do I feel on a daily basis? Is my stress temporary or chronic? Is it interfering with my ability to sleep or affecting my relationships? Have I missed work because I feel stressed out? Do I have strategies to manage my stress? Do I have a support system to turn to?

Why is my health insurance company so interested in my stress levels and what I am doing about them? Isn't the other information I provided that includes actual medical and healthy lifestyle data enough to reveal my health status? Any health psychologist would answer no to this question. It turns out, psychological stress has a dramatic impact on our lives.

According to the American Psychological Association,[1] the Mayo Clinic,[2] and many other health organizations, both short-term and long-term stress can contribute to poor health. Stress can trigger a heart attack in a person suffering from cardiovascular disease, and chronic stress is a contributing factor to the disease. Stress has also been linked to weight gain, premature aging, poor immune functioning, and even gum disease. Stress can lead to headaches, chest pain, upset stomach, fatigue, and difficulty sleeping. Not surprisingly then, stress contributes to more lasting mental health problems such as anxiety and depression-related disorders. Stress also interferes with people's ability to control their emotional states. This can exacerbate stress and resulting health problems, because when negative emotions such as fear and anxiety are not well managed people feel more stressed out. And people can get stressed about being stressed, resulting in even more distress.

Stress can also lead to behavioral outcomes associated with poor health. People who are under a lot of stress are quicker to anger, which not only is associated with cardiovascular health but also is harmful to relationships, which are a key support system. It is hard to find support from friends and family if you are not the easiest person to be around. Stress can also lead to undereating when it reduces appetite and overeating when people use food to comfort themselves. Stress is demotivating, so it can reduce the pursuit of important professional and personal goals as well as healthy behaviors that require motivation such as physical exercise. And some of the ways people cope with stress involve unhealthy choices such as frequent drug, alcohol, and tobacco use. Have you ever said to yourself, "I'm so stressed out right now; I could really use a drink"?

A certain amount of stress can be good, as long as it is productive stress. Exercise, for instance, stresses the body, but it is short-term and in the service of a healthy goal. From a physiological standpoint, it is technically "stressful," but it does not stress us out. In fact, a lot of people use exercise to manage feeling stressed.

Even some stress at work can be good if it involves manageable and stimulating challenges. Some of the pursuits that give us personal fulfillment and meaning are at least temporarily stressful, and this is fine. But a lot of the stress people deal with is the unhealthy kind. It involves financial problems, marriage or relationship difficulties, parenting challenges, being overworked, having an unhealthy work environment, not having a job, living in an unsafe neighborhood, health concerns, and so forth.

Some stress can be directly dealt with by removing the stressor. However, a lot of the time this strategy is not so easy or even possible. For example, it is hard to quit a stressful job if you need the money and can't find a suitable alternative, or to move out of a dangerous neighborhood if you lack the requisite resources. So what are people to do when they cannot easily remove or disentangle themselves from the thing making them so miserable? This is where coping resources come into play. These are the strategies, relationships, or beliefs people use to help manage stress.

There are many coping resources that do not involve supernatural beliefs. These include exercise, getting support from friends and family, taking care of a pet, engaging in a hobby such as gardening, and seeing a therapist. However, for many, religious faith is a particularly attractive and effective tool for stress management.[3]

Researchers who study religious coping have identified a number of ways that supernatural religious beliefs help people manage the many stresses of life.[4] For one, religious narratives tend to offer a positive outlook, which can be especially helpful when the world seems like it is conspiring against you. Sure, some religious narratives have a darker, more punitive, fear-focused, and apocalyptic tone, and I discuss this in the next chapter, but for the most part religious narratives are positively themed. They offer optimism and hope. They inspire people.

But do the hopeful feelings that religion encourages actually promote health? Yes. For one, optimism is inversely associated with stress.[5] People who have optimistic outlooks are less likely to get stressed out in the first place. So optimism is a stress buffer; it can help keep stress from happening or can at least make it less severe. What about people who are dealing with undeniable stressors such as serious medical problems? Is being an optimist helpful for managing stress?

Yes. Optimism serves a stress-management function for people suffering from illness and disease. For example, research shows that optimism contributes to reduced stress among women who have had surgery to treat breast cancer.[6] In fact, optimistic women experienced lower stress immediately after their surgery and at every postsurgery follow-up that researchers tracked (i.e., 3, 6, and 12 months post-surgery). Other research has found that optimism is associated with lower levels of anxiety and depression among men diagnosed with prostate cancer.[7] There have now been a number of published studies linking optimism to coping with disease diagnosis and treatment.

The benefits of optimism extend beyond health-related stress. Optimism has been linked to reduced stress and stress-related immune functioning among law students[8] and lower levels of stress among African American college students.[9] Optimism also predicts lower levels of stress and burnout among athletes.[10] And it helps new mothers cope with the financial, relationship, and personal stress associated with having a baby and even reduces the risk of postpartum depression.[11]

More generally, when people are experiencing a range of life stressors, an optimistic outlook plays a key role in maintaining psychological well-being.[12] Optimists are more energetic, persistent, and willing to tackle challenges head on.[13] In short, having a positive outlook helps people manage stress and many people report that their religious faith is the source of their positive outlook. Their faith gives them hope that they can make it through whatever challenges they are facing, that God has a plan for them and they need to do their part to stay motivated and positive.

In addition to promoting a positive life outlook, religion helps people cope with stress by making them feel connected to and protected by a higher power.[14] In chapter 1, I briefly mentioned attachment theory. If you have ever taken a high school or college introductory psychology course you probably learned about the importance of attachment security for developing infants and children and were likely introduced to some of the famous attachment research conducted by the developmental psychologist Mary Ainsworth in the late 1960s and early 1970s in a procedure called the "Strange Situation." The purpose of the procedure was to observe how infants (12 to 18 months old) engage the environment and respond to others when their mothers are and are not present.

Here is the gist. Mom and baby hang out in a laboratory room for a bit and then a stranger enters the room. At some point, mom leaves the baby in the room with the stranger. Then mom returns. Then the stranger leaves and shortly after that mom leaves, so the baby is alone. The stranger returns. Then mom returns. The whole time observers are meticulously coding the baby's emotional responses and behavior from behind a one-way glass. What is the baby doing when mom is in the room? For instance, is she happily exploring the environment? How does the baby react when mom leaves? Is she upset or not that bothered? And when mom returns, is baby easily soothed? And so on.

Based on this and related work, researchers have proposed the idea of different attachment styles. Most relevant here is the notion of a secure attachment style. This is characterized by the infant comfortably exploring the environment and interacting with the stranger when mom is in the room. The presence of the mother makes the baby feel safe enough to engage the world around it. When mom leaves the baby gets upset but is quickly comforted upon her return.

About 70% of infants fall into the securely attached category. The remaining 30% exhibit other patterns of behavior that fall into different categories of what is called insecure attachment. What is key here is that secure attachment is viewed as good for child development and health. In much of the attachment work the mother is used as the attachment figure because for much of human history moms have been the primary care-giver; this is still generally true today, though of course fathers, grandparents, and other guardians can and certainly do serve as attachment figures.

To infants, toddlers, and children, caregivers are critical attachment figures because they provide both emotional and physical security. And these feelings of security promote psychological growth because they offer a safe base from which children can comfortably explore the physical and social world. In fact, children and adults alike are more likely to try new things and be open to new ideas and opportunities when they feel safe and secure.

As we all know, parents can't provide sufficient psychological security forever. When children get older, they start to realize that their parents are fragile and mortal, and thus unable to protect them from all of the dangers of the world. But that feeling of security parents provide is so important, it is not surprising that children begin to look for other sources of protection. Religion is a common source. In fact, some psychologists have argued that God is the ultimate attachment figure.[15]

Of course, it need not be a single deity or the type of god that traditional Western religions provide that serves as a supernatural attachment figure. Indeed, research indicates that people in need of sources of emotional and social support are also more attracted to new age spiritual beliefs such as belief in astrology.[16]

We don't think of ourselves as babies, but in the way that the baby is soothed by the mother's presence in the classic attachment experiment, many of us adults, too, crave a powerful and benevolent parental figure or protective force in the universe that is looking out for humans. People can engage the world because of the feelings of security they gain from believing in this supernatural attachment figure. Supporting this idea, studies show that for people who perceive God as a source of protection, being exposed to the concept of God decreases fear and increases risk-taking.[17] Of course, some forms of risk-taking can be quite bad for people's health and safety. However, life is inherently dangerous and humans have to explore and take risks to thrive. The comforting presence of a caregiver encourages infants to explore. The comforting presence of a god or other supernatural force does the same for many religious adults.

Based on the importance of secure attachment for the regulation of psychological distress, it is not surprising that so many religious narratives describe God as a heavenly father and humans as his children. When children experience stress, they typically turn to their parents as a coping resource. Loving parents offer emotional support, which reduces stress and anxiety. The concept of a loving God serves a similar stress-mitigating function. This is demonstrated by research showing that people seek to connect with God via prayer for emotional support when coping with stress. For example, in one study, 96% of patients about to get cardiac surgery reported using prayer as a way to cope with the stress of an upcoming operation.[18]

Supernatural beliefs can also help people manage stress by making them believe their stress has grander meaning. Remember, perceptions of meaning have been directly linked to health and well-being and being able to turn a stressful situation into a meaningful challenge can be quite adaptive. Religious people facing personal struggles will often wonder if God is testing their faith and feel comforted by the belief that God would not give them a challenge he did not think they were capable of handling. And if they seek spiritual counsel from their priest, pastor, or other religious leader, they are likely to get a pep talk promoting this idea that God is giving them an opportunity to demonstrate and grow in faith, and maybe even to serve as an example to others of how religious faith can be used to navigate the many challenges of life.

Research conducted by the social psychologist and former graduate student of mine Jacob Juhl reveals that people can perceive stress through the lens of meaning and that this is quite beneficial to mental health.[19]

Critically, Juhl found that this meaning ultimately leads to greater psychological well-being. If religious individuals perceive stress as part of the important goals of testing faith, growing faith, or being an example of a faithful believer, they are able to rebrand their stress as something meaningful, and this helps them cope—which in turn improves overall well-being.

A while back I discovered the Joel Osteen XM Radio station. Osteen is a popular televangelist and author as well as the pastor of one of the largest churches in the United States. His 2004 book, *Your Best Life Now: 7 Steps to Living at Your Full Potential*, was on the New York Times Best Seller List for over 200 weeks. I knew about Joel Osteen, but I had never heard him preach until I accidentally came across his radio station when surfing channels in my car.

After listening to Osteen's sermon for just a few minutes I began to understand his popularity. He brilliantly promotes the different ways that religious faith can help people cope with the stressful challenges of life. Some religious figures have criticized Osteen's approach, arguing that it is closer to spiritual self-help than it is Christian doctrine; some have even called him a false prophet and a heretic. I am not endorsing or condemning him and am certainly not in a position to make a theological case for or against his approach or message. I am a psychologist, not a theologian or minister. I can, however, comment on how he takes advantage of the features of supernatural belief that help people in times of distress.

For one, he is beaming with optimism and this is reflected in his approach to preaching. His sermons emphasize the power of a positive attitude. Try finding a picture of Osteen on the Internet of him not smiling. Likewise, like most Christian pastors, Osteen encourages people to treat God as an attachment figure. He describes God as someone to call on for help when pursuing one's goals and dreams, just as one might ask parents for support. Perhaps more than anything, Osteen cleverly turns misery into meaning. Having financial problems? Don't let it break you. God would never give you a test you cannot pass. You just have to have faith and find that inner strength. Didn't get the job promotion you were expecting? It's fine. All part of God's plan. In fact, part of Osteen's genius is how he combines the power of optimism with the tactic of finding meaning in stress. The stressors of life are opportunities to display just how resilient your positive outlook is. When life throws its worst at you, meaning can be found in proving that your faith-based optimism can never be broken.

One fascinating study tested whether people are more inclined to engage in supernatural thinking when experiencing the stress of war.[20] In this study, participants from four Israeli cities in 1991 during the Gulf War were recruited. The researchers created two groups. Participants who lived in areas that experienced Iraqi Scud missile attacks were classified as being in a high-stress group, whereas participants who lived in cities that had not been attacked were classified as being in a low-stress group. Research assistants went to the participants' homes and administered questionnaires assessing perceived stress and a range of attitudes, some of which involved superstitions such as the belief that it is a wise idea to keep a good luck charm in the home.

Supporting the creation of this group distinction, participants in the high-stress group scored significantly higher on a stress questionnaire than participants in the low-stress group. Not surprisingly, living in a city that is under constant threat of missile attack is pretty stressful. Critically, and consistent with the other findings we've shown here, participants in the high-stress group scored higher on the measure of superstitious beliefs than participants in the low-stress condition.

Research also indicates that even among those who do not identify with any particular religion, high levels of spirituality help with stress-management.[21] Turning to any kind of supernatural belief makes stress easier to bear. Many healthcare and mental health providers are beginning to appreciate this and starting to offer more spiritual-based therapies for managing stress, and clinical research suggests that such approaches can be quite effective.[22]

SUPERNATURAL BELIEFS OFFER A BLUEPRINT FOR HEALTHY LIVING

A group of genetic researchers at the Ohio State University spent 7 years conducting a large study examining cancer rates among members of

Amish communities in Ohio.[23] Before starting the study, they made a simple prediction. Amish people would have higher rates of cancer than members of the general population. This prediction was based on the fact that the Amish have segregated themselves from mainstream society, thus leading to high rates of intermarriage within a small population. This can increase the likelihood of gene mutations that can contribute to cancer. The county of Ohio that this research was conducted in is home to over 26,000 Amish people who are all descendants of the same 100 individuals that settled that land over 200 years ago.

To their surprise, not only did the researchers not find support for their hypothesis but the opposite effect emerged. Amish people had significantly lower rates of cancer than the general population. In addition to having lower cancer rates, research shows that the Amish are less likely to be obese and suffer from diseases associated with obesity such as Type 2 diabetes.[24] The Amish also feel less stressed out and report greater mental health than members of the general public.[25]

What makes the Amish so healthy? After all, they interbreed and shun most modern technological and medical advances and these lifestyle choices can both put them at risk for certain diseases and limit their ability to effectively treat illnesses. This is true, but some of the lifestyle choices that the Amish make based on their supernatural beliefs also offer a blueprint for healthy living.

For one, the Amish believe that God desires them to be community-focused and humble. Modern conveniences can decrease people's dependence on others and lead to characteristics such as vanity and envy that ultimately push people apart and create relationship stress. So the Amish do not take advantage of most modern conveniences. They prefer the old ways that promote collaborative work and social harmony. This approach to life has many health benefits. Since they don't use much of the modern machinery and technology that makes physical labor easier, Amish people tend to be more physically active than the general population. The Amish don't need gym memberships.

This starts at an early age. Amish children engage in about twice as much physical activity as typical American children.[26] They don't have televisions, video games, and cell phones—all technologies that often pro-mote a sedentary lifestyle. They play outside and have physically demand-ing chores like most kids used to and as a result don't have the weight struggles that an increasing number of American children have.[27]

It is not the case that Amish people don't struggle at all with their weight. Their diets aren't particularly healthy and this does contribute to health-related problems. But it is in later adulthood when physical activity levels start to slow down that Amish people begin to pack on the pounds.[28] Research conducted on Amish individuals who carry what some scien-tists refer to as the "obesity gene" reveals the power of an active lifestyle. Amish adult participants who engaged in about 3 to 4 hours of moderately intense physical activity each day were not overweight, even if they had the genetic disposition to be.[29] This is an encouraging finding for those who feel shackled by their genes.

As part of their faith, Amish people also generally avoid a range of behav-iors that increase the risk of diseases such as cancer.[30] These include smok-ing, excessive alcohol consumption, and promiscuous sex. And despite spending a lot of time working outside, Amish have lower skin cancer rates than the general public because their religious tradition encourages modesty, which means they wear a lot of clothing that offers protection from solar radiation. You probably won't see any topless suntanning in an Amish community.

The Amish also prioritize family and social bonds, and a large body of research demonstrates that social connections and social support not only help reduce stress but also generally promote physical health. Indeed, loneliness is considered a significant risk factor for a number of health problems that can lead to death.[31]

The Amish are not the only example of how supernatural beliefs can offer a blueprint for healthy living. A 25-year UCLA health study found that Mormon men live on average 10 years longer than non-Mormon white men and Mormon women live about 5 years longer than non-Mormon white women.[32] Across a number of indicators of health, Mormons are doing quite well. They have low rates of cancer and cardiovascular disease. Like the Amish, the health benefits can be attributed to faith-inspired lifestyle choices. Mormons strongly believe in the Christian notion of the body being a temple. As a result, they tend to avoid alcohol and tobacco and emphasize the importance of good nutrition and an active lifestyle.

Seventh-Day Adventists are another religious group that have drawn a lot of attention from scientists seeking to understand what factors help people live long and healthy lives. Seventh-Day Adventists are an especially conservative group of Protestant Christians. They believe in the literal word of the Bible (e.g., the world was created in six days) and they are also some of the healthiest people in America. Like the Amish and Mormons, their good health can be credited to a faith-inspired lifestyle. Many Seventh-Day Adventists are vegetarian or vegan, and smoking and alcohol consumption are strongly discouraged. As a group, they are mentally very healthy and this may result from good nutrition and a spiritually driven mandate to focus on social bonds and helping others.

Beyond these specific examples, many religiously inspired beliefs offer guidelines that help people avoid unhealthy behaviors. Consider, for example, alcohol consumption. Religions often prohibit, discourage, or seek to regulate alcohol and other intoxicants. Growing up Southern Baptist, I remember that any alcohol consumption was strongly discouraged. It seemed like there was almost a fear of alcohol, as if having one drink might send you down a spiral into full-blown alcoholism. That view seemed a bit extreme to me. After all, there are plenty of people who drink responsibly and are able to balance the desire to enjoy a drink here and there with the goal of being a healthy and productive citizen. And as many people will attest, sharing a drink with friends can promote social bonding, which is vital for health and well-being.

That being said, alcohol does contribute to a number of personal and social problems that undermine health and safety. According to the Centers for Disease Control (CDC), about one-third of fatal car accidents involve alcohol-impaired driving.[33] The CDC estimates that someone is killed because of drunk driving about every 53 minutes and that alcohol-related car crashes cost about $44 billion dollars each year.

The cost of drinking is not limited to impaired driving. Hundreds of billions of dollars are spent each year as a result of people's desire to drink.

In addition to drunk driving, binge drinking and other alcohol-related accidents and crimes cost money and take lives. And this does not include the financial and health costs associated with alcohol addiction.

More and more research is also linking alcohol consumption to a range of chronic diseases. For example, studies indicate that for women, even low to moderate amounts of alcohol consumption are associated with a greater risk of cancer, particularly breast cancer.[34] This is especially concerning considering that women are drinking more than ever, now almost as much as men.[35] Many health officials see this as a major future public health epidemic, because biological differences between the sexes make women more vulnerable to the health problems associated with drinking.[36] In general, the more alcohol people drink over a long period of time, the more at risk they are of getting a number of different types of cancer.[37]

In all, alcohol consumption clearly has health and safety implications. Again, this is not to say that people can't drink responsibly. Also, a lot of health research is correlational and health-related outcomes are influenced by complex relationships between many variables. And alcohol is just one example of a potentially dangerous drug. The point is that many of the beliefs that, for many religious people, are motivated by a desire to submit to the perceived will of God are being proven by health scientists to be worthy of consideration.

More broadly, numerous studies link personal levels of religiosity to a range of health-related behaviors. For example, the teenage years are associated with a number of risky behaviors that can increase the chance of physical injury and death. Research indicates that religiosity is a protective factor. Religious teens are less likely to drink and drive, carry weapons, and get into fights, and are more likely to eat well, exercise, and get plenty of rest.[38] Religious youth are also less likely to use tobacco, alcohol, marijuana, and other drugs.[39]

Among adults, religiosity also promotes healthy behavior. For example, religious people generally follow a healthier lifestyle, which reduces their risk of mortality from causes such as cardiovascular disease.[40] These healthy lifestyle choices include lower rates of tobacco and alcohol use and higher rates of preventive health screenings.[41] The benefits of religion are not limited to the United States. For instance, a recent study of Danish Seventh-Day Adventists and Baptists found that members of these groups had considerably lower rates of sexually transmitted diseases than the general public, which could help explain their lower rates of cancers associated with human papillomavirus.[42]

Based on the large body of research linking religiosity to healthy behavior and ultimately good health and psychological well-being, psychologists have asserted that religion generally promotes self-control, which ultimately leads to healthy living.[43] But what is the secret ingredient that gives religious people better self-discipline? Again, I propose it is the supernatural aspect of religious belief.

For one, people often directly call on the supernatural through practices such as prayer when they need help resisting temptation and making healthy choices. And research indicates that prayer does boost self-control. In one study, for instance, research participants who were instructed to say a prayer prior to the start of the experiment completed a task that required self-control more successfully than participants who were not asked to pray.[44]

Even when people are not themselves asking for help from a supernatural agent they can still get assistance in the self-control department by being reminded that God is watching them. Studies demonstrate that when religious people are exposed to stimuli related to God, they are more inclined to behave in accord with their religious beliefs.[45] For example, in experiments that measured the extent to which people are able to resist temptations, participants who were first exposed to cues related to God were better able to resist.[46] This perhaps helps explain why researchers have long linked church attendance with healthy living. Weekly reminders that God is invested in your life—and is observing your behavior—may help people maintain self-discipline throughout the week. And it is not just Christians whose behavior is influenced by exposure to religious concepts. Similar results have been observed among Western and Chinese Buddhists.[47]

As discussed in chapter 5, there are growing numbers of people who do not identify with a particular religious faith but who are interested in alternative spiritual ideas and practices. Like religion, these practices often provide instruction on how to live a healthy life. They often focus on the concept of spiritual energy and emphasize the importance of healthy living for maintaining positive spiritual energy. Practices such as spiritual-based meditation are often encouraged as a way to rid the mind of distractions in order to refocus on important goals and to be mindful of the connection between one's behavior and her or his mental and physical health. And such practices have been shown to effectively promote self-control and reduce fatigue.[48]

A CLOSER LOOK AT SUPERNATURAL BELIEFS AND MENTAL HEALTH

So far in this chapter I have largely focused on physical health. It is also important to touch on the vital role that supernatural beliefs play in mental health. I did discuss the role of these beliefs in coping with stress. However, the benefits of supernatural beliefs extend far beyond stress and the mental and physical consequences of high stress and poor stress-management.

It is important to first note that some psychologists and public intellectuals have argued that believing in the supernatural is itself a form of mental illness. However, there is no compelling data to suggest that religious faith or other forms of supernatural belief represent a form of psychopathology. Diseases such as schizophrenia sometimes involve auditory and visual hallucinations that can contain supernatural-focused content. But there is no credible link between such experiences and supernatural beliefs generally.

Most humans hold supernatural beliefs, so some of the people who suffer from mental illnesses such as schizophrenia are going to be believers. However, to suggest that holding supernatural beliefs is a form of mental illness is to suggest that most of the world is mentally ill. Think about that for a moment. And for those who have equated belief in God and miracles to a form of schizophrenia either are purposely exaggerating to make a point or have no clue what schizophrenia is or how dramatically it impacts those who have it. I once worked in an outpatient clinic with clients suffering from schizophrenia, which is a serious brain disease that severely disrupts people's ability to adaptively function. It looks nothing like religious faith. If the billions of people who have a religious faith are essentially schizophrenic, how has our species made it so far? How were we ever able to spread to and dominate all corners of the Earth? The notion that to have faith in supernatural forces and deities is to be psychologically ill simply makes no sense.

The reality is that religious supernatural beliefs are typically associated with good mental health. For example, according to Gallup, people who report being very religious are less likely to have ever been diagnosed with depression than those who report being only moderately religious or not religious at all, and the very religious experience fewer daily negative emotions such as worry and anger than these other groups.[49] Religiosity is also associated with greater life happiness, which of course reduces vulnerability to mental illness.[50] And religious people are less likely to attempt suicide than nonreligious people.[51]

Research also indicates that supernatural beliefs can have a protective factor for individuals who have a high genetic risk for psychiatric illness. Researchers following the adult lives of children who had a parent who suffered from depression observed that religious faith has a powerful protective effect. These high-risk offspring were considerably less likely to develop major depressive disorder and any other psychiatric disorder if they participated in a religious faith.[52]

For people receiving mental health treatment, supernatural beliefs appear to contribute to treatment effectiveness. For example, in one study conducted in a psychiatric day-treatment program, participants who reported a belief in God came out of the treatment program much better off than nonbelievers.[53] The more patients believed in God, the greater reductions they had in depression and self-harming behavior. And they also exhibited a higher overall psychological well-being.

These are just a few examples from a large and growing body of research in support of the proposal that religious faith reduces the risk of mental health problems, helps protect people who have a genetic disposition to mental illness, and contributes to the success of many mental health therapies. These findings are completely at odds with the idea that religious supernatural beliefs are a form of mental illness. In fact, as previously discussed, atheists and agnostics are more likely than believers to hold certain paranormal beliefs such as conspiracy theories about UFOs that people often associate with paranoia and hallucinations. In the next chapter I discuss some of the ways that supernatural beliefs can harm mental and physical health, but the position that these beliefs are a form of mental illness is without merit. Ironically, atheist public intellectuals who champion the idea that many religious beliefs ignore scientific evidence are often themselves ignoring or are unaware of a large body of scientific evidence regarding the relationship between religious faith and psychological health.

THE HEALTHY ATHEIST PARADOX

Based on everything I have said thus far in this chapter, one may naturally come to the conclusion that if religion benefits health in so many ways then being an atheist is a bad idea. If supernatural religious beliefs help people cope with stress, offer the recipe for healthy living, and greatly benefit mental health, then rejecting these beliefs must put one on the path to misery and early mortality. Atheists should surely be a psychologically vulnerable and fragile group of people who are stressed out all of the time and unable to control themselves in the face of temptation. However, the relationship between religious disbelief and health is a bit more complicated.

Everything I have written here about the mental and physical health benefits of religiosity is true: higher levels of religious faith and commitment are associated with a bunch of positive health-related outcomes. But many, though certainly not all, of the studies examining the benefits of religiosity do not include atheists or at least enough of them to examine their mental and physical health. Remember, atheists are a very small group in general. Thus, most studies that reveal health benefits of religiosity are comparing people who are highly religious to those who are not particularly religious, or people who are very devoted to their faith to those who believe in God but are not particularly devoted. In other words, these studies are not specifically looking at the few individuals who reject religion entirely.

So what, then, do we know about the mental and physical health of atheists, keeping in mind the fact that research with this population has been limited?

Some studies indicate that atheists as a group are generally mentally and physically healthy. For example, in one recent study focused on mental health, atheists and believers exhibited similar levels of psychological well-being.[54] Another recent study painted a more complex picture.[55] In this research, atheists and believers were generally similar in terms of physical health. In fact, on some indicators of health such as BMI and number of chronic health conditions, atheists were healthier than believers. On indicators of mental health and well-being, however, atheists were worse off than believers. Specifically, compared to atheists and agnostics, believers reported higher levels of happiness, optimism, and self-esteem and lower levels of anxiety.

Why would atheists potentially be physically healthier on some indicators than believers if religious faith offers a blueprint for healthy living? And why do atheists sometimes seem to be doing as well mentally as believers but sometimes seem to be more psychologically vulnerable?

First, let's consider why atheists may sometimes be as physically healthy as or even healthier than believers. Atheists may enjoy certain health advantages as a result of variables unrelated to religious belief or disbelief. For one, atheists tend to be a highly educated group and education is associated with health benefits. Educated people tend to be more familiar with research on nutrition and other lifestyle factors associated with good health, and thus educated atheists may be using a more science-based blueprint for healthy living. In addition, level of education is associated with greater wealth. Therefore, educated atheists may have greater access to quality healthcare, healthy food, and other important resources. The economic benefits of being educated also buffer stress, so educated atheists might enjoy a higher quality of life and lower levels of daily stress.

As we've discussed in previous chapters, atheists may also actually be reaping some of the benefits of supernatural thinking and beliefs without realizing it. Remember, atheists experience lower death-related anxiety when given some hope of consciousness beyond death. Plus, when atheists lack a sense of meaning and are searching for it or are grappling with concerns about mortality, at least some of them turn to religious-like ideas and interests. So perhaps atheists both enjoy educational and economic advantages and use some forms of supernatural thinking to cope with psychological threats.

Now let's consider the other question. Why might atheists sometimes be less psychologically healthy than believers? First, even though some atheists turn to religious-like supernatural ideas and beliefs to counter psychologically distressing states, these ideas and beliefs are generally less socially valued. For example, belief in intelligent alien life is certainly considered more fringe than belief in a loving and powerful God. Thus, though some atheists feel the pull of supernatural beliefs when distressed, the beliefs they are drawn to may not offer sufficient existential security because they are not as valued within the broader culture. Indeed, research indicates that atheists feel less socially supported and experience a fair amount of discrimination.[56] Atheists may be turning to more fringe supernatural beliefs for the same existential reasons that believers are turning to more traditional religious beliefs but getting fewer benefits from these alternative supernatural beliefs.

This still does not explain why some studies suggest that atheists are just as psychologically healthy as believers and other studies don't. What are we missing? One key variable may be whether or not atheists are experiencing certain types of distressing life circumstances. Remember, atheists as a group tend to be well educated, and this gives them greater access to economic opportunities and the benefits associated with such opportunities. Financially successful atheists may be mentally healthy because they experience lower levels of stress and anxiety. Indeed, in a set of studies conducted in my lab, we found that economic security contributes to meaning in life.[57] People reporting that they feel financially secure perceived life as more meaningful than those reporting that their financial situation is unstable and uncertain. Similarly, presenting participants with information suggesting there may be another economic recession decreased perceptions of meaning. Economic security is a psychological buffer. Money doesn't make people happy or eliminate other personal stressors. But financial security does provide some psychological security.

By this logic, atheists with fewer resources would be more vulnerable. They don't enjoy the economic advantages that make life easier, and they also don't have culturally valued and socially connecting religious beliefs to use as a coping resource. Research supports this possibility. Specifically, a large study examining the influence of economics on well-being found that atheists and believers who lived in affluent neighborhoods had similar levels of well-being.[58] However, in poorer neighborhoods, atheists had significantly lower levels of well-being than believers.

One way to think about this issue is to treat religious faith like medicine, something people benefit from most when they are sick. People who enjoy economic prosperity, stimulating careers, and access to quality healthcare and other services are likely going to be pretty mentally healthy. Life is good for them. But for the less privileged, life can be rather uncertain and stressful. For these people, religious faith may serve as very effective medicine.

The religion-as-medicine idea also helps makes sense of global religious trends. If religion serves a medicinal function for people experiencing the stress of economic uncertainty and all of the threats that often go hand in hand with being poor, then it should be the poorest countries that are the most religious. This is certainly the case. The more economically secure a country is, the less religious it is.[59] This pattern is also true within the United States. The poorest states tend to be the most religious.

Further supporting this idea, it is in the poorest countries that religion has the most potent effect on improving well-being and reducing distress. According to Gallup, in poor countries highly religious people are much happier, less depressed, and less worried than their less religious counterparts.[60] In more affluent nations, this difference becomes much smaller.

Again, if religion is like medicine then its impact should be most observable in countries that are in need of the healing power of supernatural beliefs.

As a group then, atheists may be less in need of religious faith as medicine because they tend to live in the most prosperous places, but when these nonbelievers are down on their luck they may be particularly vulnerable to psychological distress.

This is not to say that there are not many financially successful believers. Of course, there are. In fact, as noted, religion can positively impact self-control and goal-striving, which are associated with educational and financial success. Nor is it to say that educated people who live in safe and prosperous places and who have lots of financial resources do not enjoy the many benefits of religion. Many do. Everyone needs to feel meaningful and wants to feel more than mortal. Supernatural beliefs help people, regardless of education and income, on their existential journey. This research simply reveals that supernatural beliefs play a particularly vital medicinal-like role for those who do not have as many social, educational, or economic resources that help meet basic physical and psychological needs.

The Dark Side
of Supernatural Beliefs

The 9/11 terrorist attacks took place during the first few weeks of my first year of graduate school and, as a result, very much affected my developing research interests. As a new grad student studying social psychology, I immediately became fascinated by the lengths humans would go to in order to affirm and defend a meaning- and self-transcendence-providing belief system. However, the concept of a suicide bomber truly baffled me.

This phenomenon was hard for me to make sense of because if the function of self-transcendence- and meaning-providing belief systems is to help people cope with the threat of death awareness, then how could such beliefs encourage someone to purposely die? This phenomenon suggests something quite powerful and potentially terrifying: the quest for meaning and immortality can take priority over actual physical survival. By focusing on how to be more than mortal, could a person increase the threat of actual mortality?

A willingness to take physical risks and even die for a cause is not always a bad thing. Many lives have been saved because brave individuals put their own safety on the line to help others or make the world a better place. But flying airplanes into buildings full of civilians or strapping explosives to oneself, walking into a café, and detonating those bombs does not save lives or better the world. It causes great fear and human suffering.

As a young experimental social psychologist in training, I desperately wanted to understand why, so I began to design and conduct experiments exploring these phenomena. I started to study the small ways in which everyday people prioritize cultural beliefs above physical safety and survival. The first scientific paper I ever published as the leading author tested the idea that young women who perceive physical beauty as an important source of meaning would respond to a reminder of mortality with a greater desire to suntan.[1]

Tanning is an interesting cultural phenomenon because most people are well aware of the fact that getting a good tan is accompanied by an increased risk of skin cancer. Too much exposure to natural or artificial ultraviolet (UV) rays is bad for one's health. But tanned skin is also viewed by some as physically attractive. As a result, many people, especially teenage girls and young women, purposely expose themselves to dangerous UV rays, and even spend money to do so at tanning salons. When young women think about their mortality, will they be more motivated to protect themselves from the sun's harmful rays or will they turn to meaning-providing cultural beliefs concerning female beauty?

Turns out they do both. First, for my experiment I needed women who would be inclined to perceive tanned skin as being part of their meaning system. Our self-esteem is derived from the beliefs that we find personally meaningful, so I recruited a sample of young women who had previously indicated in a survey that having tanned skin is at least somewhat important to their self-esteem.

Once these participants arrived in our lab, they were randomly assigned to a condition involving thinking about death or a control condition. We measured interest in sun-protective products immediately after participants thought about death a few minutes later, once death thoughts were no longer at the forefront of attention. Specifically, we presented participants with a bunch of different sunscreen products ranging in SPF (sun protection factor) value and asked them how interested they were in buying each product. Our goal was to assess whether they wanted high-SPF sunscreen that would protect their skin but also reduce their ability to get a tan.

For the participants who responded to the sun-protection measure immediately, thinking about death compared to a control topic increased interest in high-SPF sunscreen. But for participants who responded after a brief delay, thinking about death compared to a control topic decreased interest in the most protective products. My colleagues and I found this same effect in a number of subsequent experiments, including a study conducted at a beach in Florida.[2]

These findings indicate that women who value having tanned skin will initially respond to threatening thoughts about death with intentions to look out for their health and safety. Perfectly rational. But this attention to health is fleeting. A few minutes after being reminded of mortality, when the immediately threatening thoughts of death have faded a bit, women who value having tanned skin prioritize beauty over health. In subsequent studies, we were able to reduce a woman's desire for tanned skin not by telling her that tanning was unhealthy, but instead by convincing her that cultural standards of beauty were changing. Offering people other ways to affirm meaning is often more effective than focusing on health when seeking to reduce behaviors that are culturally valued.

A number of studies concerning health- and safety-related behaviors ranging from dieting to reckless driving tell a similar story. When people are confronted with existential threats related to death, they will often initially exhibit concerns about physical safety, but these concerns tend to quickly give way to thoughts about meaning, relationships, and legacy—all part of the human drive for immortality. It is a natural and vital instinct to respond to threats with a focus on survival. But research shows that most of us in these situations do reveal our proclivity to care about things larger and more enduring than our mortal lives.

In later research, my colleagues and I considered more dramatic ways that people might put existential needs above survival. We were specifically interested in whether a reminder of death would increase people's self-reported willingness to sacrifice themselves for their nation or religion; both represent ideologies that offer meaning and some form of self-transcendence. People die, but they can make a meaningful contribution to the longevity of cultural institutions that continue to persist long after. And, of course, religion offers a particularly powerful way to transcend death.

In these experiments, we found that thinking about death increased the belief that one's nation and religion are more important than one's own life. Thinking about death also increased willingness to die for one's nation or religion.[3,4] It is worth noting that these questionnaires were self-reported; researchers obviously cannot create situations in the lab to assess actual self-sacrifice. While there are—no doubt—many complex variables that contribute to self-sacrificial behavior, our findings suggest that existential concerns about death play a role in people's willingness to prioritize group identity and ideology over physical health and safety.

I describe all of this research because it illustrates a central point: All of us are pulled between biological motives to survive as living organisms, and existential motives to feel more than mortal. And all of us occasionally prioritize our existential ambitions over health and safety. Much of the time though, the sacrifices we make are fairly small, certainly not immediately self-destructive or harmful to others. However, sometimes the pursuit of existential goals can lead us down a dangerous and even destructive path. It is in these extreme cases that we can see the dark side of supernatural beliefs.

WHEN SCIENCE AND FAITH COLLIDE

Medicine can't heal every wound or cure every disease. But most people know someone who is alive today because of medical intervention. Maybe it is your aunt or mother who survived breast cancer because of early detection, surgery, and chemotherapy. Maybe it is your dad, who would have died from heart disease had he not had bypass surgery. Think of the number of women and infants who perished during childbirth in years past as a result of the medical limitations of the time. Or the many who have suffered and died from infectious diseases that we are now able to prevent through immunization or treat with medicines.

According to the World Health Organization (WHO), over 17 million lives have been saved since 2000 because of measles vaccinations.[5] The Centers for Disease Control and Prevention (CDC) estimates that from 1994 to 2014 childhood vaccinations prevented over 700,000 deaths and 21 million hospitalizations in the United States.[6] Mortality rates in the United States and other developed nations declined dramatically during the 20th century as a result of medicine.

People are living longer and healthier lives not just because of the medical treatment they are receiving but also because of the lifestyle choices they are making and the laws that have been passed based on medical research. Our society has slowly been able to successfully remove smoking from public places because of the science on the health consequences of secondhand smoke. And in the United States, smoking is at an all-time low, though it is still believed to be the leading cause of preventable disease and death.[7] Parents have probably always encouraged their kids to eat fruits and vegetables, but thanks to scientific research, we are learning more and more just how important a healthy diet is for both physical and mental health.

The United States is far from a science-based health utopia, though. Money and politics still influence public policy and federal guidelines. And, quite frankly, sometimes the science we use to guide our health decisions is proven wrong, or is unclear. There are still many important health-related questions that need to be tackled by scientific research and public health education. Still, science and medicine have saved millions of lives, given people hope to survive illnesses that would have killed them in decades past, and improved the quality of life for nearly everyone.

But not everyone is extolling the virtues of modern science and medicine. Though the overwhelming majority of religious Americans see no

conflict between their faith and medicine, there are religious fundamentalist groups that view the use of medical treatment as showing a lack of
faith or that consider certain medical practices and interventions to be in
opposition to Holy Scripture.

Forty-eight states allow exemptions from mandatory school immunizations for religious purposes.[8] And many states also have laws providing
some level of protection from criminal or civil prosecution for parents who
refuse medical care for their children based on religious beliefs.[9] Though
thankfully it is not a common practice, there are certainly cases in the
Untied States of parents denying their children immunizations as well as
medical treatment for a range of illnesses and injuries. Sadly, some of these
faith-based refusals have resulted in severe chronic illness and even death.

One investigation determined that between 1975 and 1995, 169
American children died as a result of parents relying on faith-healing
instead of conventional medicine.[10] In many of these cases, parents and
other members from the religious group stood over the child and prayed
while he or she slowly died in front of them, often painfully. Think about
watching your child die in this way. It is hard to imagine. That is how
powerful and dangerous supernatural beliefs can be. It is not that these
beliefs are overriding the basic motive to protect one's offspring. I suspect these parents sincerely believe they are looking out for their children's
best interests by displaying unflinching faith in their religious beliefs.
Unfortunately, good intentions aren't always enough and supernatural
beliefs can lead to bad medical decisions.

Such faith-based healing practices are not a thing of the past. For example, in 2015 a state task force in Idaho determined that in one area of
the state where members of the Followers of Christ, a Pentecostal group
that relies on faith-healing, are concentrated, the child mortality rate is 10
times that in the rest of the state.[11] Some states have gone after and successfully prosecuted parents for not seeking life-saving medical care for
their children. However, many children's rights advocates believe that the
United States is still too accommodating of faith-healing sects.[12]

Faith-based medical refusals are not a uniquely American phenomenon. Consider the case of a 28-year-old Australian woman who was

diagnosed with leukemia when she was 7 months pregnant. Doctors proposed a solution. She could have a caesarean section so the baby would
be born unharmed and then she could undergo chemotherapy to save her
own life. Doctors were optimistic because over 80% of pregnant women
with leukemia go into remission if they get treatment. However, in this
case, the woman refused this plan of action because it would involve her
receiving a blood transfusion. As a practicing Jehovah's Witness, a blood
transfusion was out of the question. The baby died in utero 3 days after her
diagnosis and the woman died less than 2 weeks after that from a stroke
and multiorgan failure. Doctors concluded that the refusal of blood products contributed to the deaths of both mom and baby.

Or consider the six (or more) HIV-positive people in the United
Kingdom who died after their pastors performed an exorcism-like ritual
and then told them that they had been completely healed and therefore no
longer needed to take their medication.[13] Even after symptoms returned
and their health deteriorated, their pastors assured them that God had
cured them. They trusted the wisdom of their religious leaders and died as
a result. The list goes on.

These types of cases inspired a series of experiments that I was involved
with, led by the social psychologist Matt Vess.[14] We proposed that existential concerns about death contribute to religious-based medical refusals
and that it would be religious fundamentalists who are most inclined to
respond to heightened death-awareness with an increased belief in the
power of faith healing as well as the right for people to refuse medicine for
religious reasons.

What do we mean precisely when we refer to someone as a religious
fundamentalist? The term is thrown around a lot in the popular media,
but what makes a fundamentalist distinct from just a deeply religious
person? Religious fundamentalism represents the extent to which people
view their religious beliefs as being uniquely true and without error. To
a fundamentalist there is only one true faith. Moreover, fundamentalists
believe in the literal word of their religious texts and, critically, their specific denominational doctrines. Thus, they are not inclined to accommo-
date other religious or nonreligious viewpoints and do not moderate their

beliefs based on changing social and cultural views or scientific discoveries that they perceive as in conflict with their religious texts or beliefs. They are the truly hardcore. It is not just that they are very religious: they have an unyielding commitment to a very specific set of beliefs. They are not prone to doubt or uncertainty. They have the answers. The problem is sometimes their answers are at odds with a scientific understanding of the world or with the beliefs and practices of other people. And this type of inflexibility makes them vulnerable to maladaptive strategies for coping with existential fears.

Like everyone else, religious fundamentalists yearn to transcend the limitations of biology. However, their path to meaning and immortality is more rigid, less open to alternatives. Most people invest in a variety of relationships, group identifications, beliefs, and personal ambitions. This is good. It reduces the likelihood of becoming obsessively focused on a single source of existential comfort. To fundamentalists, however, there is one primary source. It is not that they do not have families they love or work that they enjoy. They do. However, their approach to these connections and personal projects is dictated by their fundamentalist beliefs.

In our research, we reasoned that when mortality is on the mind, religious fundamentalists would be the people most inclined to turn to a dogmatic faith-based approach to healthcare instead of science-based medical approach. To test this, we first administered a religious fundamentalism questionnaire to research participants.[15] They rated their level of agreement with a number of statements assessing the different aspects of what it means to be a fundamentalist. This included items such as "God will punish most severely those who abandon his true religion."

Next, participants were randomly assigned to write about either death or a nondeath control topic. Subsequently, we assessed a range of attitudes and beliefs related to faith-based interventions and medical refusals.

In the first study of this series of experiments, we assessed people's endorsement of prayer as a legitimate substitute for medical treatment. Participants were asked to read a vignette about a man suffering from severe lung disease. The vignette described the man as deeply religious and indicated that despite his worsening condition he had refused the advised medical treatment. He was instead relying entirely on prayer. After reading this information, participants were asked to imagine that they were this man's doctor and to indicate to what extent they would feel compelled to tell the man that prayer is not sufficient and to insist on conventional medical treatment.

What we found was that thinking about one's own mortality influenced participants' opinions about how to handle this case. Critically, religious fundamentalism played a decisive role. For religious fundamentalists, thinking about death increased reluctance to push the idea that faith is no substitute for medicine. The opposite was true for the less dogmatic participants. For these individuals, thinking about death made them more inclined to want to push the patient to follow the conventional, science-based treatment plan.

In other words, the threat of death-awareness drove nonfundamentalists and fundamentalists in opposite directions. It made regular people, many of whom were religious, motivated to insist on science-based medicine. It is not that they were against prayer; they just did not see it as sufficient. But religious fundamentalists did. A reminder of mortality made these individuals more supportive of the stance against science-based medicine.

In a second experiment, we more directly assessed belief in the effectiveness of prayer as medicine. Participants read an article about a man refusing medical treatment for lung disease, and this article contained a personal testimony from the man, stating, "I refuse medical treatment because I know that my prayers are the best medicine available to me. My faith in the Lord will be enough to carry me through." After reading this article, participants responded to questions assessing their personal belief that faith alone would help this man's health improve as well as their belief that prayer is more effective than medical treatment.

The results looked very much the same as the results from the first study. For religious fundamentalists, thinking about death increased belief that faith alone is sufficient and more effective than medical treatment. For nonfundamentalists, the opposite pattern was observed. Thinking about death decreased the belief that faith alone would work and is more effective than conventional medicine.

In our next experiment, we turned to the issue of parents' religious right to refuse medical treatment for their children. As I've previously noted, this has been a legal issue in the United States and other countries where citizens are given protection for their religious beliefs. In this study, after completing the religious fundamentalism questionnaire and receiving the death thought or control condition, participants were given an article to read that detailed a court case in which a judge removed a young boy from his parent's home because he was suffering from pneumonia and his parents refused to seek medical care for him. Instead of seeking conventional medical treatment, they chose to rely entirely on prayer. After reading about the case, participants answered a series of questions about the judge's decision to remove the child from the home and the parents' decision to reject science-based medical treatment.

A familiar pattern emerged. Fundamentalists responded to thoughts of mortality with an increased support for religious-based medical refusals; more support for the parents and less support for the judge. Nonfundamentalists went in the opposite direction. Thinking about death made them less inclined to support the parents and more inclined to support the judge. Even in a case in which a child's health is in danger and he is completely dependent on his parents to access medical treatment, fundamentalists put faith first when grappling with the awareness of mortality.

In many of the real-world cases of people refusing medical intervention, the critical variable appears to be that the specific treatment being offered is perceived as being in direct conflict with one's religious faith. For instance, it is not the case that Jehovah's Witnesses reject all medical interventions or prefer some form of faith-healing. They specifically reject treatments that involve receiving blood based on Bible verses that instruct humans not to consume blood. Most other Christian sects do not interpret these verses as referring to medical procedures but instead understand them to be dictates to not drink blood, particularly animal blood. Jehovah's Witnesses will seek medical treatment and surgeries, while insisting on bloodless treatments.

We designed our next study based on this idea that, in some instances, medical interventions and faith are seen as being in opposition. In this study, we manipulated death thoughts as before and then assessed participants' response to a hypothetical health problem that could create a conflict between one's faith and medical treatment. We asked them, in such a situation, would they rely solely on the treatment that challenges their religious views, try to find a way to compromise so that they could benefit from the medical treatment but still feel committed to their faith, or reject the medicine and rely on faith alone.

For fundamentalists, thinking about death increased endorsement of the faith-alone approach. If science-based medicine seemed at odds with their religious views, thinking about death drove fundamentalists to reject such treatment.

This finding helps explain cases involving patients facing certain death but rejecting life-saving treatment, such as Jehovah's Witnesses who have died after refusing necessary blood transfusions. In these extreme medical situations, patients are going to be thinking about their mortality. For most people, this brush with death motivates a desire to live, and thus a desire for life-saving medical care. For many fundamentalists, faith trumps survival.

All of us, in small ways, compromise our health and safety in the service of meeting existential needs. But most of us are able to balance these goals. For certain religious fundamentalists, however, science and faith collide—and faith wins.

APOCALYPTIC VISIONS: BEATING DEATH
BY EMBRACING DEATH AND DESTRUCTION

I have always loved apocalyptic science fiction movies and books. I can't get enough of stories about the end of the world, dystopian wastelands, and the human struggle to survive when everything has gone to hell. I am not picky, either. Whether it is artificial intelligence waging war on humans, catastrophic environmental disasters, a nuclear holocaust, or a zombie virus pandemic, I love it all.

Clearly, I am not alone in my fascination with the apocalypse. Some of the most popular books, video games, television programs, and movies

have revolved around apocalyptic scenarios. For most people, a fascination with the apocalypse is perfectly healthy. In fact, pondering how life
could be stripped to the basics or end entirely as a result of technology and
science run amok or human disregard for the environment might serve as
a cautionary lesson to inspire efforts to better protect the world. Indeed,
the creators of apocalyptic fiction often claim that their stories were motivated by a desire to get the public to think and talk about real-world
environmental, technological, and sociopolitical threats. Apocalyptic narratives can be both fun and educational. But for a small number of people,
apocalyptic visions of the future are more than entertainment. They are
prophecies to be taken seriously and literally.

While two of the major world religions, Christianity and Islam, contain these types of narratives, the majority of Christians and Muslims do
not appear to be centrally focused on these aspects of their faiths. This is
where the study of religious fundamentalists again becomes critical.

As a result of being so singly focused on one source of meaning and
transcendence, fundamentalists are more inclined than their less doctri-
naire brethren to invest in apocalyptic beliefs. Consider Christianity, the
dominant religion in America. In a 2013 poll, 41% of Americans (54% of
Protestants and 77% of evangelicals) endorsed the statement "The world is
currently living in the 'end times' as described by prophecies in the Bible."[16]
This might sound a bit worrying but there is little evidence that this basic
belief alone is dangerous. For most Christians, believing the world could
end at any time appears to simply be a reminder to be a good person and
thankful for each day, to not take life for granted. In other words, most
Christians aren't really acting like they are living in end times. They are
not running around warning everyone about the approaching end times
and abandoning all worldly concerns. They are still trying to pay off their
mortgage, get that promotion at work, plan next summer's much-needed
vacation, and save for their children's college education.

It is the fundamentalists who take apocalyptic prophecies literally. They
are the ones who truly believe. My lab conducted an experiment to examine the relationship between religious fundamentalism and potentially
dangerous apocalyptic beliefs. We specifically wanted to test whether

fundamentalists turn to apocalyptic beliefs to cope with existential fears about mortality.[17] In our experiment, we first administered a questionnaire assessing religious fundamentalism, the same one previously discussed.

Next, we had half of the participants spend a few minutes writing about death. Participants in the control condition wrote about the experience of extreme physical pain. Following this manipulation, participants were instructed to read an article discussing a number of current threats to the world that could prove catastrophic. These included natural disasters, global disease pandemics, the potential for terrorist organizations to acquire nuclear weapons, and even possible threats from outer space such as solar storms and rogue asteroids, basically all the threats that big-budget Hollywood summer blockbusters have taught us about.

After reading this article, participants responded to a questionnaire assessing apocalyptic beliefs. This measure included questions representing the extent to which participants viewed the information in the article as being signs of a prophesied apocalypse such as "The events described have been foretold in the Bible and other religious writings." The questionnaire also assessed maladaptive apocalyptic beliefs such as "Taking steps to alleviate the threats described would be going against God's plan to bring about the end of the world" and "Trying to avoid or delay the end of the world is blasphemous."

Supporting the idea that fundamentalists are more invested in apocalyptic beliefs, we observed a significant positive relationship between religious fundamentalism and the belief that the phenomena described in the article are signs of a prophesied apocalypse, as well as the belief that people should not interfere or take action to prevent the coming "end of days."

Critically, we found support for the idea that apocalyptic beliefs among fundamentalists are motivated by existential concerns about death. For those scoring high on the fundamentalism questionnaire, thinking about death intensified these apocalyptic beliefs. We did not observe such an effect for nonfundamentalists, those who scored low on the fundamentalism scale. This finding demonstrates that when death-awareness is high, fundamentalists, but not regular religious believers, become even more invested in religious prophecies about the end of the world. Humans know that death is inevitable. To fundamentalists, the apocalypse is a path to enduring meaning and immortality.

There are reasons to be concerned that some people find existential comfort in fatalistic views about the end of the world. Apocalyptic beliefs may offer feelings of meaning and self-transcendence, but they can also be dangerous if they undermine people's motivation to tackle pressing social and environmental problems or prevent them from living productive lives. The fact that fundamentalists endorse the idea that people should not take action against serious threats to the planet and the people living on it is troubling. It reveals that fundamentalists are all in on one particular strategy to find meaning and death-transcendence. And this strategy poses dangers not just to them, but to all of us. Fortunately, we are talking about small numbers of people. But, of course, even one person can cause great harm to many, as is the case with suicide terrorism.

SUPERNATURAL-BASED SELF-SACRIFICE: THE CASE OF SUICIDE TERRORISM

Compared to other violent crimes, suicide terrorism is quite rare. However, it is an extremely powerful display of how existential motives can lead to dangerous outcomes. In most violent crimes, people aren't purposely trying to die. In the heat of the moment they may engage in a fist or gun fight, which could lead to injury or worse, but it is often not by design. Suicide bombers, on the other hand, spend months if not years methodically planning an attack that will kill themselves and potentially many others.

Suicide bombers are often fundamentalists, radicalized individuals who are invested in one particular path to meaning and transcendence—martyrdom. They perceive themselves as part of a meaningful and epic ideological struggle. And many of them believe they will be rewarded for their efforts in the afterlife.

Terrorist organizations often combine the existential power of apocalyptic visions with the call for martyrdom. Their religious leaders prophesy that a coming war between the followers of the true faith and their

Godless or false prophet following enemies will usher in the end times and bring glory to those willing to take up arms and sacrifice themselves for the cause.

A group of social psychologists conducted an experiment to test the proposal that existential concerns about death attract people to the idea of martyrdom.[18] The researchers recruited participants from two universities in Iran. Participants completed a death- or non-death-related writing task. After this, participants were informed that the researchers wanted to assess their impressions of some of the attitudes held by other students at their university. To do this, they were going to be shown a series of questions and read another student's responses to those questions.

What participants did not realize is that they were not actually reading opinions of fellow students; they were being randomly assigned to one of two conditions crafted by the experimenters. Half of the participants were assigned to a condition promoting a fundamentalist view of Islam that supports martyrdom attacks against the United States (a promartyrdom manipulation). For example, one of the questions was "What do you feel to be the most pressing world issue?" And the student response that participants read was "Showing the world that deaths in the name of Allah will bring an end to the imperialism practiced in the West." Another question was "Are martyrdom attacks on the United States justified?" The student response that participants read was "Yes. The United States represents the world power which Allah wants us to destroy."

The other half were assigned to a condition promoting a less fundamentalist, more tolerant and peaceful view of Islam (an antimartyrdom manipulation). For example, in this condition, the student response to the pressing world issue question was "Convincing others in the world that Islam is a peaceful religion and that Allah loves all men. The world must know that not all Muslims are motivated by the hatred and misguided beliefs that have led to many needless deaths in the name of Allah." The student response to the question about whether martyrdom attacks against the United States are justified was "No. Universally speaking, human life is too valuable to be used as a means of producing change."

These responses were created by the experimenters to see how Iranian students would respond to two very distinct Islamic worldviews when existential needs were heightened by an increased awareness of death. Are young Iranian college students susceptible to extremist viewpoints when thinking about their own mortality?

To determine this, after reading one of these two responses, participants responded to a number of questions regarding their attitudes toward the student responder and their own willingness to join the cause being promoted by those responses. These included items such as "How much do you agree with this person's opinion?" and "Rate the degree to which you would consider joining their cause."

Results in the nondeath control condition were encouraging. In this condition, favorability ratings were higher in the antimartyrdom condition than in the promartyrdom condition. In other words, Iranian students generally favored the more peaceful and tolerant Islamic view. However, this pattern flipped in the heightened death-awareness condition. For participants who first thought about death, favorability ratings were higher in the promartyrdom condition than in the antimartyrdom condition. The existential threat of death-awareness motivated sympathy for a more militant and extreme Islamic narrative.

The findings on willingness to join the cause were similar. In the nondeath condition, participants were more inclined to report a willingness to join the cause if the cause was the promotion of a more tolerant and peaceful Islam. Once again, existential threat flipped this pattern. Participants who first thought about death were more interested in joining the cause if the cause was an extreme Islamic view that favored martyrdom attacks against the United States. In fact, participants in the condition in which they thought about mortality and were then exposed to promartyrdom ideas displayed the highest level of willingness to join the cause compared to participants in all other conditions. The existential threat of death-awareness made the martyrdom message more seductive.

Thinking about death, ironically, inspired support for actions that increase the probability of dying. Earlier I talked about suntanning as an example of people putting existential motives above physical health and safety. I also noted that we all take little physical risks in the service of seeking meaning and self-transcendence. This research reveals a far more extreme way that existential pursuits can be harmful, and not just to the person engaged in the behavior. Suicide terrorism and other forms of existentially motivated violence are dangerous to all of us.

This experiment did not measure religious fundamentalism, so there is no way to know the extent to which this variable played a role. However, based on other research I discussed, it seems reasonable to predict that it would be fundamentalists who are most inclined to respond to thoughts of mortality with greater support for martyrdom attacks and a greater willingness to be personally involved in self-destructive campaigns of terror.

I am not suggesting that existential motives are the only or even primary causes of terrorism. There are undoubtedly a number of economic, social, cultural, and personality variables that contribute to the radicalization of an Islamist or other type of terrorist. Terrorism and other forms of ideological extremism are obviously complex problems. However, existential motives appear to play a role. Islamic jihadist groups promote the view that martyrs not only will be remembered and honored as heroes making a meaningful sacrifice to the cause but also will be rewarded in the afterlife. I suspect it would be much harder to convince people to sacrifice their lives for a cause if the sacrifice was not perceived as a powerful way to attain meaning and gain eternal rewards or some sense of immortality.

THE RARITY OF DANGEROUS SUPERNATURAL BELIEFS

Clearly, supernatural beliefs can take people down a dangerous path. Some maladaptive religious beliefs are so powerful that they can drive devotees to put their health at great and even mortal risk or allow their children to needlessly suffer and die. Some beliefs promote an apocalyptic vision of the world that undermines efforts to make life on Earth better for current and future generations. And some religious groups champion ideas and behaviors that can lead to horrible acts of mass violence. As a society, we must be vigilant about combating extremism for our own safety and the protection of the vulnerable.

And though I focused largely on religion, there are certainly other religious-like supernatural beliefs that have proven problematic for health. For example, people use New Age spiritual healing practices that have little or no scientific data supporting their efficacy. Some of these treatments might offer little more than psychological relief, a placebo effect. And, for most consumers, these treatments are used as supplements, not replacements, to conventional medicine. But the same reasoning applies. People may be putting their health and safety at risk if they are rejecting science-based healthcare advice and treatment because they are dogmatically invested in a New Age belief system that promises supernatural healing.

For instance, some parents involved in New Age movements do not vaccinate their children. This has contributed to states such as California having low rates of measles vaccinations, which has become a public health concern. A measles outbreak that originated in California at Disneyland motivated state legislatures to pass a new law requiring all children attending daycare or school to be fully vaccinated, regardless of the parents' religious beliefs. The passing of this surprisingly controversial bill has prompted a number of California parents to homeschool their children (homeschooled kids are exempt) or move to states that allow religious exemptions.

A critical point to remember is that, thankfully, all of these cases are rare. The religious and New Age spiritual groups that reject modern medicine are fringe, only attracting small numbers of disciples. Of course, in many less developed parts of the world supernatural-based healing practices are still very common. Some of these places do not have reliable access to modern science-based medicine. Even in places where modern medicine has been introduced, spiritual cultural traditions die hard.

It is worth noting that it is often religious-based missionary organizations that work tirelessly to bring modern medicine to these parts of the world. And the people in these countries that need this medicine are often, though certainly not always, receptive and thankful. Again, it is rare for humans to put their lives at risk by letting a supernatural belief stand in the way of science-based treatment.

The same can be said for Islamic jihadist groups. Polls indicate that only 1% of American Muslims and 3% of Muslims around the world believe that suicide bombing attacks against civilians are often justified to defend Islam.[19] Over 80% of American Muslims surveyed said such bombings are never justified for any reason, while 7% indicated that suicide bombings are sometimes justified. Of course, if this number is correct, the possibility that even 7% of American Muslims could conceive of situations in which suicide bombings are justified is reason for concern. Islam is the fastest growing world religion, and the number of Muslims living in the United States is expected to grow in the coming years.[20] Therefore, even small levels of sympathy for martyrdom terrorist attacks is worrisome. As the world continues to grapple with the threat of terrorism that is partially rooted in supernatural beliefs that promise eternal rewards, the challenge will be to honestly and rationally take on this threat without discriminating against and marginalizing the millions of law-abiding Muslims who are no more dangerous than any other thoughtful religious person. A number of moderate Muslim reformers around the world are, in fact, working to combat Islamist extremism and radicalization. They deserve our support.

The potential for religion and other supernatural beliefs to be used to radicalize individuals is always there and is not inherently specific to a single belief system. As we saw in chapter 6, supernatural beliefs are often associated with personally and socially positive outcomes. They help people cope with the hardships and uncertainties of life and provide them a way to find existential security in the face of an awareness of mortality and fears about cosmic insignificance. They give people hope and inspire them to take on difficult challenges. Unfortunately, for some, and under certain circumstances, these beliefs can also promote harmful fatalistic views of the world and inspire evil acts of great consequence.

Toward a Common Humanity

I f you aspire to be the president of the United States, it would be wise to not be an atheist. And if you are, keep it to yourself. Go to church and smile for the cameras. A recent Gallup survey found that 40% of Americans polled would not vote for an otherwise well-qualified presidential candidate if he or she were a nonbeliever.[1] Americans are more likely to vote for pretty much any other stigmatized group than they are to vote for atheists. The only group that Americans were less willing to vote for than atheists was socialists.

The dislike of atheist politicians is about trust. Americans view religious politicians as more trustworthy than atheist politicians.[2] For instance, 2016 Democratic presidential candidate Hillary Clinton scored very low on trust in many polls. Whether or not people believed her to be religious was diagnostic of whether or not they trusted her. The more people thought she was religious, the more they said they viewed her as trustworthy.[3]

Don't bring an atheist home to meet mom and dad. A survey found that of all the groups that a potential son-in-law or daughter-in-law could belong to, parents rated atheists as the least desirable.[4] Once again, trust is a key variable. For example, studies indicate that atheists are among the least trusted people in the United States, and this lack of trust influences the extent to which people think atheists make good employees.[5] In settings such as daycares, where people trust others to look after their children, religious individuals are viewed as more desirable workers than atheists. In general, many people believe that atheists are less moral than believers.[6]

Many religious leaders and politicians are working hard to ensure that the prejudice atheists face does not diminish anytime soon. Some prominent religious figures have publicly asserted that atheism is responsible for many of the social problems we face as a species. They argue, if people did not turn their backs on God, the world would be a more peaceful place and we would experience fewer tragedies such as school shootings. Some have gone so far as to assert that denying God is the cause of recent devastating natural disasters. God is punishing us for turning away from him and embracing secular values.

Notably, Reverend Jerry Falwell claimed the September 11 terrorist attacks might have been God's judgment for efforts to make the United States a secular nation. A number of conservative Christian pastors proposed that Hurricane Katrina, which killed more than 1,800 people, resulted from Americans mocking God's laws by embracing social movements that challenge traditional Christian views such as gay rights. Some have gone even further by claiming that people aren't simply rejecting God, they are embracing Satan and other dark forces. Pat Robertson, host of the "700 Club," attributed the catastrophic 2009 earthquake in Haiti to the Haitians making a pact with the devil.

Atheists are obviously not endorsing Satanism. However, religious leaders are often quick to implicate Satan as a causal force in the secular movement. Turning away from God means succumbing to the temptations of Satan. This viewpoint possibly contributes to negative views about atheists.

Some atheists have reached their breaking point and are pushing back. The New Atheist movement, in particular, appears set on not only defending atheism but also pointing the finger back at believers. Prominent atheist public intellectuals have proposed that religion is actually at the root of human suffering. They claim that religious dogma facilitates conflict between different cultural groups and serves as a barrier to accepting useful empirically derived information.

How can some people believe the Earth is less than 10,000 years old, when we have the ability now to date it as much older? How can people continue to reject the theory of evolution when the scientific evidence so overwhelmingly supports it? Whether it is attitudes about what causes sexual orientation, teen pregnancy, or the changing climate, many atheists propose that religion is keeping people ignorant and driving an unwillingness to trust secular scientific authorities.

However, as I have argued in this book, if you look beneath the surface, atheists and believers are not as different as we tend to think. Atheists may outwardly reject supernatural beliefs, but they are grappling with the same existential concerns as theists, and this often inspires some affinity for supernatural ideas, and a greater openness to exploring spiritual questions and interests. This is not to say there are no important differences between those who embrace the supernatural and those who work to reject it. But the differences are pretty apparent, frequently discussed, and, frankly, often exaggerated. What we hear less about is how believers and nonbelievers are similar.

In this final chapter, I propose a new way to think about how humans turn to supernatural thoughts and beliefs and assert that the broader distinctions made between believers and nonbelievers on many pressing social issues are often overstated or misrepresented. Most religious people, even those who endorse scientifically invalidated beliefs about topics such as the age of the Earth, do not live in a way that makes such a belief socially problematic. Plus, this view of religious people as being anti-science is oversimplistic and overblown. It ignores considerable evidence regarding the pro-science views of many believers.

And being an atheist doesn't make someone robotically rational or invulnerable to more intuitive and emotional influences. Similarly, believers are not uniquely influenced by the cognitive and ideological biases. Atheists also have blind spots.

Furthermore, being an atheist certainly doesn't make one immoral, untrustworthy, or uncaring. My hope is that by the end of this chapter, you—an atheist or believer or somewhere in between—will be able to see a common humanity that unites all people.

SHOULD WE STOP DIVIDING BELIEVERS AND NONBELIEVERS INTO GROUPS? THE SUPERNATURAL CONTINUUM

We often think and talk about psychological concepts simplistically. Take personality. You are more likely to say that you are an extrovert than to say that you score moderately high on the trait of extroversion. It is efficient and often sufficient to think in terms of categories, so we tend to do so. But many psychological characteristics are not cleanly divided into categories. They are better described as being on a continuum. Perhaps this is the case for people's propensity to engage in supernatural thinking and to hold supernatural beliefs.

It is hard to divide the world into believers and nonbelievers. Some people rarely engage in supernatural thinking and consciously reject all or nearly all forms of supernatural belief. And some folks are on the extreme other end of the continuum. They are so heavily invested in supernatural beliefs that they reject important scientific facts that clash with their beliefs. But these are extremes. And most people are not at the extreme end of either side of the continuum. They fall somewhere in between. And the intensity of people's beliefs can change over time or across situations.

Though self-identified religiosity may generally map onto this continuum pretty well, research I presented in this book suggests that we need to think beyond the traditional view of religiosity when discussing how humans approach supernatural ideas, beliefs, and interests. To review just some of the key findings:

- Relatively nonreligious trained scientists and nonreligious community members in the United States and Finland engage in certain types of supernatural thinking (seeing design and purpose in nature), particularly when they are making quick (intuitive) decisions and thus not carefully thinking through an idea.
- Atheists have a hard time not using teleological language (describing events as meant to be) when describing life events.
- Atheists exhibit physiological signs of distress when challenging God to cause harm.
- Atheists are more likely than theists to endorse certain religious-like supernatural-lite beliefs such as the belief that intelligent alien life is monitoring and influencing human behavior.
- Atheists who lack meaning and are seeking it are most inclined to endorse supernatural-lite beliefs.
- Though most people who call themselves atheists do not believe in God, there is disagreement between atheists on other spiritual and metaphysical issues.
- Some atheists endorse spiritual beliefs and practices.
- When thinking about mortality, atheists are less inclined to turn to secular beliefs that provide meaning if they are exposed to information suggesting that there is continued consciousness beyond death.
- As traditional religious identification decreases in a society, interest in nontraditional supernatural and supernatural-lite concepts and beliefs increases.

If atheists sometimes see the world through the lens of design and purpose, experience physiological distress indicative of a fear of angering God, believe in phenomena (e.g., UFOs) that lack empirical support, and become more intuitive, spiritual, and interested in supernatural concepts when thinking about the threat of death or the potential meaninglessness of life, perhaps we should stop labeling people as believers or nonbelievers and instead embrace a broader view that accepts supernatural interests as a natural part of the human condition. At a minimum, we should move past the view that atheists are like Spock, from *Star Trek*, completely rational, never moved by emotional intuitions, and believers are like Kirk, always following their hearts. Most of us are a little bit of both.

To help make this point, let's think about this issue another way. If you are an atheist, do this little thought exercise. Imagine attending a concert by your favorite music artist or group. When you were enjoying the live music, hearing some of your favorite songs, what were you thinking? Were you rationally and thoughtfully deconstructing the music, focusing on the technical details of the sound? Or were you "feeling the music," letting it move you? My guess is the latter, unless you are a music critic or technician tasked with evaluating the performance. Music is most enjoyed in a more intuitive mindset.

Another example. Ever watched a movie and had the hairs on your arm stand up because you were so touched by a particularly emotional scene of personal triumph, joy, loss, or sadness? During that experience did you stop yourself, purposely short-circuiting your intuitive feelings so that you could objectively evaluate the logistics of the scenario, acting, cinematography, or quality of the audio? Again, unless you had some specific reason to do so, I suspect you just enjoyed the scene and the emotional journey it took you on. This isn't to say that people are never analytically critical of movies. But, for example, when fans watch fantasy and science fiction movies that defy physical laws of the universe, they enjoy them most when they just go along, letting the story move them, as opposed to analytically challenging the realism.

Atheists are familiar with religious experiences; they just might not realize it. When Christians talk about the spirit moving them or feeling the presence of God, it is a similar phenomenon as enjoying a beautiful sunset, experiencing the feeling of love, or being emotionally touched by music or some other form of art. Religious experiences are often about subjective feelings. Thus, religious experiences involve a willingness to trust intuition. Most of the time, there is nothing problematic about these intuitive experiences. They can be quite healthy as well as psychologically rewarding and enriching. Remember, it is in these intuitive mindsets that people, religious and nonreligious alike, feel the greatest sense of meaning in life.[7]

Traditional religious identification may be on the decline, but clearly people are looking for opportunities to have spiritual experiences that involve finding meaning through intuitive processes. In the modern world, there are simply more options for people to choose from and explore as well as a greater social acceptance for people to shop around and mix and match a variety of supernatural ideas and beliefs. However, as we previously considered, the extent to which these alternative spiritual explorations provide the same level of existential comfort and as traditional religious faiths remains unclear. More research is needed to explore the short and long-term psychological and health implications of people shifting from more traditional to less traditional spiritual beliefs and interests.

It is also worth noting that religiosity is not always about intuitive feelings. Clearly, there is a deep scholarly and philosophical component of religion. Also, many see religious doctrines as outlining a sensible way of living, a guidebook for how to be a good person. As a result, they thoughtfully base important life choices on these doctrines. As discussed in chapter 6, religious beliefs often inspire healthy lifestyles and adaptive ways of coping with some of life's challenges. Thus, I would not argue that the entire religious enterprise is based on intuitive feelings. Many smart theologians and philosophers have made strong arguments for the moral and social value of religion. However, intuitive thinking is a key component of religious experiences that invoke the supernatural. Faith in religious supernatural forces demands a willingness to suspend a skeptical mindset and embrace or at least be open to ideas outside of our known understanding of the laws of nature.

I suspect many atheists will understand this illustration comparing religious experiences to secular experiences that involve more intuitive cognitive processes, but would also be quick to point out that going to a concert, watching a movie, or appreciating a piece of art or natural beauty is not a belief. It is merely a temporary experience. True. The conscious belief in God or other supernatural agents is more than a passing psychological state. But it is similar and gets us back to my argument that we need to move beyond simple categories.

Psychologists often distinguish between states and traits. States are passing feelings. They can change depending on a number of circumstances. A trait, however, is more enduring. It is a stable psychological characteristic, something not easily moved around. For instance, the state of positive mood is something people experience when they are in a situation that makes them happy, such as watching a funny movie, going out with friends, or spending time with a romantic partner or spouse. Positive mood is a state in this context because it is temporary, an emotion triggered by a particular stimulus.

The trait of positive mood is something else. It means to be chronically in a good mood, even in situations that others may not find particularly pleasant. In other words, high trait positive mood means that one experiences the state of positive mood frequently. Low trait positive mood means that one experiences the state of positive mood less frequently. But at the end of the day, we're still talking about the same experience.

Enduring religious beliefs such as a belief in God are more like traits. They transcend situations. I propose that even some atheists are "believers" in the sense that they are high in trait spirituality and hold nontraditional supernatural beliefs. These atheists frequently rely on intuitive experiences and feelings and are thus naturally attracted to supernatural ideas, just less conventional ones that are typically not associated with religion. In fact, the reason some atheists have rejected God in the first place is more intuitive than rational because it comes from a feeling of anger toward God as opposed to a more analytical rejection of the supernatural.[8] In other words, some atheists are best described as emotional atheists, not rational atheists.

Other people are generally more skeptical. Their supernatural thinking is rare because they rely less frequently on intuition. But just like the scientists at top research universities who exhibited teleological thinking, particularly when they were not given much time to react and thus had to rely on intuition, even hardcore skeptics occasionally experience the state of supernatural thinking.

The desire to divide atheists and theists into distinct categories may be partially the result of Western culture. In individualistic nations like the United States, we tend to view religiosity and spirituality as personal choices that people freely make, whereas those in more collectivist cultures often, though not always, view these characteristics as similar to personality traits.

But people don't choose their personalities. Likewise, spirituality may be more of an innate trait than a personal choice.

For the last several semesters in the cultural psychology course that I teach I have asked my students to respond to this idea that spirituality is more of a personality trait than a choice. I suggest that some people are naturally more spiritual than others, they tend to more frequently have spiritual experiences and are thus more likely to be attracted to occupations and personal interests that capitalize on this spirituality just as an extrovert is more likely to gravitate toward occupations and interests that allow her or him to be social.

The overwhelming majority of my students reject this idea. Some of them will at least partially acknowledge the notion that some people seem to be better than others at being spiritual, but they almost always attribute it to effort, not natural disposition. In our individualistic culture in which so many of us have been taught that faith is a personal choice, it is easy to divide believers and nonbelievers into different groups and to have negative feelings toward those in the other group because we believe they freely chose and are thus personally responsible for their faith or lack of it.

However, cognitive science does tend to support the view that religiosity and spirituality are traits that are at least partially based on natural dispositions. As we explored previously, researchers have linked traits such as theory of mind (imagining the thoughts and feelings of others) and moral concern to belief in God. We also considered how such traits help explain why women tend to be more religious and spiritual than men. Survey after survey shows that, compared to men, women are more likely to believe in God, pray, go to church, and engage in church-related activities. Women are also the target audience for many self-help spirituality books and magazines as well as New Age spiritual practices.

Other research highlights another inherent cognitive determinant of supernatural thinking. Remember that intuitive thinking is associated with religion and spirituality, and people tend to find meaning using intuitive, not analytic, processes. Though all people engage in both intuitive and analytic thought processes, there are also inherent trait differences in the tendency to use one style of thinking over the other. And these trait cognitive differences predict a range of supernatural beliefs,[9,10] including religious beliefs.[11] Those who score higher on trait intuitive thinking tend to believe in the supernatural more than those who score low on this trait.

In short, there are natural differences that make people more or less inclined to engage in supernatural thinking and hold supernatural beliefs. However, not being naturally inclined for spirituality does not mean one never engages in supernatural thinking or benefits from it.

Not everyone is a natural artist or athlete, but that does not mean we can't all enjoy making art or playing sports. For most pursuits, it takes a combination of dedication and natural ability to excel. But would we say Michael Phelps made a choice to have ideal physical characteristics for being an Olympic swimmer? No. Nor would most people say that not having the ideal swimmer's body prevents them from occasionally enjoying a good swim.

Not everyone is naturally inclined to be spiritual or religious. This doesn't mean that they don't ever feel the pull of the supernatural, as I have shown in this book. Likewise, not everyone is naturally inclined to be an atheist, but this does not mean that natural theists are incapable of being skeptical about the supernatural or taking a more analytic approach to important life questions. And again, most people are not at the extreme ends of these positions. It simply is not that black and white.

That being said, people have a tendency to make simple group distinctions. It is human nature. Considering this, another way to move toward a better understanding of similarities between those who consciously reject the supernatural and those who embrace it is to consider common stereotypes and beliefs about each of these supposed groups, and how these stereotypes and beliefs exaggerate differences, making the distinctions between believers and nonbelievers appear more consequential than they really are.

ARE RELIGIOUS PEOPLE ANTI-SCIENCE?

Many atheists claim that one of their main problems with religion is that to be religious mandates a rejection of science and that this rejection is harmful not only to believers but also to society as a whole. Science not only has allowed us to have a better understanding of how the world works but also has dramatically improved the lives of humans. Of course, science can be used to cause great harm and destruction. But I suspect most would agree that science has, on the whole, been very beneficial to humans. Some atheists are, not surprisingly, concerned about any religious perspective that would challenge the validity and utility of science.

But the truth is, most believers are not anti-science. The view promoted by a few vocal atheists that religious people, particularly Christians, do not like, understand, or believe in science may actually be part of the problem by driving some Christians away from having an interest and pursuing careers in science. For example, one series of recent studies found that Christian and non-Christian participants both indicated a similarly high awareness of the stereotypes that Christians are not good at and don't trust science. However, whereas Christians reported these stereotypes to be incorrect, non-Christians endorsed them as true.[12] Many atheists would be surprised to learn that most Christians know that they are viewed as anti-science but do not feel that this view fairly represents them.

It is true that certain religious beliefs are at odds with our current scientific understanding of the world. And this can become problematic if such beliefs serve as barriers to scientific progress. However, much of the time I suspect they do not. The theory of evolution is often cited as the most controversial conflict between science and religion. As discussed earlier in the book, many people struggle with some of the potential implications of humans as evolved animals, that we are no more significant or purposeful than any other organism.

However, many religious people have tried to align their personal faith with science. Pope Francis professed that both the "Big Bang" and evolution are not in conflict with religious teaching and are, in fact, central to appreciating God. He actively calls on Christians to embrace science. Though there are certainly religious groups that reject this view, many Christians and believers from other faiths do not, or at least do not let their personal beliefs on the matter influence the science-based views that are more important to modern living.

In fact, according to Pew survey data from 2013, religious Americans' views on evolution are more complex than what stereotypes about Christians suggest.[13] The majority of Catholics and mainline Protestants believe in evolution, they are just divided in the extent to which they believe God played a role. These groups are about evenly split on whether they side with the view that humans did evolve but that God guided the process or the view that evolution is entirely due to natural processes.

White evangelical Protestants are the most inclined to reject evolution. Almost two-thirds of this group believes humans and animals have always existed in their present form. However, surveys also indicate that many people of faith are uncertain about what they believe, suggesting an openness to learning more about evolution and considering how it could be compatible with their religious beliefs.[14]

Nonprofit organizations such as BioLogos are championing a Christian view of evolution, that one can believe in science and be a person of faith. Many Christians are sincerely and thoughtfully working to embrace scientific ideas and discoveries while maintaining their faith. Promoting the idea that religious people reject science is counterproductive.

What about actual scientists? Religious people may support science at some level, but, as some have suggested, does becoming a trained scientist turn people away from religion? This would suggest that religion and science are ultimately at odds.

Scientists are more likely to be atheists than are nonscientists;[15] however, nearly 50% of scientists identify as religious.[16] The founder of

BioLogos and current head of the National Institute of Health, Francis Collins, is not only an accomplished physician-geneticist (he led the Human Genome Project) but also a devout Christian. Echoing survey data, Collins has stated in essays and interviews that there are many working scientists who see no conflict between religion and science. Collins's assertion that science and religion are compatible may be helping efforts to improve the religion and science dialogue, as a recent experiment found that participants who learned about Collins as a man of faith and science became more open to the idea that science and religion are not in conflict.[17]

More generally, despite the fact that some argue that science and religion are adversaries, most scientists do not believe there is an inherent conflict.[18] In one large survey of university professors, scientists in the fields of physics, biology, chemistry, sociology, economics, political science, and psychology were asked to indicate which of three views about religion best describes their own views: "there is very little truth in religion," "there are basic truths in many religions," and "there is the most truth in only one religion." The majority of scientists in every field chose the second option, that many religions have basic truths. The percentage of scientists who chose this option ranged from 63.5% at the low end (physics professors) to 76.2% at the high end (sociology professors) for an average of 71% across fields.[19]

Another survey found that only 15% of scientists indicated believing that science and religion are always in conflict.[20] And a large international survey found that the majority of scientists in many countries such as the United States, France, Italy, and Taiwan believe that science and religion speak to distinct realties, and thus are not in conflict.[21] In the same international survey, less than 25% of scientists in every surveyed country said that science has made them less religious.

In sum, despite the fact that some have asserted that religion opposes science, there are many religious people involved in science. In addition, the majority of scientists think religions offer basic truths and do not see science as in conflict with religion. Clearly, the relationship between religion and science is not as contentious as some would like to believe.

More broadly, religious people are not an uneducated class of people. In addition to labeling them anti-science, some outspoken secularists/atheists suggest that religious people are intellectually simple and poorly educated. They argue that better education would reduce people's tendency to turn to what they view as primitive supernatural religious beliefs. It is true that research tends to find a small but reliable negative correlation between religiosity and general intelligence.[22] However, this argument that believers are unintelligent and/or uneducated fails to account for the considerable amount of evidence that religion goes hand in hand with educational success. For one, religious youth are more likely to graduate from high school and enroll in college than their nonreligious peers.[23]

Moreover, according to Pew, in the United States, atheists are actually less likely to have a college education than members of a number of religious groups including Hindus, Buddhists, Unitarian Universalists, and Christians from Episcopalian, Anglican, and United Church of Christ denominations.[24] Roughly 43% of atheists have college degrees. Interestingly, only 24% of religious "nones" have college degrees, which is a lower percentage than the total US average (27%), and the percentage of college-educated people from a range of religious backgrounds such as Muslims, Mormons, Methodists, Lutherans, and Catholics.

Of course, there are a number of demographic and social factors having little to do with religion that influence those numbers. Clearly though, it is incorrect to suggest that religious people just lack education. There is no compelling reason to associate religion with ignorance and a lack of educational achievement.

If atheists are concerned about some of the more antiquated, nonscientific views typically found among the religious-right, they should perhaps be equally (or more) concerned about the growing anti-science views from parts of the academic-left. Scholars in disciplines such as sociology, cultural anthropology, and gender studies have vocally rejected empiricism in favor of more postmodern-based methodologies. They argue that science is a social construct and reject analytic and quantitative methods in favor of approaches that rely more on people's intuitive feelings and personal opinions than systematic, data-based research. I would argue that the constructivists on the left are more dangerous than the creationists on the right. Creationists may reject certain scientific theories, but constructivists reject the entire scientific enterprise. And while creationists have little authority on college campuses, postmodern professors have considerable influence in what students are taught, at least in certain fields in the social sciences and humanities.

DOES RELIGION CAUSE HATE AND VIOLENCE?

The other big concern that some atheists express about religion is the idea pushed by a small group of atheist activists that religion is the cause of many of the wars and other acts of collective violence that have plagued our species. The problem with this position is that it ignores a fair amount of what we know about human psychology, as well as the many wars and genocides that have little or nothing to do with religious faith. As discussed in the previous chapter, religious fundamentalism is concerning because fundamentalists are often unwilling to compromise and are prone to socially dangerous positions. But again, most religious folks aren't fundamentalists. And fundamentalism can most certainly take a secular form.

The proclivity to form groups, favor members of one's own group, and engage in discriminatory and even violent acts against members of other groups is not a religious problem, it is a human problem. For decades, social psychologists have studied the conditions that contribute to social conflict. In fact, many of the early social psychologists became interested in this topic because they themselves fled Europe during World War II or had family members displaced or killed in the war.

If you have ever taken an introductory psychology class you are probably familiar with some of the classic research that was very much sparked by the horrors of World War II. The Milgram obedience studies were among the most famous. These were experiments conducted to determine the extent to which regular citizens would obey an authority figure (the experimenter) even if this meant causing serious physical pain to a total stranger. Many participants complied with the experimenter's command to administer electric shock to the stranger, even when he screamed out in pain. Of course, there was no actual electric shock, but the research participants did not know this.

We learned a lot from these studies on obedience. Regular people, when they are directed by authorities and when they do not feel personally responsible for their decisions, will sometimes hurt others. These experiments have been criticized for a number of reasons. For one, they were in an artificial lab setting. Participants weren't hitting, stabbing, or shooting anyone. True. But the amount of coercion being used to get participants to obey was also quite weak. It was just an experiment at a university lab, so participants knew they could refuse the commands of the experimenter and walk out at any time. Some did. But many—a surprising number—did not.

It is not hard to imagine that many people could be pressed to commit unethical acts and even horrible violence if they feared for their livelihood, social status, or their own safety and the safety of their family. And this has nothing to do with religion. Some psychologists have offered alternative explanations of Milgram's results, and there are certainly a number of personal and environmental factors that influence this kind of behavior. Critical though is that people are capable of causing harm to others for reasons that have absolutely no connection to religion or any other supernatural belief.

A fair amount of violent conflict occurs over competition for scarce resources. Religion is sometimes implicated in these struggles between coalitions, but it is often little more than a symbolic marker of which tribe one belongs to. The real fight is over desirable land, water, oil, and other valuable resources. Social psychologists have also shown that people will show favoritism toward their own group even if the characteristics that define their group are quite inconsequential such as the type of art people like or the sports team they support. Many of the groups that people fight for are, of course, not inconsequential, but they are also not necessarily religious or supernatural-related (e.g., one's nation).

Humans don't need supernatural beliefs to insult, exclude, hate, or kill one another. Some people exploit religiosity to harness hate. But religious doctrines that promote hatred and violence are created by hateful and violent people, not vice versa. Extremists and fundamentalists can take many forms. And the psychological factors that drive some to evil are not inherently tied to the supernatural.

To atheists who think that religion is the cause of human suffering and violence, consider the following questions. Do you honestly think if religion disappeared tomorrow we would suddenly or even eventually have world peace? Can you explain how so much pain, suffering, and death was caused at the hands of secular communist nations or tyrannical dictatorships? Have you not seen the human characteristics of greed, ego, and a desire for power and control present in those who have no religious faith?

In addition, many of the efforts to promote peace, feed hungry people, cure diseases, and improve the living conditions of the impoverished are spearheaded by religious organizations. Large national survey data sets provide strong evidence that religiosity is positively associated with charitable giving.[25] If religion inherently leads to hate and conflict, why is it so often associated with acts of kindness, generosity, and sacrifice?

Moreover, numerous studies directly link religious practices to prosocial behavior. For example, researchers found across multiple studies that having people pray for others decreased anger and aggression following a provocation.[26] In another study researchers found that having Muslim Palestinian youth participants think from the perspective of Allah (God) reduced bias against Jewish Israelis.[27] We should be worried about religious extremism. But we should be equally worried about the pain and suffering caused by factors unrelated to religion.

In short, don't fall for the arguments made by a small but vocal group of atheists that religion is a primitive tribalism that is not only anti-science, but also inherently divisive. For every cult leader, Islamic extremist, Christian white supremacist, and religious dictator there are many more peaceful, thoughtful, caring, and generous believers who use religion as a source of meaning, inspiration, and social guidance in their own life, a way to connect to and empathize with others, not a means to dominate or cause pain. The tribal psychology that can lead to conflict will continue with or without the existence of religion. Bad people use religion to do bad, and good people often use religion to do good. And as decades of social and behavioral science research has shown, all of us can be influenced by the economic, social, cultural, and self-serving forces that contribute to conflict between groups.

ARE ATHEISTS ANTI-RELIGION?

Just as some atheists see religious people as anti-science, some religious believers think atheists are anti-religion. This notion is also an overstatement. As I have already pointed out, there are certainly some vocal atheists who have made a lot of waves (and perhaps a lot of money) bashing religion. But the vast majority of atheists are not bothered by their religious counterparts. In one study, researchers found that less than 6% of atheist scientists are actively anti-religion.[28]

I am a researcher who studies the psychology of belief and disbelief, so I have spent a considerable amount time among both believers and nonbelievers. When talking to atheists, I rarely hear an outright disdain for religion. Some atheists express concerns about the more problematic stances that certain religious groups have taken and worry about religion influencing public policy. Some also are quick to note some of the scandals and abuses of power that have occurred within religious organizations. And some have even expressed a certain level of envy toward religious people. They don't feel inspired to be religious but recognize that it helps many people find comfort, meaning, and a sense of community.

Also, many religious "nones" do not reject the idea of religion, but instead the human corruption of it. A Pew poll found that 22% of "nones" describe themselves as being opposed specifically to organized religion.[29] Common complaints among the religious unaffiliated are that religious institutions are power hungry, too involved with politics, and focus too much on rules. Of course, these concerns are not specific to atheists and agnostics. Many self-identified religious people have expressed frustration with religious organizations. Despite their concerns about religion, many "nones" still see it as having value: the vast majority of religious unaffiliated view religious institutions as being good for the community, playing an important role in helping the poor, and strengthening morality.[30]

More than anything, many nonbelievers feel socially marginalized. As discussed at the start of this chapter, atheists are one of the most unpopular and least trusted social groups. Interestingly, the more prevalent atheists are, or at least are believed to be, in a society, the less people distrust them.[31] When people see atheists playing prominent roles in their culture, they may be less likely to perceive them as the mysterious other.

The truth is that since atheists are such a small group, little is known about them. It is only in very recent years that social and behavioral scientists have started to think about the social and psychological lives of atheists. Atheists can sometimes seem defensive or antagonistic toward religion, but this might reflect a sense of insecurity about how they are viewed and treated more than an active dislike of religion or religious people.

In fact, as we've previously discussed, some atheists participate in religious activities such as attending church because they have a religious spouse, want their kids to receive religious education, or are looking to connect to a community. If these atheists were adamantly anti-religion, it is doubtful they would be so willing to commune with religious folks.

Many atheists are also very interested in learning about religion and especially how different faith traditions are similar and distinct. Humanist atheists in particular often turn to religious teachings for inspiration on how to approach spiritual practices. Atheists may not believe in God, but they see value in many of the moral guidelines and humanitarian principles that many religions promote. Believe it or not, some atheists pray.[32] They don't believe that a supernatural force is listening to their prayers, but they find the activity to be helpful for finding calm and focus. Of course, most atheists don't pray but more and more of them are interested in activities that have a spiritual quality such as meditation.

DO ATHEISTS LACK A MORAL CODE?

Perhaps the most common belief about atheists is that they lack a moral code.[33] This belief is based on the notion that human morality comes from religion. Indeed, all religions provide guidelines for living a moral life.

As a kid growing up in a Southern Baptist church, I was certainly taught that the path to being a good person was to believe in God and follow the teachings of Jesus Christ. Rejecting God and Jesus was essentially giving up any hope of being a decent human being. The Christian faith describes humans as born sinners who need God's guidance and forgiveness. The best we can do, according to Christian teachings, is work hard to follow the example of Christ and be willing to admit sins and ask God to forgive them.

Religious or not, most people would agree with the basic idea that humans are naturally going to make mistakes and cause harm to themselves and others in the process. Most people would also recognize that people can be selfish, arrogant, and cruel. Acknowledging these vulnerabilities is good. Humility, a willingness to admit wrong, and ambitions to be a better person are all important attributes. And they are not found only among believers.

However, many religious individuals find the belief that God is monitoring the lives of humans to be an important component of self-improvement. In fact, experiments have shown that religious people are more honest and helpful when they are reminded of their religious faith or the idea that God is watching them.[34] The general finding that reminders of one's religious faith inspires good behavior is not specific to Christianity. It has been observed across a number of religions.

For example, in one clever experiment, researchers had Muslim participants listen to one of two audio recordings. For one group of participants, the Muslim call to prayer could be heard in the background of the audio recording. The other group listened to the same audio recording without the call to prayer in the background. Later in the experiment, all participants completed tasks that allowed the experimenter to measure cheating behavior. Muslim participants who could hear the Muslim call to prayer in the background were more honest on the subsequent tasks than Muslim participants who listened to the same audio recording but without the call to prayer being audible.[35]

Another study examined the idea that religion is important to morality in a unique way by testing for a relationship between the number of people in a society that believe in hell (i.e., God's punishment) and crime statistics.[36] The more people in a nation that believed in hell, the lower that nation's crime rates. Statistical analyses revealed that this effect could not be explained by economic factors. The belief that humans answer to a supernatural power has powerful implications for social behavior.

What about those who do not believe? Are there good reasons to distrust them, to question their morality? No, not really. It is true, as just discussed, that religiosity has been empirically linked to prosocial behavior. However, some have argued that much of this research did not actually compare religious people to atheists.[37] As I noted earlier, many studies do not have a sufficient number of atheists to make meaningful comparisons between believers and nonbelievers and tend to treat low levels of religiosity as similar to no religiosity. This is a problem because there may be important differences between those who believe in God but do not have a strong religious commitment and those who do not at all believe in God. In other words, low religiosity is not identical to atheism.

Atheists may turn to other cultural and social structures for moral guidance or even embrace some of the teachings of religion without holding specific supernatural beliefs. Remember, some atheists attend church because they want their children to get a religious education. Few atheists would argue that religion has no social value. But what do we actually know about the moral behavior of atheists? To answer this question, researchers conducted a study with over 1,200 participants from diverse demographic and geographic backgrounds within the United States and Canada.[38] In total, 43% of the sample reported being nonreligious and 56% reported some degree of religiousness, most of which involved some denomination of Christianity. In this study, participants were randomly alerted five times each day to complete questions on their smartphones. They were specifically asked if they had committed, were the target of, or had witnessed a moral or immoral act within the past hour. For each act reported, participants were instructed to describe the event. They also completed questions about their emotions during the event.

The researchers found no significant difference between religious and nonreligious participants in the number of moral or immoral acts they committed, were the target of, or witnessed. Thus, there was no evidence that the moral and immoral experiences in the daily lives of religious and nonreligious people are all that different.

However, the researchers did observe some interesting differences on emotional reactions to these experiences. Religious people reported feeling guiltier, more embarrassed, and more disgusted than nonreligious people when they had engaged in immoral behavior. Religious people also felt a greater sense of pride and gratefulness than nonreligious people when they committed a moral act. In other words, though no behavioral difference was observed in terms of morality, religious people appeared more emotionally impacted by the behaviors they engaged in that implicated morality.

How do we know that atheists and believers were telling the truth about their moral and immoral behavior? We don't. This is a weakness of these kinds of survey studies. However, consider the fact that there are very few atheists in prison. According to the Bureau of Prisons, only one out of 1,000 prison inmates identify as atheist, a much lower percentage than what is found in the general population.[39]

Obviously, this does not directly prove that atheists are more moral than believers. They may simply have a number of educational, social, and economic advantages that reduce their likelihood of engaging in criminal behavior or at least their likelihood of being caught and imprisoned. That being said, it is clear that prisons aren't teaming with Godless heathens.

Moreover, many evolutionary and social psychologists have argued that moral behavior is inherent to human psychology, not something that comes entirely from social learning. Social learning does play an important role. Kids need role models and instruction. That being said, humans are naturally social animals. We rely on one another to survive and thrive. Thus, moral behavior is adaptive. People are at their best when they work together in groups in the service of shared goals. People who don't play well with others are often marginalized, ostracized, or punished by the group. We all engage in selfish behavior, but we also naturally pursue a social contract with others. You help me and I will help you.

An evolutionary perspective explains why people are most inclined to help family members before strangers. We naturally favor our kin. And the more we appear to have in common with others, the more we feel inclined to help them. This is how our minds work. Kinship starts with actual genetic relatedness but then appears to symbolically extend out to those who share common characteristics, including political and religious beliefs. As I've said, we naturally form groups and favor those in our group. This can be good. It helps us work toward common goals. But it can also lead to distrust and conflict between groups. Thus, our ability to peacefully and productively coexist with others relies, in part, on our ability to create a superordinate group, a common humanity.

HOW TO IMPROVE RELATIONSHIPS: COMMON HUMANITY

I have a challenge for you. Don't unfriend Facebook friends whose views on politics, religion, and so forth, make you so angry that you want to scream. If someone is abusive or horribly prejudiced, sure, get rid of them. But try really hard not to curate your social network so that you are only connected to those who see the world pretty much as you do. This challenge can extend beyond cyberspace as well. If you are deeply religious, in your daily life, don't separate yourself from those who are not. Likewise, if you are a nonbeliever, don't segregate yourself from people of faith. Listen. Learn. Try to connect.

I took on this challenge myself. On Facebook and Twitter I am friends with or follow people representing all sorts of beliefs: conservatives, liberals, libertarians, atheists, traditional Christians, Muslims, spiritual seekers, skeptics, and so on. Sometimes I can't believe the views some people hold. How can they think that way? But I typically won't unfriend or unfollow them. In fact, I have made it my mission to pay more attention to their posts. What are they into? What is important to them? Likewise, in my daily life I try to cultivate relationships with people who hold all sorts of views and I resist the urge to distance myself from people whose beliefs are in opposition to my own.

Why torture yourself with such a challenge, and what have I accomplished with this cruel exercise? A lot, actually. First, it really isn't torture. In fact, I would argue that life is more interesting and educational when you seek out relationships with people who have different viewpoints. I personally find it quite stimulating. Doing so also serves as an important reminder of the fact that a lot of smart people hold a lot of diverse and interesting beliefs.

Critically though, interacting with people holding diverse views helps me better realize just how similar most of us actually are. The people I disagree with on a range of social, cultural, and political topics are also people who are proud of their children's humble accomplishments such as making the honor roll or winning a school citizen of the month award. These are people who volunteer at animal rescue shelters and adult literacy programs. These are people looking for a low-fat cake recipe or who want to start training for a triathlon. They loved the new *Star Wars* movie and can't wait for the next season of *Game of Thrones*. Sure, I don't always agree with their stances on important topics. But guess what? They feel the same way.

In addition, I very sincerely believe that I have grown a lot from these efforts. I have even changed some of my views on big issues, beliefs I have held for much of my adult life. By listening to and learning about the views of others, I have become better at appreciating that many issues are complex and all of us have biased and irrational views on certain topics and more rational and empirically supported views on other topics. And maybe sometimes there simply is not a "correct" vantage point. But regardless of who is right or wrong, or if there is even a right or wrong, below the surface these people are not so different from me. And forcing myself to remain connected to them helps me see this fact.

At the core, we all, or at least the vast majority of us, are driven by the same motives and have the same basic priorities. We love our family and friends. We have a sense of morality that compels us to care about the welfare of others, even if we express it in different ways. We have goals, things we want to improve or change about ourselves or our life circumstances. And we want to have fun, to enjoy life.

We also have the same vulnerabilities. We fear loss and social rejection. We have self-doubts and are sometimes envious of what others have, or at least of what we think they have. We can be selfish and unsympathetic to the plight of others. We sometimes let our egos get in the way of acting fairly and rationally. In short, we have the same strengths and the same insecurities.

Yes, people have different personalities, and some people have traits that make them immoral and antisocial. But these pathological characteristics are rare. Most of us are just doing the best we can to fulfill our obligations and live a life of meaning and value.

Recently, our local mosque hosted a number of open house events to provide members of our largely Christian community a chance to ask questions and familiarize themselves with the Muslim faith and the people who subscribe to it. In a time of escalating anxiety about terrorism and inflammatory political rhetoric, the leaders of the mosque believed such an event would help ease tensions and show members of a largely White and Christian city that at the core people are people. We need more of these kinds of opportunities to connect us as humans. We might disagree with some of the beliefs others hold and cultural practices they support, but the battle of ideas should not prevent us from seeing a common humanity.

In this book, I offered a motivational analysis of the human proclivity to engage in supernatural thinking and hold supernatural beliefs. Specifically, I put forward a case based on decades of scientific research that humans are naturally pulled to the supernatural because we are existential animals, uniquely aware of our mortality and driven to find some sense of self-transcendent meaning. Unlike any other animal, humans have to confront the knowledge that we are born destined to die. As a result, we struggle with the meaning of our existence and we have to live our whole lives haunted by the ever-present threat of death. How do we cope with that knowledge? How do we get up each day and live productive lives? What keeps us from the paralyzing anxiety that could result from the realization that we will die and can die at any moment? What prevents us from being chronically depressed about how little and fragile our lives are in the grand scheme of things?

At the core of my argument is that our supernatural tendencies unite us as a species. Sure, people differ from one another on supernatural thoughts and beliefs. Some people consciously reject the world of the supernatural, whereas others embrace it. My argument though is that beneath the surface each of us engages in a certain level of supernatural thinking whether we realize it or not and that one reason we do is because of the existential insecurities and questions about death and the meaning of life that we all need answered.

And if we can understand this about ourselves, that we are united in our struggle to be more than mortal, to have lives that have enduring meaning, we can perhaps strive to connect to one another in a way that will reduce the distrust and conflict that so often divides our species.

CHAPTER 1
1. Cohen, F., Sullivan, D., Solomon, S., Greenberg, J., & Ogilvie, D. M. (2011). Finding everland: Flight fantasies and the desire to transcend mortality. *Journal of Experimental Social Psychology, 47,* 88–102. doi:10.1016/j.jesp.2010.08.013
2. Schredl, M. (2007). Personality correlates of flying dreams. *Imagination, Cognition, and Personality, 27,* 129–137. doi:10.2190/IC.27.2.d
3. Solomon, S., Greenberg, J., & Pyszczynski, T. (1991). A terror management theory of social behavior: The psychological functions of self-esteem and cultural worldviews. *Advances in Experimental Social Psychology, 24,* 93–159. doi:10.1016/S0065-2601(08)60328-7
4. Goldenberg, J. L., Pyszczynski, T., Greenberg, J., Solomon, S., Kluck, B., & Cornwell, R. (2001). I am not an animal: Mortality salience, disgust, and the denial of human creatureliness. *Journal of Experimental Psychology: General, 130,* 427–435. doi: 10.1037//0096-3445.130.3.427
5. Rach, J. A. (2013, April 5). Survey reveals women feel comfortable to break wind in front of partners 7.5 months into a relationship. Retrieved from http://lifestyle.one/closer/celebrity/news/survey-reveals-women-feel-comfortable-break-wind-front-partners-7-5-months-relationship/
6. Cox, C. R., Goldenberg, J. L., Arndt, J., & Pyszczynski, T. (2007). Mother's milk: An existential perspective on negative reactions to breast-feeding. *Personality and Social Psychology Bulletin, 33,* 110–122. doi:10.1177/0146167206294202
7. Roberts, T.-A., Goldenberg, J. L., Power, C., & Pyszczynski, T. (2002). "Feminine protection": The effects of menstruation on attitudes toward women. *Psychology of Women Quarterly, 26,* 131–139. doi:10.1111/1471-6402.00051
8. Motyl, M., Hart J., & Pyszczynski, T. (2010). When animals attack: The effects of mortality salience, infrahumanization of violence, and authoritarianism on support for war. *Journal of Experimental Social Psychology, 46,* 200–203. http://dx.doi.org/10.1016/j.jesp.2009.08.012
9. Goldenberg, J. L., Cox, C., Pyszczynski, T., Greenberg, J., & Solomon, S. (2002). Understanding human ambivalence about sex: The effects of

stripping sex of its meaning. *Journal of Sex Research, 39,* 310–320. doi:10.1080/00224490209552155

10. Beatson, R. M., & Halloran, M. J. (2007). Humans rule! The effects of creatureliness reminders, mortality salience and self-esteem on attitudes towards animals. *British Journal of Social Psychology, 46,* 619–632. doi:10.1348/014466606X147753

11. Beatson, R., Loughnan, S., & Halloran, M. J. (2009). Attitudes toward animals: The effect of priming thoughts of human-animal similarities and mortality salience on the evaluation of companion animals. *Society and Animals, 17*(1), 72–89. doi: 10.1163/156853009X393774

12. Tracy, J. L., Hart, J., & Martens, J. P. (2011). Death and science: The existential underpinnings of belief in intelligent design and discomfort with evolution. *PLoS ONE 6*(3): e17349. doi:10.1371/journal.pone.0017349

CHAPTER 2

1. Hicks, J. A., & Routledge, C. (Eds.). (2013). *The experience of meaning in life: Classical perspectives, emerging themes, and controversies.* New York, NY: Springer. http://www.springer.com/us/book/9789400765269

2. Mascaro, N., & Rosen, D. H. (2005). Existential meaning's role in the enhancement of hope and prevention of depressive symptoms. *Journal of Personality, 73,* 985–1014.

3. Ungar, T., Ungar, A., & Kim, M. (2011). Comments on meaninglessness and suicidal risk. *International Forum for Logotherapy, 34,* 72–75.

4. Kinnier, R. T., Metha, A. T., Keim, J. S., & Okey, J. L. (1994). Depression, meaninglessness, and substance abuse in "normal" and hospitalized adolescents. *Journal of Alcohol and Drug Education, 39,* 101–111.

5. Russo-Netzre, P., Schulenberg, S. E., & Batthyany, A. (Eds.). (2016). *Clinical perspectives on meaning: Positive and existential psychotherapy.* New York, NY: Springer.

6. Park, C. L. (2011). Meaning, coping, and health and well-being. In S. Folkman (Ed.), *The Oxford handbook of stress, health, and coping* (pp. 227–241). New York, NY: Oxford University Press.

7. Hill, P. L., & Turiano, N. A. (2014). Purpose in life as a predictor of mortality across adulthood. *Psychological Science, 25,* 1482–1486.

8. Kim, E. S., Strecher, V. J., & Ryff, C. D. (2014). Purpose in life and use of preventive health care services. *Proceedings of the National Academy of Sciences, 111,* 16331–16336. doi:10.1073/pnas.1414826111

9. Bower, J. E., Kemeny, M. E., Taylor, S. E., & Fahey, J. T. (2003). Finding positive meaning and its association with natural killer cell cytotoxicity among participants in a bereavement-related disclosure intervention. *Annals of Behavioral Medicine, 25,* 146–155.

10. Koole, S. L., & Van Den Berg, A. E. (2005). Lost in the wilderness: Terror management, action orientation, and nature evaluation. *Journal of Personality and Social Psychology, 88,* 1014–1028. doi:10.1037/0022-3514.88.6.1014

11. Vess, M., Hicks, J., Routledge, C., & Hoeldtke, R. (2017). Awe and meaning: Elucidating divergent effects of awe on perceptions of meaning in life. Unpublished manuscript.

12. Kelemen, D., Rottman, J., & Seston, R. (2013). Professional physical scientists display tenacious teleological tendencies: purpose-based reasoning as a cognitive default. *Journal of Experimental Psychology: General, 142*, 1074–1083.

13. Jarnefelt, E., Canfield, C. F., & Kelemen, D. (2015). The divided mind of a disbeliever: Intuitive beliefs about nature as purposefully created among different groups of non-religious adults. *Cognition, 140*, 72–88. doi: 10.1016/j.cognition.2015.02.005. Epub 2015 Apr 13.

14. Heywood, B. T., & Bering, J. M. (2014). "Meant to be": How religious beliefs and cultural religiosity affect the implicit bias to think teleologically. *Religion, Brain, and Behavior, 4*, 183–201. http://dx.doi.org/10.1080/2153599X.2013.782888

15. Norenzayan, A., & Willard, A. K. (2013). Cognitive biases explain religious belief, paranormal belief, and belief in life's purpose. *Cognition, 129*, 379–391. http://dx.doi.org/10.1016/j.cognition.2013.07.016

16. Davis, W., Juhl, J., & Routledge, C. (2011). Death and design: The terror management function of teleological beliefs. *Motivation and Emotion, 35*, 98–104.

17. Schimel, J., Hayes, J., Williams, T. J., & Jahrig, J. (2007). Is death really the worm at the core? Converging evidence that worldview threat increases death-thought accessibility. *Journal of Personality and Social Psychology, 92*, 789–803.

18. Fetterman, A. K., & Robinson, M. D. (2013). Do you use your head or follow your heart? Self-location predicts personality, emotion, decision-making and performance. *Journal of Personality and Social Psychology, 105*, 316–334. doi.org/10.1037%2Fa0033374

19. Heintzelman, S. J., & King, L. A. (2015). Meaning in life and intuition. *Journal of Personality and Social Psychology, 110*, 477–492. doi: 10.1037/pspp0000062

20. Fetterman, A. K., Juhl, J. T., Meier, B. P., Abeyta, A. A., Routledge, C., & Robinson, M. D. (2017). The path to God is through the heart: Metaphoric self-location as a robust predictor of religiosity. Unpublished manuscript.

21. Pennycook, G., Cheyne, J. A., Seli, P., Koehler, D. J., & Fugelsang, J. A. (2012). Analytic cognitive style predicts religious and paranormal belief. *Cognition, 123*, 335–346. doi.org/10.1016/j.cognition.2012.03.003

22. Shenhav, A., Rand, D. G., & Greene, J. D. (2012). Divine intuition: Cognitive style influences belief in god. *Journal of Experimental Psychology: General, 141*, 423–428. doi:10.1037/a0025391

23. McCrae, R. R. (1984). Situational determinants of coping responses: Loss, threat, and challenge. *Journal of Personality and Social Psychology, 46*, 919–928. http://dx.doi.org/10.1037/0022-3514.46.4.919

CHAPTER 3

1. Holt-Lunstad, J., Smith, T. B., Baker, M., Harris, T., & Stephenson, D. (2015). Loneliness and social isolation as risk factors for mortality: A meta-analytic review. *Perspectives on Psychological Science, 10*, 227–237. doi:10.1177/1745691614568352

2. Kwilecki, S. (2011). Ghosts, meaning, and faith: After-death communications in bereavement narratives. *Death Studies, 35*, 219–243. doi:10.1080/07481187.2010.511424

3. Ecklund, E. H., & Lee, K. S. (2011). Atheists and agnostics negotiate religion and family. *Journey for the Scientific Study of Religion, 50,* 728–743. https://doi.org/10.1111/j.1468-5906.2011.01604.x

4. Acklin, M. W., Brown, E. C., & Mauger, P. A. (1983). The role of religious values in coping with cancer. *Journal of Religion and Health, 22,* 322–333. doi:10.1007/BF02279928

5. Tarakeshwar, N., Vanderwerker, L. C., Paulk, E., Pearce, M. J., Kasl, S. V., & Prigerson, H. G. (2006). Religious coping is associated with the quality of life of patients with advanced cancer. *Journal of Palliative Medicine, 9,* 646–657. doi:10.1089/jpm.2006.9.646

6. Koenig, H. G., Larson, D. B., & Larson, S. S. (2001). Religion and coping with serious medical illness. *Annals of Pharmacotherapy, 35,* 352–359. doi:10.1345/aph.10215

7. Pyszczynski, T., Solomon, S., & Greenberg, J. (2003). *In the wake of 9/11: The psychology of terror.* Washington, DC: American Psychological Association.

8. Ellis, L., Wahab, E. A., & Ratnasingan, M. (2013). Religiosity and fear of death: A three-nation comparison. *Mental Health, Religion, and Culture, 16,* 179–199. http://dx.doi.org/10.1080/13674676.2011.652606

9. Nelson, L. D., & Cantrell, C. H. (1980). Religiosity and death anxiety: A multi-dimensional analysis. *Review of Religious Research, 21,* 148–157. doi:10.2307/3509880

10. Norenzayan, A., & Hansen, I. G. (2006). Belief in supernatural agents in the face of death. *Personality and Social Psychology Bulletin, 32,* 174–187. doi:10.1177/0146167205280251

11. Grossman, C. L. (2010). Poll: 83% say god answers prayers, 57% favor national prayer day. *USA Today.* Retrieved from http://usatoday30.usatoday.com/news/religion/2010-05-05-prayer05_ST_N.htm

12. Schimel, J., Hayes. J., Williams, T., & Jahrig, J. (2007). Is death really the worm at the core? Converging evidence that worldview threat increases death-thought accessibility. *Journal of Personality and Social Psychology, 92,* 789–803. doi:10.1037/0022-3514.92.5.789

13. Routledge, C., Roylance, C., & Abeyta, A. A. (2015). Miraculous meaning: Threatened meaning increases belief in miracles. *Journal of Religion and Health, 56,* 776–783. doi: 10.1007/s10943-015-0124-4

14. Routledge C., Arndt, J., Wildschut, T., Sedikides, C., Hart, C., Juhl, J., . . . Scholtz, W. (2011). The past makes the present meaningful: Nostalgia as an existential resource. *Journal of Personality and Social Psychology, 101,* 638–652.

15. Routledge, C., Abeyta, A., & Roylance, C. (2016). An existential function of evil: The effects of religiosity and compromised meaning on belief in magical evil forces. *Motivation and Emotion, 40,* 681–688. doi.org/10.1007/s11031-016-9571-9

16. Van Tongeren, D. R., & Green, J. D. (2010). Combating meaninglessness: On the automatic defense of meaning. *Personality and Social Psychology Bulletin, 36,* 1372–1384. doi: 10.1177/0146167210383043

17. Stetzer, E. (2015, June 12). The rapid rise of nondenominational christianity: My most recent piece at CNN. *Christianity Today.* Retrieved from http://www.

christianitytoday.com/edstetzer/2015/june/rapid-rise-of-non-denominational-christianity-my-most-recen.html

CHAPTER 4

1. Lipka, M. (2016, June 1). 10 facts about atheists. *Pew Research Center.* Retrieved from http://www.pewresearch.org/fact-tank/2016/06/01/10-facts-about-atheists/
2. Ecklund, E. H., & Long, E. (2011). Scientists and spirituality. *Sociology of Religion, 72,* 253–274. doi:10.1093/socrel/srr003
3. Norenzayan, A., Gervais, W. M., & Trzesniewski, K. H. (2012). Mentalizing deficits constrain belief in a personal god. *PLoS ONE, 7,* e36880. https://doi.org/10.1371/journal.pone.0036880
4. Norenzayan, A., & Willard, A. K. (2013). Cognitive biases explain religious belief, paranormal belief, and belief in life's purpose. *Cognition, 129,* 379–391. http://dx.doi.org/10.1016/j.cognition.2013.07.016
5. Jack, A. I., Friedman, J. P., Boyatzis, R. E., & Taylor, S. N. (2016). Why Do You Believe in God? Relationships between Religious Belief, Analytic Thinking, Mentalizing and Moral Concern. *PLoS ONE, 11*(5), e0155283. https://doi.org/10.1371/journal.pone.0155283
6. Harms, W. (2012, April 18). Belief in god rises with age, even in atheist nations. *UChicagoNews.* Retrieved from https://news.uchicago.edu/article/2012/04/18/belief-god-rises-age-even-atheist-nations
7. Jong, J., Halberstadt, J., & Bluemke, M. (2012). Foxhole atheism, revisited: The effects of mortality salience on explicit and implicit religious belief. *Journal of Experimental Social Psychology, 48,* 983–989. http://dx.doi.org/10.1016/j.jesp.2012.03.005
8. Lindeman, M., Heywood, B., Riekki, T., & Makkonen, T. (2014). Atheists become emotionally aroused when daring god to do terrible things. *International Journal for the Psychology of Religion, 24,* 124–132. http://dx.doi.org/10.1080/10508619.2013.771991
9. Harmon-Jones, E., Simon, L., Greenberg, J., Pyszczynski, T., Solomon, S., & McGregor, H. (1997). Terror management theory and self-esteem: Evidence that increased self-esteem reduces mortality salience effects. *Journal of Personality and Social Psychology, 72,* 24–36. doi:10.1037/0022-3514.72.1.24
10. Vail, K. E., Rothschild, Z. K., Weise, D., Solomon, S., Pyszczynski, T., & Greenberg, J. (2010). A terror management analysis of the psychological functions of religion. *Personality and Social Psychology Review, 14,* 84–94. doi:10.1177/1088868309351165
11. Heflick, N. A., & Goldenberg, J. L. (2012). No atheists in foxholes: arguments for (but not against) afterlife beliefs buffer mortality salience effects for atheists. *British Journal of Social Psychology, 52,* 385–392.
12. Dechesne, M., Pyszczynski, T., Arndt, J., Ransom, S., Sheldon, K. M, van Knippenberg, A., & Janssen, J. (2003). Literal and symbolic immortality: The effect of evidence of literal immortality on self-esteem striving in response to mortality salience. *Journal of Personality and Social Psychology, 84,* 722–737. doi:10.1037/0022-3514.84.4.722

CHAPTER 5

1. Lipka, M. (2015, November 11). *Religious "nones" are not only growing, they're becoming more secular.* Retrieved from http://www.pewresearch.org/fact-tank/2015/11/11/religious-nones-are-not-only-growing-theyre-becoming-more-secular/
2. Lipka, M. (2015, November 11). *Religious "nones" are not only growing, they're becoming more secular.* Retrieved from http://www.pewresearch.org/fact-tank/2015/11/11/religious-nones-are-not-only-growing-theyre-becoming-more-secular/
3. Pew Research Center. (2015, May 12). *America's changing religious landscape.* Retrieved from http://www.pewforum.org/2015/05/12/americas-changing-religious-landscape/
4. Harper Elixer. HarperOne. http://harperone.hc.com/harperelixir/
5. Astin, J. A. (1998). Why patients use alternative medicine: Results of a national study. *JAMA, 279,* 1548–1553. doi:10.1001/jama.279.19.1548
6. Pew Research Center. (2009, December 9). *Many Americans mix multiple faiths.* Retrieved from http://www.pewforum.org/2009/12/09/many-americans-mix-multiple-faiths/#ghosts-fortunetellers-and-communicating-with-the-dead
7. Spelgel, L. (2013, February 8). *Spooky number of Americans believe in ghosts.* Retrieved from http://www.huffingtonpost.com/2013/02/02/real-ghosts-americans-poll_n_2049485.html
8. Lipka, M. (2015, October 30). *18% of Americans say they've seen a ghost.* Retrieved from http://www.pewresearch.org/fact-tank/2015/10/30/18-of-americans-say-theyve-seen-a-ghost/
9. Hakansson, A. (2015, October 30). *Belief in ghosts rises across secular Sweden.* Retrieved from http://www.thelocal.se/20151030/belief-in-ghosts-rises-in-secular-sweden
10. Routledge, C. (2016, May). *Beyond religion: Finding meaning in nontraditional magical beliefs.* Paper presented at the annual American Psychological Society Conference at Chicago, IL.
11. Kennedy, J. E., Kanthamani, H., & Palmer, J. (1994). Psychic and spiritual experiences, health, well-being, and meaning in life. *Journal of Parapsychology, 58,* 353–383.
12. Norenzayan, A., & Willard, A. K. (2013). Cognitive biases explain religious belief, paranormal belief, and belief in life's purpose. *Cognition, 129,* 379–391. http://dx.doi.org/10.1016/j.cognition.2013.07.016
13. Routledge, C., Roylance, C., & Abeyta, A. A. (2015). Miraculous meaning: Threatened meaning increases belief in miracles. *Journal of Religion and Health, 56,* 776–783.doi: 10.1007/s10943-015-0124-4
14. Routledge, C., Abeyta, A., & Roylance, C. (in press). An existential function of evil: The effects of religiosity and compromised meaning on belief in magical evil forces. *Motivation and Emotion, 40,* 681–688. doi:10.1007/s11031-016-9571-9
15. Miller, J. W. (2013, October 27). What could be scarier than a paranormal hot dog stand? Haunted house business isn't just for Halloween anymore. *Wall Street Journal.* Retrieved from http://www.wsj.com/articles/SB10001424052702304799404579155510452280906
16. DiBlasio, N. (2012, June 26). A third of Earthlings believe in UFOs, would befriend aliens. *USA Today.* Retrieved from http://usatoday30.usatoday.com/news/nation/story/2012-06-26/ufo-survey/55843742/1

17. Spelgel, L. (2013, September 11). *48 percent of Americans believe UFOs could be ET visitations*. Retrieved from http://www.huffingtonpost.com/2013/09/11/48-percent-of-americans-believe-in-ufos_n_3900669.html

18. Rickman, D. (2015). *More people believe in aliens and ghosts than God*. Retrieved from http://indy100.independent.co.uk/article/more-people-believe-in-aliens-and-ghosts-than-god--xJ3xFtsaIe

19. Swami, V., Chamorro-Premuzic, T., & Shafi, M. (2010). Psychology in outer-space: Personality, individual difference, and demographic predictors of beliefs about extraterrestrial life. *European Psychologist, 15,* 220–228. doi:10.1027/1016-9040/a000023

20. Routledge, C. (2016, May). *Beyond religion: Finding meaning in nontraditional magical beliefs*. Paper presented at the annual American Psychological Society Conference at Chicago, IL.

21. Shermer, M. (2011). *The believing brain*. New York, NY: St. Martin's Griffin.

22. Routledge, C., Abeyta, A. A., & Roylance, C. (2017). We are not alone: The meaning motive, religiosity, and belief in extraterrestrial intelligence. *Motivation and Emotion, 41,* 135–146.

23. Routledge, C. (2017, July 21). Don't believe in God? Maybe you'll try U.F.O.s. *New York Times*. Retrieved from https://www.nytimes.com/2017/07/21/opinion/sunday/dont-believe-in-god-maybe-youll-try-ufos.html?_r=0

24. Lifshin, U., Greenberg, J. Soenke, M., Darrel, A., Pyszczynski, T. (in press). Mortality salience, religiosity, and indefinite life extension: Evidence of a reciprocal relationship between afterlife beliefs and support for forestalling death. *Religion, Brain, and Behavior*. http://dx.doi.org/10.1080/2153599X.2016.1238841

25. Lifshin, U., Greenberg, J., Weise, D., & Soenke, M. (2016). It's the end of the world and I feel fine: Soul belief and perceptions of end-of-the-world scenarios. *Personality and Social Psychology Bulletin, 42,* 104–117. doi:10.1177/0146167215616800

26. Linssen, C., & Lemmens, P. (2016). Embodiment in whole-brain emulation and its implications for death anxiety. *Journal of Evolution and Technology, 26*(2), 1–15.

27. Mormon Transhumanist Association. (2014). *Member survey results*. Retrieved from http://transfigurism.org/pages/about/member-survey-results/

28. Church of Perpetual Life. http://www.churchofperpetuallife.org

29. Vail, K. E., & Soenke, M. (in press). The impact of mortality salience on meaning in life among religious and atheists. *Religion, Brain, and Behavior,* http://dx.doi.org/10.1080/2153599X.2016.1238845

CHAPTER 6

1. American Psychological Association. (2013). *How stress affects your health* [Fact sheet]. Retrieved from http://www.apa.org/helpcenter/stress.aspx

2. Mayo Clinic Staff. (2016, April 28). *Stress symptoms: Effects on your body and behavior*. Retrieved from http://www.mayoclinic.org/healthy-lifestyle/stress-management/in-depth/stress-symptoms/art-20050987

3. Ano, G. G., & Vasconcelles, E. B. (2005). Religious coping and psychological adjustment to stress: A meta-analysis. *Journal of Clinical Psychology, 61,* 461–480. doi: 10.1002/jclp.20049

4. Koenig, H. G., King, D. E., & Carson, V. B. (2012). *Handbook of religion and health*. New York, NY: Oxford University Press.

5. Carver, C. S., Scheier, M. F., & Segerstrom, S. C. (2010). Optimism. *Clinical Psychology Review, 30*, 879–889. http://dx.doi.org/10.1016/j.cpr.2010.01.006

6. Carver, C. S., Pozo, C., Harris, S. D., Noriega, V., Scheier, M. F., Robinson, D. S., . . . Clark, K. C. (1993). How coping mediates the effect of optimism on distress: A study of women with early stage breast cancer. *Journal of Personality and Social Psychology, 65*, 375–390. doi:10.1037/0022-3514.65.2.375

7. Bjorck, J. P., Hopp, D. P., & Jones, L. W. (1999). Prostate cancer and emotional functioning: Effects of mental adjustment, optimism, and appraisal. *Journal of Psychosocial Oncology, 17*, 71–85. http://dx.doi.org/10.1300/J077v17n01_05

8. Segerstrom, S. C., Taylor, S. E., Kemeny, M. E., & Fahey, J. L. (1998). Optimism is associated with mood, coping, and immune change in response to stress. *Journal of Personality and Social Psychology, 74*, 1646–1655. http://dx.doi.org/10.1037/0022-3514.74.6.1646

9. Baldwin, D. R., Chambliss, L. N., & Towler, K. (2003). Optimism and stress: An African-American college student perspective. *College Student Journal, 37*, 276–285.

10. Gustafsson, H., & Skoog, T. (2012). The mediational role of perceived stress in the relation between optimism and burnout in competitive athletes. *Anxiety, Stress and Coping, 25*, 183–199. doi:10.1080/10615806.2011.594045

11. Grote, N. K., & Bledsoe, S. E. (2007). Predicting postpartum depressive symptoms in new mothers: The role of optimism and stress frequency during pregnancy. *Health and Social Work 32*, 107–118. doi:10.1093/hsw/32.2.107

12. Chang, E. C. (1998). Does disposition optimism moderate the relationship between perceived stress and psychological well-being? A preliminary investigation. *Personality and Individual Differences, 25*, 233–240. http://dx.doi.org/10.1016/S0191-8869(98)00028-2

13. Carver, C. S., Scheier, M. F., & Segerstrom, S. C. (2010). Optimism. *Clinical Psychology Review, 30*, 879–889. http://dx.doi.org/10.1016/j.cpr.2010.01.006

14. Koenig, H. G., King, D. E., & Carson, V. B. (2012). Handbook of religion and health. New York, NY: Oxford University Press.

15. Kirkpatrick, L. A. (2005). *Attachment, evolution, and the psychology of religion*. New York, NY: Guilford Press.

16. Rogers, P. (2013). Investigating the relationship between adult attachment and belief in the paranormal: Results from two studies. *Imagination, Cognition, and Personality, 32*, 393–425. doi:10.2190/IC.32.4.e

17. Kupor, D. M., Laurin, K., & Levav, J. (2015). Anticipating divine protection? Reminders of god can increase nonmoral risk taking. *Psychological Science, 26*, 374–384. doi:10.1177/0956797614563108

18. Saudia, T. L., Kinney, M. R., Brown, K. C., & Young-Ward, L.(1991). *Heart and Lung: The Journal of Critical Care, 20*, 60–65.

19. Juhl, J., Routledge, C. Hicks, J., & Sedikides, C. (2017). Can affectively negative experiences contribute to wellbeing? The affectively negative need-fulfillment

model. In M. D. Robinson & M. Eid (Eds.), *The happy mind: Cognitive contributions to well-being* (pp. 389–407). New York, NY: Springer.

20. Keinan, G. (1994). Effects of stress and tolerance for ambiguity on magical thinking. *Journal of Personality and Social Psychology, 67,* 48–55. doi:10.1037/0022-3514.67.1.48

21. Kim, Y., & Seidlitz, L. (2002). Spirituality moderates the effect of stress on emotional and physical adjustment. *Personality and Individual Differences, 32,* 1377–1390. doi:10.1016/S0191-8869(01)00128-3

22. Tuck, I., Alleyne, R., & Thinganjana, W. (2006). Spirituality and stress management in healthy adults. *Journal of Holistic Nursing, 24,* 245–253. doi:10.1177/0898010106289842

23. Westman, J. A., Ferketich, A. K., Kauffman, R. M., MacEachern, S. N., Wilkins, J. R., III, Wilcox, P. P., . . . Bloomfield, C. D. (2010). Low cancer incidence rates in Ohio Amish. *Cancer Causes and Control, 21*(1), 69–75. doi:10.1007/s10552-009-9435-7

24. Hsueh, W. C., Mitchell, B. D., Aburomia, R., Pollin, T. I., Sakul, H., Ehm, M. G., . . . Shuldiner, A. R. (2000). Diabetes in the old order Amish: Characterization and heritability analysis of the Amish family diabetes study. *Diabetes Care, 23,* 595–601. doi:10.2337/diacare.23.5.595

25. Miller, K., Yost, B., Flaherty, S., Hillemeier, M. M., Chase, G. A., Weisman, C. S., & Dyer, A. (2007). Health status, health conditions, and health behaviors among Amish women: Results from the central Pennsylvania women's health study. *Women's Health Issues, 17,* 162–171. http://dx.doi.org/10.1016/j.whi.2007.02.011

26. University of Maryland Medical Center. (2012, October 23). Amish children are twice as physically active as non-Amish children are, study finds. *ScienceDaily.* Retrieved from www.sciencedaily.com/releases/2012/10/121023152317.htm

27. Hairston, K. G., Ducharme, J. L., Treuth, M. S., Hsueh, W. C., Jastreboff, A. M., Ryan, K. A., . . . Snitker, S. (2013). Comparison of BMI and physical activity between old order Amish children and non-Amish children. *Diabetes Care, 36,* 873–878. doi:10.2337/dc12-0934

28. Hairston, K. G., Ducharme, J. L., Treuth, M. S., Hsueh, W. C., Jastreboff, A. M., Ryan, K. A., . . . Snitker, S. (2013). Comparison of BMI and physical activity between old order Amish children and non-Amish children. *Diabetes Care, 36,* 873–878. doi:10.2337/dc12-0934

29. Wanjek, C. (2008, September 16). How Amish avoid obesity. *Live Science.* Retrieved from http://www.livescience.com/5087-amish-avoid-obesity.html

30. Westman, J. A., Ferketich, A. K., Kauffman, R. M., MacEachern, S. N., Wilkins, J. R., III, Wilcox, P. P., . . . Bloomfield, C. D. (2010). Low cancer incidence rates in Ohio Amish. *Cancer Causes and Control, 21*(1), 69–75. doi:10.1007/s10552-009-9435-7

31. Holt-Lunstad, J., Smith, T. B., Baker, M., Harris, T., & Stephenson, D. (2015). Loneliness and social isolation as risk factors for mortality: A meta-analytic review. *Perspectives on Psychological Science, 10,* 227–237. doi:10.1177/1745691614568352

32. Enstrom, J. E., & Breslow, L. (2008). Lifestyle and reduced mortality among active California Mormons, 1980–2004. *Preventative Medicine, 46,* 133–136. doi:10.1016/j.ypmed.2007.07.030

33. Centers for Disease Control and Prevention. (2016, April 15). *Impaired driving* [Fact sheet]. Retrieved from http://www.cdc.gov/motorvehiclesafety/impaired_driving/impaired-drv_factsheet.html

34. Allen, N. E., Beral, V., Casabonne, D., Kan, S. W., Reeves, G. K., Brown, A., & Green, J. Moderate alcohol intake and cancer incidence in women. *Journal of the National Cancer Institute, 101,* 296–305. doi:10.1093/jnci/djn514

35. White, A., Castle, I. P., Chen, C. M., Shirley, M., Roach, D., & Hingson, R. (2015). Converging patterns of alcohol use and related outcomes among females and males in the United States, 2002 to 2012. *Alcoholism: Clinical and Experimental Research, 39,* 1712–1726. doi:10.1111/acer.12815

36. National Institute on Alcohol Abuse and Alcoholism. (1999, December). *Are women more vulnerable to alcohol's effects?* Retrieved from http://pubs.niaaa.nih.gov/publications/aa46.htm

37. National Cancer Institute. (2013, June 24). *Alcohol and cancer risk* [Fact sheet]. Retrieved from http://www.cancer.gov/about-cancer/causes-prevention/risk/alcohol/alcohol-fact-sheet#r18

38. Wallace, J. M., & Forman, T. A. (1998). Religion's role in promoting health and reducing risk among American youth. *Health Education and Behavior, 25,* 721–741. doi:10.1177/109019819802500604

39. Yeung, J. W. K., Chan, Y. C., & Lee, B. L. K. (2009). Youth religiosity and substance use: A meta-analysis from 1995 to 2007. *Psychological Reports, 105,* 255–266. doi:10.2466/PR0.105.1.255-266

40. Powell, L. H., Shahabi, L., & Thoresen, C. E. (2003). Religion and spirituality: Linkages to physical health. *American Psychologist, 58*(1), 36–52. http://dx.doi.org/10.1037/0003-066X.58.1.36

41. Aldwin, C. M., Park, C. L., Jeong, Y. J., & Nath, R. (2014). Differing pathways between religiousness, spirituality, and health: A self-regulation perspective. *Psychology of Religion and Spirituality, 6*(1), 9–21. http://dx.doi.org/10.1037/a0034416

42. Korup, A. K., Thygesen, L. C., Christensen, R. deP., Johansen, C., Sondergaard, J., & Hvidt, N. C. (2016). Association between sexually transmitted disease and church membership: A retrospective cohort study of two Danish religious minorities. *BMJ Open, 6.* doi:10.1136/bmjopen-2015-e010128

43. McCullough, M. E., & Willoughby, B. (2009). Religion, self-regulation, and self-control: Associations, explanations, and implications. *Psychological Bulletin, 135*(1), 69–93. http://dx.doi.org/10.1037/a0014213

44. Friese, M., & Wanke, M. (2014). Personal prayer buffers self-control depletion. *Journal of Experimental Social Psychology, 51,* 56–59. http://dx.doi.org/10.1016/j.jesp.2013.11.006

45. Shariff, A. F., Willard, A. K., Andersen, T., & Norenzayan, A. (2016). Religious priming: A meta-analysis with a focus on prosociality. *Personality and Social Psychology Review, 20*(1), 27–48. doi: 10.1177/1088868314568811

46. Laurin, K., Kay, A. C., & Fitzsimons, G. M. (2012). Divergent effects of activating thoughts of God on self-regulation. *Journal of Personality and Social Psychology, 102*(1), 4–21. http://dx.doi.org/10.1037/a0025971

47. Clobert, M., Saroglou, V., & Hwang, K. K. (2015). Buddhist concepts as implicitly reducing prejudice and increasing prosociality. *Personality and Social Psychology Bulletin, 41,* 513–525. doi:10.1177/0146167215571094

48. Tang, Y. Y., Ma, Y., Wang, J., Fan, Y., Feng, S., Lu, Q., . . . Posner, M. I. (2007). Short-term meditation training improves attention and self-regulation. *Proceedings of the National Academy of Sciences, 104,* 17152–17156. doi:10.1073/pnas.0707678194104

49. Newport, F., Agrawal, S., & Witters, D. (2010, December 1). *Very religious Americans report less depression, worry.* Retrieved from http://www.gallup.com/poll/144980/religious-americans-report-less-depression-worry.aspx

50. Pew Research Center. (2016, April 12). *Religion in everyday life.* Retrieved from http://www.pewforum.org/2016/04/12/religion-in-everyday-life/

51. Gearing, R. E., & Lizardi, D. (2009). Religion and suicide. *Journal of Religion and Health, 48,* 332–341. doi:10.1007/s10943-008-9181-2

52. Kasen, S., Wickramaratne, P., Gameroff, M. J., & Weissman, M. M. (2012). Religiosity and resilience in persons at high risk for major depression. *Psychological Medicine, 42,* 509–519. doi:10.1017/S0033291711001516

53. Rosmarin, D. H., Bigda-Peyton, J. S., Kertz, S. J., Smith, N., Rauch, S. L., & Bjorgvinsson, T. (2013). A test of faith in God and treatment: The relationship of belief in God to psychiatric treatment outcomes. *Journal of Affective Disorders, 146,* 441–446. http://dx.doi.org/10.1016/j.jad.2012.08.030

54. Moore, J. T., & Leach, M. M. (2016). Dogmatism and mental health: A comparison of the religious and secular. *Psychology of Religion and Spirituality, 8*(1), 54–64. http://dx.doi.org/10.1037/rel0000027

55. Hayward, R. D., Krause, N., Ironson, G., Hill, P. C., & Emmons, R. (2016). Health and well-being among the non-religious: Atheists, agnostics, and no preference compared with religious group members. *Journal of Religion and Health, 55,* 1024–1037. doi:10.1007/s10943-015-0179-2

56. Weber, S. R., Pargament, K. I., Kunik, M. E., Lomax, J. W., II, & Stanley, M. A. (2012). *Journal of Religion and Health, 51*(1), 72–86. doi:10.1007/s10943-011-9541-1

57. Abeyta, A., Routledge, C., Kersten, M., & Cox, C. R. (2017). The existential cost of economic insecurity: Threatened financial security undercuts meaning. *Journal of Social Psychology, 157,* 692–702. http://dx.doi.org/10.1080/00224545.2016.1270892

58. Hoverd, W. J., & Sibley, C. G. (2013). Religion, deprivation, and subjective well-being: Testing a religious buffering hypothesis. *International Journal of Wellbeing, 3,* 182–196. doi:10.5502/ijw.v3i2.5

59. Barber, N. (2011). A cross-national test of the uncertainty hypothesis of religious belief. *Cross-Cultural Research, 45,* 318–333. doi:10.1177/1069397111402465

60. Crabtree, S., & Pelham, B. (2009, March 6). Religion provides emotional boost to world's poor. *Gallup.* Retrieved from http://www.gallup.com/poll/116449/Religion-Provides-Emotional-Boost-World-Poor.aspx

CHAPTER 7

1. Routledge, C., Arndt, J., & Goldenberg, J. L. (2004). A time to tan: Proximal and distal effects of mortality salience on intentions to sun-tan. *Personality and Social Psychology Bulletin, 30,* 1347–1358. doi:10.1177/0146167204264056

2. Cox, C., Cooper, D. P., Vess, M., Arndt, J., Goldenberg, J. L., & Routledge, C. (2009). Bronze is beautiful but pale can be pretty: The effects of appearance standards and mortality salience on sun-tanning outcomes. *Health Psychology, 28,* 746–752. doi:10.1037/a0016388

3. Routledge, C., Juhl, J., Abeyta, A. A., & Roylance, C. (2014). Using the past to promote a peaceful future: Nostalgia proneness mitigates existential threat induced nationalistic and religious self-sacrifice. *Social Psychology, 45,* 339–346. doi:10.1027/1864-9335/a000172

4. Routledge, C., & Arndt, J. (2008). Self-sacrifice as self-defense: Mortality salience increases efforts to affirm a symbolic immortal self at the expense of the physical self. *European Journal of Social Psychology, 38,* 531–541. doi:10.1002/ejsp.442

5. World Health Organization. (2015, November 12). *Measles vaccination has saved an estimated 17.1 million lives since 2000.* Retrieved from http://www.who.int/mediacentre/news/releases/2015/measles-vaccination/en/

6. Center for Disease Control and Prevention. (2014, April 24). *Report shows 20-year US immunization program spares millions of children from diseases.* Retrieved from http://www.cdc.gov/media/releases/2014/p0424-immunization-program.html

7. Center for Disease Control and Prevention. (2016, December 1). *Current cigarette smoking among adults in the United States.* Retrieved from https://www.cdc.gov/tobacco/data_statistics/fact_sheets/adult_data/cig_smoking/

8. National Conference of State Legislatures. (2016, August 23). *States with religious and philosophical exemptions from school immunization requirements.* Retrieved from http://www.ncsl.org/research/health/school-immunization-exemption-state-laws.aspx

9. National District Attorney Association. (2015, February 11). *Religious exemptions to child neglect.* Retrieved from http://www.ndaa.org/pdf/2-11-2015%20Religious%20Exemptions%20to%20Child%20Neglect.pdf

10. Asser, S. M., & Swan, R. (1998). Child fatalities from religion-motivated medical neglect. *Pediatrics, 101,* 625–629. doi:10.1542/peds.101.4.625

11. Governor's Task Force on Children and Risk. (2015). http://idahochildren.org/wp-content/uploads/2014/12/IDCARTFtoOtter.pdf

12. Glauser, W. (2011). United States still too lenient on "faith healing" parents, say children's rights advocates. *Canadian Medical Association Journal, 183,* E709–E710. doi:10.1503/cmaj.109-3944

13. *6 Deaths as British Churches Claim to Cure HIV with Prayer.* (2011, November 27). Retrieved from http://www.ibtimes.com/6-deaths-british-churches-claim-cure-hiv-prayer-375144

14. Vess., M., Arndt, J., Cox, C., Routledge, C., & Goldenberg, J. L. (2009). Exploring the existential function of religion: The effects of religious fundamentalism and mortality salience on faith-based medical refusals. *Journal of Personality and Social Psychology, 97,* 334–350. doi:10.1037/a0015545

15. Altemeyer, B., & Hunsberger, B. (1992). Authoritarianism, religious fundamentalism, quest, and prejudice. *International Journal for the Psychology of Religion, 2,* 113–133. http://dx.doi.org/10.1207/s15327582ijpr0202_5

16. Chumley, C. K. (2013, September 12). *4 in 10 American adults: We're living in the end time*. Retrieved from http://www.washingtontimes.com/news/2013/sep/12/4-in10-american-adults-were-living-end-times/

17. Routledge, C., Abeyta, A. A., & Roylance, C. (in press). Death and end times: The effects of mortality salience and religious fundamentalism on apocalyptic beliefs. *Religion, Brain, and Behavior*. http://dx.doi.org/10.1080/2153599X.2016.1238840

18. Pyszczynski, T., Abdolhossein, A., Solomon, S., Greenberg, J., Cohen, F., & Weise, D. (2006). Mortality salience, martyrdom, and military might: The great Satan versus the axis of evil. *Personality and Social Psychology Bulletin, 32*, 525–537. doi:10.1177/0146167205282157

19. Pew Research Center. (2013, April 30). *Appendix A: U.S. Muslims: Views on religion and society in a global context*. Retrieved from http://www.pewforum.org/2013/04/30/the-worlds-muslims-religion-politics-society-app-a/?beta=true&utm_expid=53098246-2.Lly4CFSVQG2lphsg-KopIg.1&utm_referrer=http%3A%2F%2Fwww.pewforum.org%2F2013%2F04%2F30%2Fthe-worlds-muslims-religion-politics-society-overview%2F%3Fbeta%3Dtrue

20. Mohamed, B. (2016, January 6). A new estimate of the U.S. Muslim population. *Pew Research Center*. Retrieved from http://www.pewresearch.org/fact-tank/2016/01/06/a-new-estimate-of-the-u-s-muslim-population/

CHAPTER 8

1. McCarthy, J. (2015, June 22). *In U.S., socialist presidential candidates least appealing*. Retrieved from http://www.gallup.com/poll/183713/socialist-presidential-candidates-least-appealing.aspx

2. Clifford, S., & Gaskins, B. (2016). Trust me, I believe in God: Candidate religiousness as a signal of trustworthiness. *American Politics Research, 44*, 1066–1097. doi:10.1177/1532673X15608939

3. Clifford, S., & Gaskins, B. (2016). Trust me, I believe in God: Candidate religiousness as a signal of trustworthiness. *American Politics Research, 44*, 1066–1097. doi:10.1177/1532673X15608939

4. Edgell, P., Gerteis, J., & Hartmann, D. (2006). Atheists as "other": Moral boundaries and cultural membership in American society. *American Sociological Review, 71*, 211–234. doi:10.1177/000312240607100203

5. Gervais, W. M., Shariff, A. F., & Norenzayan, A. (2011). Do you believe in atheists? Distrust is central to anti-atheist prejudice. *Journal of Personality and Social Psychology, 101*, 1189–1206. doi:10.1037/a0025882

6. Clifford, S., & Gaskins, B. (2016). Trust me, I believe in God: Candidate religiousness as a signal of trustworthiness. *American Politics Research, 44*, 1066–1097. doi:10.1177/1532673X15608939

7. Heintzelman, S. J., & King, L. A. (2016). Meaning in life and intuition. *Journal of Personality and Social Psychology, 110*, 477–492. doi:10.1037/pspp0000062

8. Exline, J. J., Park, C. L., Smyth, J. M., & Carey, M. P. (2011). Anger toward God: Social-cognitive predictors, prevalence, and links with adjustment to bereavement and cancer. *Journal of Personality and Social Psychology, 100*, 129–148. doi:10.1037/a0021716

9. Genovese, J. E. C. (2005). Paranormal beliefs, schizotypy, and thinking styles among teachers and future teachers. *Personality and Individual Differences, 39,* 93–102. http://dx.doi.org/10.1016/j.paid.2004.12.008

10. Aarnio, K., & Lindeman, M. (2005). Paranormal beliefs, education, and thinking styles. *Personality and Individual Differences, 39,* 1227–1236. http://dx.doi.org/10.1016/j.paid.2005.04.009

11. Pennycook, G., Ross, R. M., Koehler, D. J., & Fugelsang, J. A. (2016). Atheists and agnostics are more reflective than religious believers: Four empirical studies and a meta-analysis. *PLoS ONE, 11.* doi:10.1371/journal.pone.0153039

12. Rios, K., Cheng, Z. H., Totton, R. R., & Shariff, A. F. (2015). Negative stereotypes cause Christians to underperform in and disidentify with science, *Social Psychological and Personality Science, 6,* 959–967. doi:10.1177/1948550615598378

13. Masci, D. (2014, October 30). 5 facts about evolution and religion. *Pew Research Center.* Retrieved from http://www.pewresearch.org/fact-tank/2014/10/30/5-facts-about-evolution-and-religion/

14. Hill, J. (2014). National study of religion and human origins. *BioLogos.* Retrieved from https://biologos.org/uploads/projects/nsrho-report.pdf

15. Pew Research Center. (2009, November 5). *Scientists and belief.* Retrieved from http://www.pewforum.org/2009/11/05/scientists-and-belief/

16. Ecklund, E. H. (2011, May 25). *What scientists think about religion.* Retrieved from http://www.huffingtonpost.com/elaine-howard-ecklund-phd/the-contours-of-what-scie_b_611905.html

17. Scheitle, C. P., & Ecklund, E. H. (2015). The influence of science popularizers on the public's view of religion and science: An experimental assessment. *Public Understanding of Science, 26*(1), 25–39. doi:10.1177/0963662515588432

18. Ecklund, E. H., Park, J. Z., & Sorrell, K. L. (2011). Scientists negotiate boundaries between religion and science. *Journal for the Scientific Study of Religion, 50,* 552–569. doi:10.1111/j.1468-5906.2011.01586.x

19. Ecklund, E. H., & Scheitle, C. P. (2007). Religion among academic scientists: Distinctions, disciplines, and demographics. *Social Problems, 54,* 289–307. doi:10.1525/sp.2007.54.2.289

20. Ecklund, E. H., Park, J. Z., & Sorrell, K. L. (2011). Scientists negotiate boundaries between religion and science. *Journal for the Scientific Study of Religion, 50,* 552–569. doi:10.1111/j.1468-5906.2011.01586.x

21. Ecklund, E. H., Johnson, D. R., Scheitle, C. P, Matthews, K. R. W., & Lewis, S. W. (2016). Religion among scientists in an international context: A new study of scientists in eight regions. *Socius: Sociological Research for a Dynamic World, 2,* 1–9. doi:10.1177/2378023116664353

22. Zuckerman, M., Silberman, J., & Hall, J. A. (2013). The relation between intelligence and religiosity: A meta-analysis and some proposed explanations. *Personality and Social Psychology Review, 17,* 325–354. doi:10.1177/1088868313497266

23. Erickson, L. D., & Phillips, J. W. (2012). The effect of religious-based mentoring on educational attainment: More than just a spiritual high? *Journal for the Scientific Study of Religion, 51,* 568–587. doi:10.1111/j.1468-5906.2012.01661.x

24. Murphy, C. (2016, November 4). The most and least educated U.S. religious groups. *Pew Research Center.* Retrieved from http://www.pewresearch.org/

fact-tank/2016/11/04/the-most-and-least-educated-u-s-religious-groups/?utm_content=buffereb4dd&utm_medium=social&utm_source=twitter.com&utm_campaign=buffer

25. Margolis, M. F., & Sances, M. W. (2016). Partisan differences in nonpartisan activity: The case of charitable giving. *Political Behavior.* doi:1007/s11109-016-9382-4

26. Bremner, R. H., Koole, S. L., & Bushman, B. J. (2011). "Pray for those who mistreat you": Effects of prayer on anger and aggression. *Personality and Social Psychology Bulletin, 37,* 830–837. doi:10.1177/0146167211402215

27. Ginges, J., Sheikh, H., Atran, S., & Argo, N. (2016). Thinking from God's perspective decreases biased valuation of the life of a nonbeliever. *Proceedings of the National Academy of Sciences, 113,* 316–319. doi:10.1073/pnas.1512120113

28. Ecklund, E. H. (2011, May 25). *What scientists think about religion.* Retrieved from http://www.huffingtonpost.com/elaine-howard-ecklund-phd/the-contours-of-what-scie_b_611905.html

29. Lipka, M. (2016, August 24). Why America's "nones" left religion behind. *Pew Research Center.* Retrieved from http://www.pewresearch.org/fact-tank/2016/08/24/why-americas-nones-left-religion-behind/

30. Pew Research Center. (2012, October 9). *"Nones" on the rise: One-in-five adults have no religious affiliation.* Retrieved from http://www.pewforum.org/files/2012/10/NonesOnTheRise-full.pdf

31. Gervais, W. M. (2011). Finding the faithless: Perceived atheist prevalence reduces anti-atheist prejudice. *Personality and Social Psychology Bulletin, 37,* 543–556. doi:10.1177/0146167211399583

32. Boorstein, M. (2013, June 24). Some nonbelievers still find solace in prayer. *Washington Post.* Retrieved from https://www.washingtonpost.com/local/non-believers-say-their-prayers-to-no-one/2013/06/24/b7c8cf50-d915-11e2-a9f2-42ee3912ae0e_story.html

33. Simpson, A., & Rios, K. (2017). The moral contents of anti-atheist prejudice (and why atheists should care about it). *European Journal of Social Psychology.* doi:10.1002/ejsp.2219

34. Shariff, A. F., Willard, A. K., Andersen, T., & Norenzayan, A. (2015). Religious priming: A meta-analysis with a focus on prosociality. *Personality and Social Psychology Review, 20*(1), 27–48. doi:10.1177/1088868314568811

35. Aveyard, M. E. (2014). A call to honesty: Extending religious priming of moral behavior to Middle Eastern Muslims. *PLoS ONE, 9.* doi:10.1371/journal.pone.0099447

36. Shariff, A. F., & Rhemtulla, M. (2012). Divergent effects of beliefs in heaven and hell on national crime rates. *PLoS ONE, 7.* doi:10.1371/journal.pone.0039048

37. Galen, L. W. (2012). Does religious belief promote prosociality? A critical examination. *Psychological Bulletin, 138,* 876–906. http://dx.doi.org/10.1037/a0028251

38. Hofmann, W., Wisneski, D. C., Brandt, M. J., & Skitka, L. J. (2014). Morality in everyday life. *Science, 345,* 1340–1343. doi:10.1126/science.1251560

39. Chalabi, M. (2015, March 12). *Are prisoners less likely to be atheists?* Retrieved from http://fivethirtyeight.com/features/are-prisoners-less-likely-to-be-atheists/